Undergraduate Topics in Computer Science

Undergraduate Topics in Computer Science (UTiCS) delivers high-quality instructional content for undergraduates studying in all areas of computing and information science. From core foundational and theoretical material to final-year topics and applications, UTiCS books take a fresh, concise, and modern approach and are ideal for self-study or for a one- or two-semester course. The texts are all authored by established experts in their fields, reviewed by an international advisory board, and contain numerous examples and problems. Many include fully worked solutions.

For further volumes:
http://www.springer.com/series/7592

Gerard O'Regan

Introduction
to Software Process
Improvement

 Springer

Dr. Gerard O'Regan
11 White Oaks
Mallow, Co. Cork
Ireland
oregang@yahoo.com

Undergraduate Topics in Computer Science ISSN 1863-7310
ISBN 978-0-85729-171-4   e-ISBN 978-0-85729-172-1
DOI 10.1007/978-0-85729-172-1
Springer London Dordrecht Heidelberg New York

British Library Cataloguing in Publication Data
A catalogue record for this book is available from the British Library

Printed on acid-free paper

Springer is part of Springer Science+Business Media (www.springer.com)

To my two wonderful godchildren
Cian and Niamh

Preface

Overview

The objective of this book is to give an introduction to the software process improvement field to computer science students. The well-known Capability Maturity Model Integration (CMMI[1]) is used as the vehicle for software process improvement as it has become the de facto standard[2] for implementing best practice in software engineering. The reader is guided through the steps in setting up a CMMI improvement initiative; implementing the various CMMI process areas and maturity levels; and conducting appraisals. Appraisals are an essential part of the continuous improvement cycle as they allow the organization to understand its current software engineering process maturity, to prioritize future process improvements, and to confirm that the process improvements made have been effective.

The Software Engineering Institute (SEI) and many other quality experts believe that there is a close relationship between the quality and maturity of the underlying software processes and the quality of the delivered software product. The implementation of the CMMI brings best practice in software and systems engineering into the organization, thereby enhancing its software engineering effectiveness and enabling it to achieve more consistent results.

The implementation of the CMMI enables the organization to design and develop software following sound software engineering principles, i.e. the requirements are clearly defined and documented; a software design is produced that is valid with respect to the requirements. The software code implements the design and peer reviews and testing are employed to verify that the implementation is valid with respect to the requirements and the design. Sound project management practices are employed during the project, and this enables a high-quality software solution to be delivered on time and on budget to the customer.

---

[1] Specifically, the CMMI Development Model, CMMI-Dev, V1.2 is used as the vehicle for software process improvement in this book.

[2] Other approaches that are popular include the ISO/IEC 15504 standard (SPICE) and ISO 9001.

The steps involved in setting up a CMMI improvement initiative in an organization are described. This includes a discussion of the typical teams that will need to be involved as well as their roles and responsibilities. Guidance is provided to assist in the implementation of processes to satisfy the CMMI requirements, and this includes examples of typical deliverables produced to implement specific and generic practices in the various process areas. Tools to support the organization in enhancing its software engineering effectiveness are also described.

The software engineering maturity of an organization is determined objectively by an appraisal, and the organization is typically assigned a maturity level to reflect the extent of its implementation of the CMMI. Large organizations will often be interested in achieving a particular CMMI maturity level (e.g. CMMI level 2 or level 3) to allow benchmarking against competitor organizations, and this is determined by a formal SCAMPI Class A appraisal. Small organizations will often have a limited budget for process improvement initiatives, and formal appraisals may not be a priority. Instead, the focus may be on improvements to provide a tangible return on investment and to make a difference to software quality, on-time delivery, and so on.

Software process improvement should provide a tangible return on investment. These initiatives typically take place in order to achieve certain business goals such as improving software quality, reducing the time to market, improving productivity, reducing the cost of poor quality. Companies will measure the return on investment achieved to judge its effectiveness.

Organization and Features

The first chapter provides motivation for software process improvement. It discusses the benefits that may be gained and models that are available to support software process improvement.

Chapter 2 provides a broad overview of software engineering and includes a discussion on software life cycles and the phases in software development. It includes discussion on requirements elicitation, software design, implementation, testing, and maintenance.

Chapter 3 gives an overview of the CMMI model and discusses the five maturity levels and their constituent process areas.

Chapter 4 describes the activities and teams required to set up a CMMI improvement initiative for an organization. These include the CMMI Steering Group, the SEPG team, and process-specific teams. A continuous improvement cycle is described, as software process improvement is continuous.

Chapter 5 focuses on the implementation of CMMI level 2 in a typical organization. It includes an overview of each of the level 2 process areas as well as typical deliverables produced in a level 2 implementation.[3]

---

[3]These are typical deliverables produced and the CMMI needs to be interpreted appropriately to meet the needs of the organization.

Chapter 6 focuses on the implementation of CMMI level 3 in an organization. It includes an overview of each of the level 3 process areas as well as typical deliverables produced.

Chapter 7 gives an overview on the implementation of CMMI level 4 and 5 in an organization. Many organizations are more focused on CMMI level 2 and 3 implementation rather than on the higher maturity levels.[4]

Chapter 8 discusses various tools to support the organizations in improving their software engineering maturity. The focus is first to define the process and then to find tools to support the process.

Chapter 9 discusses the SCAMPI appraisal methodology. This includes the formal SCAMPI Class A appraisal often employed by large organizations to obtain a CMMI rating that allows them to benchmark itself against other organizations, and SCAMPI Class B and C appraisals that are less expensive and time consuming but may not be used for benchmarking.

Audience

This main audience of this book are computer science students who are interested in learning about software process improvement, and in how it can assist software companies in achieving high-quality and reliable software on-time and on budget. It will also be of interest to software engineers, quality professionals, and software managers who are involved in software process improvement programmes as well as the motivated general reader.

---

[4]The exception to this may be companies in India where the marketing benefit of CMMI level 4 and level 5 maturity is significant. Many software companies in India need to be appraised at CMMI level 5 to be taken seriously as well as to attract and retain high-calibre staff.

Acknowledgements

I am deeply indebted to family and friends who supported my efforts in this endeavour. I wish to express a special thanks to former colleagues in industry and academia. I thank Dr. Micheal Mac An Airchinnigh, Dr. Andrew Butterfield, and Dr. Hugh Gibbons for a wonderful experience at Trinity College Dublin; Dr. Richard Messnarz for an interesting CMM assessment at Friedrichshafen, Germany; Dr. David Parnas (a grandfather of computer science) for sharing his interesting theoretical world of software quality (I do not see it solving the problem of delivering high-quality software on-time and on-budget); Rohit Dave of Motorola who was superb at the corporate quality game; John Murphy of DeCare Systems Ireland; John Wall of Lecan; Linda Booth, Charlie Smith, Mike Bew, and Neil Hawthorn of Allianz in the UK for a wonderful cultural experience in England; Uinsionn O'Connor and the team in EirGrid for an interesting CMMI level 3 implementation in Dublin; and Sarah Farrell of the Centre of Software Engineering, Dublin.

Cork, Ireland   Gerard O'Regan

Contents

Motivation for Software Process Improvement

1

Key Topics

> Software Process
> Software Process Improvement
> Process Mapping
> Benefits of Software Process Improvement
> CMMI
> ISO/IEC 15504 (SPICE)
> ISO 9000
> Six Sigma

1.1
Introduction

The information society and knowledge economy is an integral part of the world we live in, and software is at the heart of modern business and is pervasive throughout society. New technologies such as the World Wide Web and mobile phones have transformed our lives, and software is an integral part of these technologies. Companies have changed their way of doing business to take advantage of new technologies, and major changes have been made to the business processes in banks, insurance companies, and the travel industry.

Modern automobiles use software to enhance the driving experience, and the software is used to fly airplanes safely throughout the world. Software is used to control nuclear power stations as well as missile and defence systems; it is used to control manufacturing plants, and everyday items such as televisions and washing machines are all driven by software.

The success of business today is highly influenced by the functionality and quality of the software that it uses. It is essential that the software used is safe, reliable, of a high quality,

G. O'Regan, *Introduction to Software Process Improvement*, Undergraduate Topics in Computer Science, DOI 10.1007/978-0-85729-172-1_1,
© Springer-Verlag London Limited 2011

and fit for purpose. Companies may develop their own software internally or they may acquire software solutions off-the-shelf or from bespoke software development. Software development companies need to deliver high-quality and reliable software consistently on time to their customers.

Cost is a key driver in most organizations and it is essential that software is produced as cheaply and efficiently as possible, and that waste is reduced or eliminated in the software development process. In a nutshell, companies need to produce software that is *better, faster, and cheaper* than their competitors in order to survive in the marketplace. That is, companies need to continuously work smarter to improve their businesses.

Software process improvement initiatives are aligned to business goals and play a key role in helping companies achieve their strategic goals. It is invaluable in the implementation of best practice in organizations and allows companies to focus on fire prevention rather than firefighting. It allows companies to problem solve key issues to eliminate quality problems and to critically examine their current processes to determine the extent to which it meets their needs, as well as identifying how the process can be improved, and where waste can be minimized or eliminated.

It allows companies to identify the root causes of problems (e.g. using the five why tool) and to determine appropriate solutions to the root causes of problems. The benefits of successful process improvement include the consistent delivery of high-quality software, improved financial results, and increased customer satisfaction.

Software process improvement initiatives lead to a focus on the process and on ways to improve the process. This is important since most problems are caused by defective processes rather than by people, and a focus on the process helps to avoid a blame culture that occurs when blame is apportioned to individuals rather than the process. The focus on the process leads to a culture of openness in discussing problems and their solutions and in instilling process ownership in the process practitioners.

Software process improvement allows companies to mature their software engineering processes and to achieve their business goals more effectively. It helps software companies to deliver the agreed software on time and on budget, as well as improving the quality of the delivered software, reducing the cost of development, and improving customer satisfaction with the software. It has become an indispensable tool for software engineers and managers to achieve their goals and provides a return on investment to the organization.

1.2
What Is a Software Process?

A software development process is the process used by software engineers to design and develop computer software. It may be an undocumented ad hoc process as devised by the team for a particular project or it may be a standardized and documented process used by various teams on similar projects. The process is seen as the glue that ties people, technology, and procedures coherently together.

The processes employed in software development include processes to determine the requirements; processes to design and develop the software; processes to verify that the software is fit for purpose; and processes to maintain the software.

A software process is a set of activities, methods, practices, and transformations that people use to develop and maintain software and the associated work products.

DEFINITION 1.1 (SOFTWARE PROCESS)
A *process* is a set of practices or tasks performed to achieve a given purpose. It may include tools, methods, material, and people.

An organization will typically have many processes in place for doing its work, and the object of process improvement is to improve these to meet business goals more effectively.

The Software Engineering Institute (SEI) believes that there is a close relationship between the quality of the delivered software and the quality and maturity of the underlying processes employed to create the software. The SEI adopted and applied the principles of process improvement employed in the manufacturing field to develop process maturity models such as the CMM and its successor the CMMI. These maturity models are invaluable in maturing software processes in software intensive organizations.

The process is an abstraction of the way in which work is done in the organization and is seen as the glue that ties people, procedures, and tools together (Fig. 1.1).

A process is often represented by a process map which details the flow of activities and tasks. The process map will typically include the inputs to each activity as well as the output from an activity. Often, the output from one activity will become an input to the next activity. A simple example of a process map for creating the system requirements specification is described in Fig. 1.2. The input to the activity to create the systems requirements specification will typically be the business requirements, whereas the output is the systems requirements specification document itself.

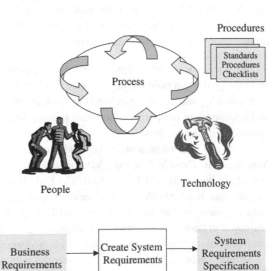

Fig. 1.1 Process as glue for people, procedures, and tools

Fig. 1.2 Sample process map

As a process matures it is defined in more detail and documented. It will have clearly defined entry and exit criteria, inputs and outputs, an explicit description of the tasks, verification of the process, and consistent implementation throughout the organization.

1.3
What Is Software Process Improvement?

Software process improvement is concerned with practical action to improve the processes in the organization to ensure that they meet business goals more effectively. For example, the goal may be to improve process performance to allow projects to be delivered faster and with higher quality. The origins of the software process improvement field go back to the manufacturing sector and to Walter Shewhart's work in the 1930s on statistical process control.

His work was later refined by Deming and Juran and they argued that high-quality processes are essential to the delivery of a high-quality product. They argued that the quality of the end product is largely determined by the processes used to produce and support it, and that therefore needs to be an emphasis on the process as well as the product.

These quality gurus argued that product quality will improve as variability in process performance is reduced [Dem:86], and their approach was effective in transforming manufacturing companies with quality problems to companies that could consistently deliver high-quality products. Further, improvements to quality led to cost reductions and higher productivity as less time was spent in re-working defective products.

The work of Deming and Juran was later applied to the software quality field by Watt Humphries and others at the SEI leading to the birth of the software process improvement field.

DEFINITION 1.2 (SOFTWARE PROCESS IMPROVEMENT)
A program of activities designed to improve the performance and maturity of the organization's software processes and the results of such a program.

Software process improvement initiatives support the organization in achieving its key business goals such as delivering software faster to the market, improving quality, reducing or eliminating waste. The objective is to work smarter and to build software better, faster, and cheaper than competitors. Software process improvement makes business sense and provides a return on investment.

There are international standards and models available to support software process improvement. These include the CMMI model, the ISO 9001 standard, and the ISO 15504 (popularly known as SPICE) standard. The CMMI model was developed by the Software Engineering Institute (SEI). It includes best practice for processes in software and systems engineering. The ISO 9001 standard is a quality management system that may be employed in hardware or software development companies. The ISO 15504 standard is an international standard for software process improvement and process assessment.

Software process improvement is concerned with defining the right processes and following them consistently. It involves training all staff on the new processes, refining the processes, and continuously improving the processes.

1.4
What Are the Benefits of Software Process Improvement?

Many organizations have problems with developing high-quality software consistently on time to their customers. There are problems with budget and schedule overruns, late delivery of the software, spiralling costs, problems with the quality of the delivered software, customer complaints with the functioning of the software, and staff morale.

Software process improvement can assist in dealing with these problems. It requires an investment but there are cost benefits and it provides a return on the investment made. Specifically, the benefits from software process improvement include

- Improvements to quality
- Reductions in the cost of poor quality
- Improvements in productivity
- Reductions to the cost of software development
- Improvements to on-time delivery
- Improved consistency in budget and schedule delivery
- Improvements to customer satisfaction
- Improvements to employee morale

The Software Engineering Institute maintains data on the benefits that organizations have achieved from using the CMMI. It has measured the improvements in several categories such as cost, schedule, productivity, quality, customer satisfaction, and the return on investment.

The results in Table 1.1 are from 25 organizations and are from publicly available conference presentations, published papers, and individual collaborations [SEI:06].

For example, *Northrop Grumman Defense Systems* met every milestone (25 in a row) with high quality and customer satisfaction; *Lockheed Martin* reported an 80% increase in software productivity over a 5-year period when it achieved CMM level 5 and obtained further increases in productivity as it moved to CMMI level 5. *Siemens (India)* reported an improved defect removal rate from over 50% before testing to over 70% before testing and a post-release defect rate of 0.35 defects per KLOC. *Accenture* reported a 5:1 return on investment from software process improvement activities.

Table 1.1 Benefits of software process improvement (CMMI)

Improvements	Median	# Data points	Low	High
Cost	20%	21	3%	87%
Schedule	37%	19	2%	90%
Productivity	62%	17	9%	255%
Quality	50%	20	7%	132%
Customer satisfaction	14%	6	−4%	55%
ROI	4.7:1	16	2:1	27:1

1.5
What Models Are Used in Software Process Improvement?

A process model[1] such as the CMMI defines best practice for software processes in an organization. It describes what the processes should do rather than how they should be done, and this allows the organization to use professional judgment to choose the most appropriate process implementation to meet its needs. The process model will need to be interpreted and tailored to the particular organization.

A process model provides a place to start an improvement initiative and it provides a common language and shared vision for improvement. It provides a framework to prioritize actions and allows the benefits of the experience of other organizations to be shared. There are several popular process models used in software process improvement including

- Capability Maturity Model Integration (CMMI)
- ISO 9001 Standard
- ISO 15504
- PSP and TSP
- Six Sigma
- IEEE standards
- Root Cause Analysis
- Balanced Scorecard

The CMMI was developed by the Software Engineering Institute and is the successor to the older software CMM which was released in the early 1990s. The latter was specific to the software field and was influenced by Watt Humphrey's work at IBM [Hum:89]. The CMMI is a suite of products used for improving processes, and it includes models, appraisal methods, and training material. The CMMI models address three areas of interest:

- CMMI for Development (CMMI-DEV)
- CMMI for Services (CMMI-SVC)
- CMMI for Acquisition (CMMI-ACQ)

The CMMI Development Model is the vehicle used for software process improvement in this book and is discussed in Chapter 3. It is a framework that allows organizations to improve their maturity by improvements to their underlying processes. It provides a structured approach and allows the organization to set improvement goals and priorities. It provides a clearly defined roadmap for improvement and it allows the organization to improve at its own pace. Its approach is evolutionary rather than revolutionary, and it recognizes that a balance is required between project needs and process improvement needs. It allows the processes to evolve from ad hoc immature activities to disciplined mature processes.

---

[1] There is the well-known adage "All models are wrong, some are useful".

The CMMI practices may be used for the development, acquisition, and maintenance of products and services. A SCAMPI appraisal determines the process maturity of an organization and allows it to benchmark itself against other organizations.

ISO 9001 is an internationally recognized quality management standard and is customer and process focused. It applies to the processes that an organization uses to create and control products and services, and it emphasizes continuous improvement.[2] The standard is designed to apply to any product or service that an organization supplies.

The implementation of ISO 9001 involves understanding the requirements of the standard and how the standard applies to the organization. It requires the organization to identify its quality objectives, define a quality policy, produce documented procedures, and carry out independent audits to ensure that the processes and procedures are followed. An organization may be certified against the ISO 9001 standard to gain recognition to its commitment to quality and continuous improvement. The certification involves an independent assessment of the organization to verify that it has implemented the ISO 9001 requirements properly and that the quality management system is effective. It will also verify that the processes and procedures defined are consistently followed and that appropriate records are maintained. The ISO 9004 standard provides guidance for continuous improvement.

The ISO/IEC 15504 standard (popularly known as ISO SPICE) is an international standard for process assessment. It includes guidance for process improvement and for process capability determination, as well as guidance for performing an assessment. It includes an exemplar process assessment model for software life cycle processes and also an exemplar process assessment model for systems life cycle processes. There is a version of SPICE termed "Automotive SPICE" that is used in the automotive sector.

ISO/IEC 15504 can be used in a similar way to the CMMI and its exemplar models (for either software or systems life cycles) may be employed to implement best practice in process definition. Assessments may be performed to identify strengths and opportunities for improvement.

The Personal Software Process (PSP) is a disciplined data-driven software development process that is designed to help software engineers understand and to improve their personal software process performance. It was developed by Watt Humphrey at the SEI, and it helps engineers to improve their estimation and planning skills and to reduce the number of defects in their work. This enables them to make commitments that they can keep and to manage the quality of their projects.

The Team Software Process (TSP) was developed by Watt Humphries at the SEI and is a structured approach designed to help software teams understand and improve their quality and productivity. Its focus is on building an effective software development team, and it involves establishing team goals, assigning team roles as well as other teamwork activities. Team members must already be familiar with the PSP.

Six Sigma (6σ) was developed by Motorola as a way to improve quality and reduce waste. Its approach is to identify and remove the causes of defects in processes by minimizing process variability. It uses quality management techniques and tools such as the

---

[2]The ISO 9004 standard provides guidance on continuous improvement.

five whys, business process mapping, statistical techniques, and the DMAIC and DMADV methodologies. There are several roles involved in six-sigma initiatives such as Champions, Black Belts, and Green Belts, and each role requires knowledge and experience and is awarded on merit subject to training and certification. Sponsorship and leadership is required from top management to ensure the success of a Six-Sigma initiative. Six Sigma was influenced by earlier quality management techniques developed by Shewhart, Deming, and Juran.

A Six-Sigma project follows a defined sequence of steps and has quantified targets. These targets may be financial, quality, customer satisfaction, and cycle time reduction.

1.6
Process Mapping

The starting point for improving a process is first to understand the process as it is currently performed. This involves participation from the process stakeholders to reach a common understanding of how the process is actually performed and to identify how it may be improved. The process as currently performed is then sketched pictorially, with activities and their inputs and outputs recorded graphically. This graphical representation is termed a "process map" and is an abstract description of the process "as is".

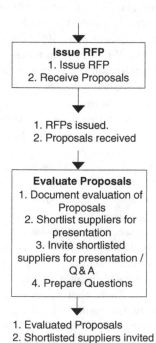

Fig. 1.3 Sample process map

The process map is an abstraction of the way that work is done, and it may be critically examined to determine how effective it really is and to identify weaknesses in the process. The process thinking by the process practitioners leads to modifications to the definition of the current process, and the proposed definition is sketched in a new process map to yield the process "to be". Once the team has agreed on the new process the templates required to support the process become clear from an examination of the input and output of the various activities. Procedures or guidelines will be documented to provide details on how the process is to be carried out.

For example, the following is a simple process map that is part of supplier selection (Fig. 1.3).

There are two activities listed in this process map. These are the "Issue RFP" activity that has two tasks and the "Evaluate Proposals" activity that has four tasks associated with it. There are other approaches to process mapping but the approach adopted here aims to keep the process map as simple and as abstract as possible.

A more detailed process map would specify standards to support the process and the roles involved in carrying out the tasks and activities. Entry and exit criteria could be specified as well as any verification steps and measures.

1.7
Process Improvement Initiatives

The need for a software process improvement initiative often arises from the realization that the organization is weak in some areas in software engineering and that it needs to improve to achieve its business goals more effectively. The starting point of any improvement initiative is an examination of the business goals of the organization and these may include

- Delivering high-quality products on time
- Delivering products faster to the market
- Reducing the cost of software development
- Improving software quality

There is more than one approach to the implementation of the CMMI. A small organization has fewer resources available and team members involved in the initiative will typically be working part-time. Larger organizations may be able to assign people full time on the improvement activities. The software process improvement initiative should be designed to enable the organization achieve its business goals more effectively.

Once the organization needs have been identified the improvement initiative commences. This involves conducting an appraisal to determine the current strengths and weaknesses of the processes; analysing the results to formulate a process improvement plan; implementing the plan; piloting the improved processes and verifying that they are effective; rolling out the new processes. The improvements are monitored for effectiveness and the cycle repeats. The philosophy suggested in this book is

- The improvement initiative should be based on business needs.
- Improvements should be planned based on an objective understanding of the strengths and weaknesses of the current processes in the organization.
- The CMMI Development Model (V1.2) is employed as the vehicle for improvement.
- The improvements need to be prioritized (as it is not possible to do everything at once).
- The improvement initiative should be planned and managed as a standard project.
- The results achieved need to be reviewed at the end of the period and a new improvement cycle started for continuous improvement.
- Software process improvement requires people to change their behaviour and so organization culture needs to be considered.
- There needs to be a Process Champion to drive the process improvement initiative in the organization.
- Senior management need to be 100% committed to the success of the initiative.
- Staff need to be involved in the improvement initiative and there needs to be a balance between project needs and the improvement activities.

The continuous improvement cycle suggested in this book is influenced by the IDEAL^{SM} model and by Deming's Plan-Do-Check-Act (PDCA) process improvement cycle. It is described in Chapter. 4.

1.8
Barriers to Success

Software process improvement initiatives are not always successful, and occasionally an improvement initiative is abandoned. Some of the reasons for failure are

- Unrealistic expectations
- Trying to do too much at once
- Lack of senior management sponsorship
- Focusing on a maturity level
- Poor project management of the initiative
- Not run as a standard project
- Insufficient involvement of staff
- Insufficient time to work on improvements
- Inadequate training on software process improvement
- Lack of pilots to validate new processes
- Inadequate rollout of new processes

It is essential that a software process improvement initiative be treated as a standard project with a project manager assigned to manage the initiative. Senior management need to be 100% committed to the success of the initiative, and they need to make staff available to work on the improvement activities. It needs to be clear to all staff that the improvement initiative is a priority to the organization. All staff need to receive appropriate training on software process improvement and on the process maturity model.

The CMMI project manager needs to consider the risks of failure of the initiative and to manage them accordingly.

1.9
Review Questions

1. What is a software process?
2. What is software process improvement?
3. What are the benefits of software process improvement?
4. Describe the various models available for software process improvement.
5. Draw the process map for the process of cooking your favourite meal.
6. Describe how a process improvement initiative may be run.
7. What are the main barriers to successful software process improvement initiatives and how can they be overcome?

1.10
Summary

The success of business is highly influenced by software, and companies may develop their own software internally or they may acquire software solutions off-the-shelf or from bespoke software development. Cost is a key driver in most organizations and it is essential that software is produced as cheaply and efficiently as possible, and that waste is reduced or eliminated in the software development process. Companies need to produce software that is *better, faster, and cheaper* than their competitors in order to survive in the marketplace.

Software process improvement plays a key role in helping companies to achieve their strategic goals and is invaluable in the implementation of best practice in organizations. It allows companies to focus on fire prevention rather than firefighting and to critically examine their processes to determine the extent to which they meet their needs. It enables them to identify how the process may be improved and how waste can be minimized or eliminated.

Software process improvement initiatives lead to a focus on the process and this focus on process thinking is important since most problems are caused by defective processes rather than by people. A focus on the process rather than people leads to a culture of openness in discussing problems and instils process ownership in the process practitioners.

Software process improvement allows companies to mature their software engineering processes and to achieve their business goals more effectively. It helps software companies to deliver the agreed software on time and on budget, as well as improving the quality of the delivered software, reducing the cost of development, and improving customer satisfaction. It has become an indispensable tool for software engineers and managers to achieve their goals and provides a return on investment to the organization.

The next chapter gives an overview of software engineering including project management, software life cycles, and various engineering activities such as requirements development and management, design and implementation, software inspections and testing.

Software Engineering

2

2.1
Introduction

The NATO Science Committee organized two famous conferences on software engineering in the late 1960s. The first conference was held in Garmisch, Germany, in 1968 and this was followed by a second conference in Rome in 1969. Over 50 people from 11 countries attended the Garmisch conference, and the attendees included the eminent Dutch computer scientist, Edsger Djkstra, who did important theoretical work on formal specification and verification. The NATO conferences highlighted problems that existed in the software sector in the late 1960s, and the term "software crisis" was coined to refer to these problems. These included budget and schedule overruns, as well as problems with the quality and reliability of the delivered software.

The conference led to the birth of *software engineering* as a discipline in its own right and the realization that programming is quite distinct from science and mathematics.

G. O'Regan, *Introduction to Software Process Improvement*, Undergraduate Topics
in Computer Science, DOI 10.1007/978-0-85729-172-1_2,
© Springer-Verlag London Limited 2011

Programmers are like engineers in that they build software products, and they therefore need education on traditional engineering as well as the latest technologies. The education of a classical engineer includes product design and mathematics. However, often computer science education places more emphasis on the latest technologies rather than the key engineering principles of designing and building high-quality products that are safe to use.

Programmers therefore need knowledge of sound engineering principles to enable them to build products that are safe for the public to use. This includes a solid foundation on design and the mathematics required for building safe software products. Mathematics plays a key role in engineering and may assist software engineers in the delivery of high-quality software products. Several mathematical approaches that can assist software engineers are described in [ORg:06].

There are parallels between the software crisis and serious problems with bridge construction in the nineteenth century. Several bridges collapsed or were delivered late or over-budget. The root cause of the problem was that many people who presented themselves as qualified to design and construct bridges did not have the required knowledge and expertise. Consequently, many bridges collapsed leading to loss of life or endangering the lives of the public.

This led to legislation requiring engineers to be licensed by the Professional Engineering Association prior to practicing as engineers. The engineering associations identify a core body of knowledge that the engineer is required to possess, and the licensing body verifies that the engineer has the required qualifications and experience. This helps to ensure that only personnel competent to design and build products actually do so, thereby leading to products that are safe for the public to use. Engineers have a responsibility to ensure that products are properly built and are safe for the public to use.

The Standish group has conducted research (Fig. 2.1) on the extent of problems with IT projects since the mid-1990s. This study was conducted in the United States, but there is no reason to believe that European or Asian companies perform any better. The results indicate serious problems with on-time delivery of projects or projects being cancelled.[1] However, the comparison between 1995 and 2009 suggests that there have been some improvements with a greater percentage of projects being delivered successfully and a reduction in the percentage of projects being cancelled.

Fred Brooks argues that software is inherently complex, and that there is no silver bullet that will resolve all of the problems associated with software development such as schedule or budget overruns and software quality problems [Brk:75, Brk:86]. The problems with poor software quality and poor software design can lead to software flaws that at best cause minor irritation or at worse can seriously disrupt the work of an organization or individual.

---

[1] It should be noted that these are IT projects covering diverse sectors including banking, telecommunications rather than pure software companies. My experience is that software companies following maturity frameworks such as the CMMI achieve more consistent project results. Mathematical approaches to software quality are focused on technical mathematical ways to achieve software quality. There is also the need to focus on the management side of software engineering, as this is essential for project success.

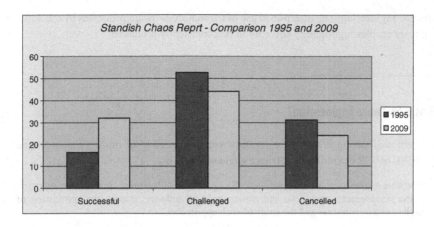

Fig. 2.1 Standish report – results of 1995 and 2009 survey

It is therefore essential that software development organizations place sufficient emphasis on quality throughout the software development life cycle.

The Y2K problem was caused by the 2-digit representation of dates and it required major re-work of legacy software to enable the software to function correctly in the new millennium. Clearly, well-designed programs would have hidden the representation of the date and would have required minimal changes for year 2000 compliance. Instead, companies spent vast sums of money to rectify the Y2K problem.

The quality of software produced by some companies is impressive.[2] These companies employ mature software processes and are committed to continuous improvement. Today, there is a lot of industrial interest in software process maturity for software organizations, and various approaches to assess and mature software companies are described in [ORg:02].[3] These focus mainly on improving the effectiveness of the management, engineering, and organization practices related to software engineering.

The focus of this book is to show how the CMMI may be employed in software process improvement to enhance the software engineering effectiveness of organizations. The objective is to mature software processes with the introduction of best practice in

---

[2] I recall projects at Motorola that regularly achieved 5.6σ quality in a L4 CMM environment (i.e. approx 20 defects per million lines of code. This represents very high quality).

[3] Approaches such as the CMM or SPICE (ISO 15504) focus mainly on the management and organizational practices required in software engineering. The emphasis is on defining software processes that are fit for purpose and consistently following them. The process maturity models focus on what needs to be done rather than on how it should be done. This gives the organization the freedom to choose the appropriate implementation to meet its needs. The models provide useful information on practices to consider in the implementation.

software engineering. The disciplined use of the mature software processes by the software engineers enables high-quality software to be consistently produced.

2.2
What Is Software Engineering?

Software engineering involves the multi-person construction of multi-version programs. The IEEE 610.12 definition of software engineering is

Software engineering is the application of a systematic, disciplined, quantifiable approach to the development, operation, and maintenance of software; that is, the application of engineering to software, and the study of such approaches.

Software engineering includes

1. Methodologies to design, develop, implement, and test software to meet customers' needs.
2. Software is engineered. That is, the software products are properly designed, developed, and tested in accordance with engineering principles.
3. Quality and safety are properly addressed.
4. Mathematics may be employed to assist with the design and verification of software products. The level of mathematics employed will depend on the safety-critical nature of the product. Systematic peer reviews and rigorous testing will often be sufficient to build quality into the software, with heavy mathematical techniques reserved for safety- and security-critical software.
5. Sound project management and quality management practices are employed.
6. Support and maintenance of the software is properly addressed.

Software engineering is not just programming. It requires the engineer to state precisely the requirements that the software product is to satisfy and then to produce designs that will meet these requirements. The project needs to be planned and delivered on time and budget. The requirements must provide a precise description of the problem to be solved, i.e. it should be evident from the requirements what is and what is not required. The requirements need to be rigorously reviewed to ensure that they are stated clearly and unambiguously and are exactly what the customer wants. The next step is then to create the design that will solve the problem, and it is essential to validate the correctness of the design. Next, the software to implement the design is written, and peer reviews and software testing are employed to verify and validate the correctness of the software.

The verification and validation of the design is rigorously performed for safety-critical systems, and it is sometimes appropriate to employ mathematical techniques for these systems. However, it will usually be sufficient to employ peer reviews or software inspections to verify and validate the design as these methodologies provide a high degree of rigour. Peer reviews may include approaches such as Fagan inspections [Fag:76], Gilb inspections [Glb:94], or the Prince2 approach to quality reviews [OGC:04].

The term "engineer" is a title that is awarded on merit in classical engineering. It is generally applied only to people who have attained the necessary education and competence to be called engineers and who base their practice on classical engineering principles. The title places responsibilities on its holder such as to behave professionally and ethically. Often in computer science the term "software engineer" is employed loosely to refer to anyone who builds things, rather than to an individual with a core set of knowledge, experience, and competence.

Several computer scientists (such as Parnas [4]) have argued that computer scientists should be educated as engineers to enable them to apply appropriate scientific principles to their work. They argue that computer scientists should receive a solid foundation in software engineering to enable them to perform as engineers in building high-quality products that are safe for the public to use.

Software engineers need education[5] on specification, design, turning designs into programs, software inspections, and testing. The education should enable the software engineer to produce well-structured programs that are fit for purpose.

Parnas has argued that software engineers have responsibilities as professional engineers.[6] They are responsible for designing and implementing high-quality and reliable software that is safe to use. They are also accountable for their own decisions and actions[7] and have a responsibility to object to decisions that violate professional standards.

---

[4]Parnas has made important contributions to computer science. He advocates a solid engineering approach with the extensive use of classical mathematical techniques to software development. He also introduced information hiding in the 1970s which is now a part of object-oriented development.

[5]Software companies that are following approaches such as the CMM or ISO 9001 consider the education and qualification of staff prior to assigning staff to performing specific tasks. The appropriate qualifications and experience for the specific role are considered prior to appointing a person to carry out the role. Most mature companies place significant emphasis on the education and continuous development of their staff and on introducing best practice in software engineering into their organization.

[6]The concept of accountability is not new; indeed the ancient Babylonians employed a code of laws ca. 1750 BC known as the Hammurabi code. This code included the law that if a house collapsed and killed the owner then the builder of the house would be executed.

[7]However, it is unlikely that an individual programmer would be subject to litigation in the case of a flaw in a program causing damage or loss of life. A comprehensive disclaimer of responsibility for problems rather than a guarantee of quality accompanies most software products. Software engineering is a team-based activity involving many engineers in various parts of the project, and it would be potentially difficult for an outside party to prove that the cause of a particular problem is due to the professional negligence of a particular software engineer, as there are many others involved in the process such as reviewers of documentation and code and the various test groups. Companies are more likely to be subject to litigation, as a company is legally responsible for the actions of their employees in the workplace, and a company is also a more wealthy entity than one of its employees. The legal aspects of licensing software may protect software companies from litigation including those companies that are not focused on software quality. However, greater legal protection for the customer can be built into the contract between the supplier and the customer for bespoke software development.

Engineers are required to behave professionally and ethically with their clients. The membership of the professional engineering body requires the member to adhere to the code of ethics[8] of the profession. Engineers in other professions are licensed, and therefore Parnas argues that a similar licensing approach be adopted for professional software engineers.[9] This would provide extra confidence that the software engineer has the right competence for the particular assignment. Professional software engineers are required to follow best practice and the defined software processes.[10]

Most mature software companies invest heavily in training as they realise that the education and knowledge of its staff are essential to delivering high-quality products and services to their customers. Employees in these companies receive professional training related to the roles that they are performing. This includes training on disciplines such as project management, service management, and software testing. The fact that the employees are professionally qualified increases confidence in the ability of the company to deliver high-quality products and services. Otherwise, a company that pays little attention to the competence and continuous development of its staff will obtain a poor reputation in the market and a loss of market share.

2.3
Challenges in Software Engineering

The challenge in software engineering is to deliver high-quality software on time and on budget to customers. The Standish Group research [ORg:02] (Fig. 2.2) on project cost overruns in the USA during 1998 indicated that 33% of projects are between 21 and 50% overestimate, 18% of projects are between 51 and 100% overestimate, and 11% of projects are between 101 and 200% overestimate.

The accurate estimation of project cost, effort, and schedule is a challenge in software engineering. Consequently, organizations and project managers need to determine how good their estimation process actually is and to make improvements as appropriate. The use of software metrics is an objective mechanism to determine how good the estimation actually is, and improvements in estimation will be evident from a reduced variance between estimated and actual effort. The project manager will compute the actual project effort

---

[8]Most mature software companies have a defined code of ethics that employees are expected to adhere. Larger companies will wish to project a good corporate image and to be respected worldwide.

[9]The British Computer Scientist (BCS) has introduced a qualification system for computer science professionals that it used to show that professionals are properly qualified. The most important of these is the BCS Information Systems Examination Board (ISEB) which allows IT professionals to be qualified in service management, project management, software testing, and so on.

[10]Software companies that are following the CMMI or ISO 9000 standards will employ audits to verify that the processes and procedures have been followed. Auditors report their findings to management and the findings are addressed appropriately by the project team and affected individuals.

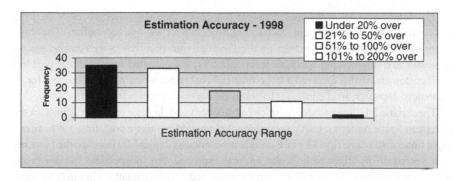

Fig. 2.2 Standish 1998 report – estimation accuracy

versus estimated project estimate as well as the actual project schedule versus estimated project schedule.

Risk management is an important part of project management, and the objective is to identify potential risks early and throughout the project and to manage them appropriately. It involves determining the probability of each risk occurring, assessing the impact of each risk should it materialize, monitoring the risks during project execution, and managing each risk appropriately. Actions are identified to reduce the probability of the risk occurring or reducing the impact of the risk should it materialize.

It is a challenge to consistently deliver high-quality software on time and on budget. Software quality needs to be properly planned to enable the project to deliver a quality product. Flaws with poor quality software will at best cause irritation to clients and lead to a negative impact on customer satisfaction. At worse the credibility of the company may be severely damaged with a subsequent loss of market share.

There is a strong economic case to delivering high-quality software to the client, as it reduces the time and cost of re-working defective software. The cost of poor quality (COPQ) should be measured and targets set for its reductions. Quality needs to be built into the software and this requires software processes that are fit for purpose. It is also important that lessons are learned during the project and acted upon appropriately. This helps to promote a culture of continuous improvement.

There are a number of high-profile software failures in the literature. They include the millennium bug (Y2K) problem; the floating-point bug in the Intel microprocessor; the European Space Agency Ariane-5 disaster . These have caused embarrassment to the organizations as well as the cost of replacement and correction.

The millennium bug is now a part of computer science folklore. The event itself on 1 January 2000 had minimal impact throughout the world as most companies had invested heavily in correcting the problem. It was due to the use of two digits to represent dates rather than four digits. The solution involved finding and analysing all code that had a Y2K impact; planning and making the necessary changes; and verifying the correctness of the changes. The worldwide cost of correcting the millennium bug is estimated to have been in billions of dollars.

The Intel response to the mathematical bug in its Pentium microprocessor in 1994 embarrassed the company and had a negative impact on its reputation. The Intel Corporation was slow to acknowledge the floating-point problem in its Pentium microprocessor and in providing adequate information on the potential impact of the problem to its customers. It also incurred a large financial cost in replacing microprocessors for its customers. However, Intel continues to dominate the microprocessor market.

The Ariane-5 failure caused major embarrassment and damage to the credibility of the European Space Agency (ESA). Its maiden flight ended in failure on 4 June 1996, after a flight time of 40 s. The first 37 s of the flight proceeded as expected. However, the launcher then veered off its flight path, broke up, and exploded. An independent inquiry board investigated the cause of the failure, and its report and recommendations are in [Lio:96].

The inquiry noted that the failure of the inertial reference system was followed immediately by a failure of the backup inertial reference system. The problem was traced to a software failure due to an operand error. Specifically, the problem was the conversion of a 64-bit floating-point number to a 16-bit signed integer value number. The floating-point number was too large to be represented as a 16-bit number and this resulted in the resulting operand error. The inertial reference system and the backup reference system reported failure owing to the software exception.

The operand error occurred owing to an exceptionally high value related to the horizontal velocity, and this was due to the fact that the early part of the trajectory of Ariane-5 was different from the earlier Ariane-4, as it required a higher horizontal velocity. The inquiry board made a series of recommendations to prevent a re-occurrence of similar problems in the future. However, the disaster did not cause long-term damage to the ESA.

These failures indicate that quality needs to be carefully considered when designing and developing software for all modern organizations. The effect of software failure may result in huge costs to correct the software (e.g. poorly designed legacy software in the case of the Y2K problem); the negative perception of a company and possible loss of market share in the case of the floating-point problem (e.g. Intel microprocessor problem); or the loss of a valuable communications satellite (e.g. Ariane-5).

2.4
Software Processes and Life Cycles

Organizations vary by size and complexity and the processes employed for doing work will vary from one organization to another. The development of software involves many processes such as those for defining requirements; processes for project management and estimation; and processes for design, implementation, testing.

It is important that the processes employed are fit for purpose and a key premise in the software quality field is that the quality of the resulting software is influenced by the quality and maturity of the underlying processes and compliance to them. Therefore, it is necessary to focus on the quality of the processes as well as the quality of the resulting software.

There is, of course, little point in having high-quality processes unless their use is institutionalized in the organization. That is, all staff need to follow the processes consistently. This requires that all affected staff are trained on the new processes and that process discipline is instilled by an appropriate audit strategy.

Mature software companies will establish high-quality processes for the various software management and engineering activities. All affected staff will then be trained on the new processes and audits will be conducted to ensure that the process is followed. Data will be collected to improve the process. The software process assets in an organization generally consist of

- A software development policy for the organization
- Process maps that describe the flow of activities
- Procedures and guidelines that describe the processes in more detail
- Checklists to assist with the performance of the process
- Templates for the performance of specific activities (e.g. design, testing)
- Training materials

The processes employed to develop high-quality software generally include processes for

- Project management process
- Requirements process
- Design process
- Coding process
- Peer review process
- Testing process
- Supplier selection and management processes
- Configuration management process
- Audit process
- Measurement process
- Improvement process
- Customer support and maintenance processes

The software development process has an associated life cycle that consists of various phases. There are several well-known life cycles employed such as the waterfall model [Roy:70], the spiral model [Boe:88], and the Rational Unified Process (RUP). These are described in more detail in the following sections.

2.4.1
Waterfall Life Cycles

The waterfall model   is described pictorially in Fig. 2.3. It starts with requirements gathering and definition. It is followed by the functional specification, the design and implementation of the software, and comprehensive testing. The testing generally includes unit,

Fig. 2.3 Waterfall life cycle
model

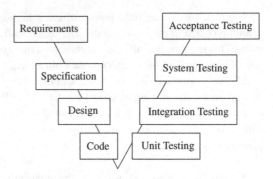

system, and user acceptance testing. The waterfall model is employed for projects where the requirements can be identified early in the project life cycle or are known in advance. It is also called the "V" life cycle model, with the left-hand side of the "V" detailing requirements, specification, design, and coding and the right-hand side detailing unit tests, integration tests, system tests, and acceptance testing. Each phase has entry and exit criteria that must be satisfied before the next phase commences. There are several variations to the waterfall model.

Most companies employ a set of templates to enable the performance of activities in the various phases to be consistently performed. Templates may be employed for project planning and reporting; requirements definition; design; testing; and so on. These templates may be based on the IEEE standards.

2.4.2
Spiral Life Cycles

The spiral model is useful where the requirements are not fully known at project initiation. The requirements evolve as a part of the development life cycle. The development proceeds in a number of spirals, where each spiral typically involves updates to the requirements, design, code, testing and a user review of the particular iteration or spiral.

The spiral is, in effect, a reusable prototype with the business analysts and the customer reviewing the current iteration and providing feedback to the development team. The feedback is then analysed and addressed in subsequent spirals. This approach is often used in joint application development for web-based software development as usability and the look and feel of the application is a key concern. The implementation of part of the system helps in gaining a better understanding of the requirements of the system, and this feeds into subsequent development cycle in the spiral. The process repeats until the requirements and the software product are fully complete.

There are several variations of the spiral model including Rapid Application Development (RAD); Joint Application Development (JAD); and the Dynamic Systems Development Method (DSDM) models. Agile methods have become popular in recent

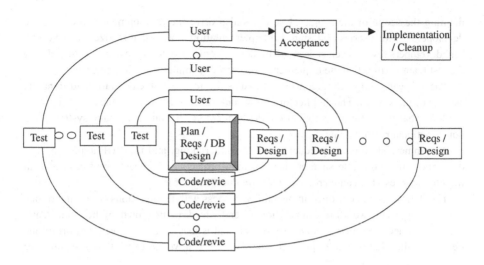

Fig. 2.4 Spiral life cycle model

years and these generally employ sprints (or iterations) of 2 weeks duration to implement a number of user stories. A sample spiral model is shown in Fig. 2.4.

There are other life cycle models, for example, the iterative development process that combines the waterfall and spiral life cycle model. The Cleanroom approach developed by Harlan Mills at IBM includes a phase for formal specification and its approach to software testing is based on the predicted usage of the software product. The Rational Unified Process has become popular in recent years and it is discussed in the next section.

2.4.3
Rational Unified Process

The Rational Unified Process [Jac:99] was developed at the Rational Corporation (now part of IBM), and it uses the Unified Modelling Language (UML) as a tool for specification and design. UML was developed by Rumbaugh, Booch, and Jacobson [ORg:06]. It is a visual modelling language for software systems and provides a means of specifying, constructing, and documenting the object-oriented system. This facilitates the understanding of the architecture and complexity of the system.

The unified process is use case driven, architecture centric, iterative, incremental and includes cycles, phases, workflows, risk mitigation, quality control, project management, and configuration control. Software projects may be very complex, and there are risks that requirements may be missed in the process or that the interpretation of a requirement may differ between the customer and the project team.

Requirements are gathered as *use cases*, and the use cases describe the functional requirements from the point of view of the user of the system. They describe what the system will do at a high level and ensure that there is an appropriate focus on the user when defining the scope of the project. Use cases also drive the development process, as the developers create a series of design and implementation models that realize the use cases. The developers review each successive model for conformance to the use case model, and the test team verifies that the implementation correctly implements the use cases.

The software architecture concept embodies the most significant static and dynamic aspects of the system. The architecture grows out of the use cases and factors such as the platform that the software is to run on, deployment considerations, legacy systems, and non-functional requirements.

A commercial software product is a large undertaking, and the RUP approach is to decompose the work into smaller slices or mini-projects, where each mini-project is an iteration that results in an increment to the product (Fig. 2.5).

The iterations are controlled in the unified process with the iterations consisting of one or more steps in the workflow. An iteration generally leads to the growth of the product, and if there is a need to repeat an iteration then all that is lost is the misdirected effort of one iteration rather that the entire product. That is, RUP is a way to mitigate risk in software engineering (Fig. 2.6).

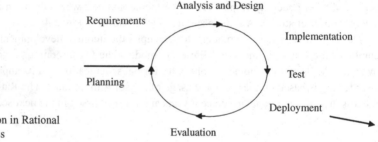

Fig. 2.5 Iteration in Rational Unified Process

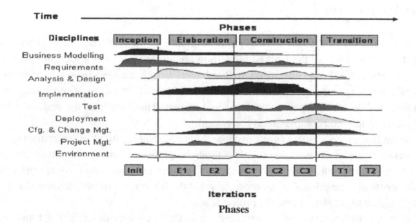

Fig. 2.6 Phases and workflows in Rational Unified Process

The waterfall life cycle is often used in software development. However, it has the disadvantage that the risk is greater towards the end of the project where it is expensive to correct mistakes from earlier phases. An iterative software development process applies the waterfall steps iteratively. That is, the system is developed in a series of increments rather than being developed in one step. An increment is a subset of the system functionality and the software development involves selecting an increment to develop, and then another, and so on. The earliest iterations address the areas of greatest risk to the project. Each iteration produces an executable release and includes integration and testing activities.

The unified process consists of four phases. These are inception, elaboration, construction, and transition. Each phase consists of one or more iterations and an iteration consists of several workflows. The workflows may be requirements, analysis, design, implementation, and test. Each phase terminates in a milestone with one or more project deliverables.

The inception phase identifies and prioritizes the most important risks. It is concerned with the initial project planning and cost estimation and initial work on the architecture and functional requirements for the product. The elaboration phase specifies most of the use cases in detail, and the system architecture is designed. The construction phase is concerned with building the product. At the end of this phase, the product contains all of the use cases that management and the customer have agreed for the release. The system is ready for transfer to the user community. The transition phase covers the period during which the product moves into the customer site and includes activities such as training customer personnel, providing on-site assistance, and correcting defects found after delivery.

2.4.4
Agile Development

There has been a growth of popularity among software developers in lightweight methodologies such as Agile. This is a *software development* methodology that claims to be more responsive to customer needs than traditional methods such as the waterfall model. The waterfall development model is similar to a wide and slow-moving value stream and halfway through the project 100% if the requirements are typically 50% done. However, for agile development 50% of requirements are typically 100% done halfway through the project.

This methodology has a strong collaborative style of working and its approach includes the following:

- Aim is to achieve a narrow fast-flowing value stream
- Feedback and adaptation employed in decision-making
- User stories and sprints are employed
- Stories are either done or not done
- Iterative and incremental development is employed
- A project is divided into iterations
- An iteration has a fixed length (i.e. Timeboxing is employed)

- Entire software development life cycle is employed for the implementation of each story
- Change is accepted as a normal part of life in the Agile world
- Delivery is made as early as possible
- Maintenance is seen as part of the development process
- Refactoring and evolutionary design employed
- Continuous integration is employed
- Short cycle times
- Emphasis on quality
- Stand-up meetings
- Plan regularly
- Direct interaction preferred over documentation
- Rapid conversion of requirements into working functionality
- Demonstrate value early
- Early decision-making

Ongoing changes to requirements are considered to be normal in the Agile world, and it is believed to be more realistic to change requirements regularly throughout the project rather than attempting to define all of the requirements at the start of the project. The methodology includes controls to manage changes to the requirements, and good communication and early regular feedback are an essential part of the process.

A story may be a new feature or a modification to an existing feature. It is reduced to the minimum scope that can deliver business value, and a feature may give rise to several stories. Stories often build upon other stories and the entire software development life cycle is employed for the implementation of each story. Stories are either done or not done, i.e. there is no such thing as a story being 80% done. The story is complete only when it passes its acceptance tests. Stories are prioritized based on a number of factors including

- Business value of story
- Mitigation of risk
- Dependencies on other stories

Sprint planning is performed before the start of an iteration. The goal is to assign stories to the iteration to fill the available time. The estimates for each story and their priority are determined, and the prioritized stories are assigned to the iteration.

A short morning stand-up meeting is held daily during the iteration and attended by the project manager and the project team. It discusses the progress made the previous day, problem reporting and tracking, and the work planned for the day ahead. A separate meeting is conducted for issues that require more detailed discussion.

Once the iteration is complete the latest product increment is demonstrated to an audience including the product owner. This is to receive feedback as well as identifying new requirements. The team also conducts a retrospective meeting to identify what went well and what went poorly during the iteration. This is to identify improvement actions for future iterations.

Agile employs pair programming and a collaborative style of working with the philosophy that two heads are better than one. This allows multiple perspectives in decision-making and a broader understanding of the issues.

Software testing is very important and Agile generally employs automated testing for unit, acceptance, performance, and integration testing. Tests are run often and aim to catch programming errors early. They are generally run on a separate build server to ensure all dependencies are checked. Tests are re-run before making a release. Agile employs test-driven development with tests written before the code. The developers write code to make a test pass with ideally developers only coding against failing tests. This approach forces the developer to write testable code.

Refactoring is employed in Agile as a design and coding practice. The objective is to change how the software is written without changing what it does. Refactoring is a tool for evolutionary design where the design is regularly evaluated and improvements implemented as they are identified. The automated test suite is essential in showing that the integrity of the software is maintained following refactoring.

Continuous integration allows the system to be built with every change. Early and regular integration allows early feedback to be provided. It also allows all of the automated tests to be run, thereby identifying problems earlier.

2.5
Life Cycle Phases

The waterfall software development life cycle consists of various phases including

- Business requirements definition
- Specification of system requirements
- Design
- Implementation
- Unit testing
- System testing
- UAT Testing
- Support and maintenance

2.5.1
Business Requirements Definition

The requirements specify what the customer wants and define what the software system is required to do as distinct from how this is to be done. They are the foundation for the system, and if the requirements are incorrect then the implemented system will be incorrect. Prototyping may be employed to assist in the definition and validation of the requirements.

The prototype will include key parts of the system and the users may examine the prototype to clarify the requirements and to give early feedback. The prototype may be thrown away once the prototyping is complete or it may be reused in the development of the system. The following are characteristics of good requirements (Table 2.1):

Table 2.1 Characteristics of good requirements

No.	Characteristics of good requirements
1.	The requirements are numbered to facilitate traceability
2.	Each requirement is clear and unambiguous
3.	Each requirement is testable
4.	Each requirement has a priority to indicate its importance
5.	Each requirement may be implemented
6.	The requirements have been analysed and any conflicts between the requirements are resolved
7.	Each requirement is broken down as fully as possible
8.	Each requirement is consistent with the project's objectives
9.	Each requirement is necessary
10.	Each requirement is stated as a stakeholder need (i.e. premature design/solution or implementation information is not included)
11.	The requirements are complete and consistent
12.	The requirements are correct
13.	The business requirements are traceable to the system requirements and vice versa
14.	The technical constraints have been identified

The proposed system may be composed of several sub-systems, and the system requirements may therefore be composed of sub-system requirements. The specification of the requirements needs to be unambiguous to ensure that all parties involved in the development of the system understand fully what is to be developed and tested.

The implications of the proposed set of requirements need to be considered, as the choice of a particular requirement may affect the choice of another requirement. For example, one key problem in the telecommunications domain is feature interaction. The problem is that two features may work correctly in isolation, but when present together they interact in an undesirable way. Therefore, feature interactions need to be identified and investigated at the requirements phase to determine how interactions should be resolved.

- Requirement Gathering and Prototyping
  This involves meetings with the stakeholders to gather all relevant information for the proposed product. This includes interviews and requirements workshops to elicit the requirements from the various stakeholders. Prototyping may be employed and this early working system helps to identify gaps and misunderstandings between developers and users. The prototype may also serve as a basis for writing the specification. It involves the following:

  – Define prototype objectives
  – Decide which functional requirements will be prototyped

- Develop the prototype
- Evaluate the prototype

- Requirement Consolidation and Documentation
  This involves the consolidation of the collected information into a coherent set of requirements. In some cases the customer will explicitly produce the requirements, whereas in other cases they will be produced by business analysts in the software organization with an appropriate level of participation from the customers.

  One or more requirements workshops take place with the stakeholders to discuss and prioritize the requirements, as well as identifying and resolving any conflicting requirements. The requirements document is updated accordingly with the agreed requirements for the system.
- Requirements Review and Validation
  This involves validation by the stakeholders to ensure that the defined requirements are actually those desired. This may involve several reviews of the requirements by the stakeholders with updates made by the author until all stakeholders are ready to approve the document as a statement of the requirements of the system.

  The validation of the requirements will ensure that they are complete, consistent, realizable and reflect the needs of the customer.
- Technical Analysis
  This involves analysis to verify the feasibility of the implementation of the requirements and the proposed product.
- Developer/Client Contract
  This involves a written contract between the client and the developer. For bespoke development this will be a legal contract accompanied by a statement of work. For software being developed in-house the contract is essentially the signed off business requirements document which is then subject to formal change control.
- Changes to Requirements
  Changes to the requirements often occur during the software development cycle. It is essential that any proposed changes are evaluated and that the impacts on schedule, effort, budget, and technical areas are fully considered prior to approval of the proposed changes.

  Requirements may change for various reasons such as business or regulatory changes or further desirable requirements only becoming apparent to the customer at a late stage of development or when the system is nearing completion.
- Requirements Specification Notations
  The requirements for a system are generally documented in a natural language such as "English". Natural language is inherently ambiguous and care therefore needs to be taken to ensure precision in the definition of the requirements. It is essential that there is no ambiguity in the specification due to the use of natural language, and this has led to interest in notations to express requirements unambiguously, although these notations are not widely used at this time.

For example, the safety-critical or security-critical fields often employ formal mathematical notations for increased rigour in the specification of the requirements. This includes the use of formal specification languages such as *Z* or *VDM*. The advantage of these mathematical languages is that they are precise and amenable to proof, and mathematical analysis may be employed to debug[11] the requirements. This provides increased confidence in the correctness and validity of the requirements. The disadvantage of the use of formal methods is that many clients would not understand a formal mathematical specification and would be reluctant to accept it as the system contract.

Other notations to express the requirements include the visual modelling language UML [Rum:99] which has become popular in recent years.

2.5.2
Specification of System Requirements

This phase of the software life cycle involves a detailed specification of the system requirements of the product, and it is essentially a statement of what the software development organization will provide to meet the business requirements. That is, the detailed business requirements are a statement of what the customer wants, whereas the specification of the system requirements is a statement of what will be delivered by the software development organization.

It is essential that the system requirements are valid with respect to the business requirements. Traceability is employed to show that the business requirements are addressed by the system requirements, and the system requirements are reviewed by the stakeholders to ensure that they are valid with respect to the business requirements.

There are two categories of system requirements: namely, functional requirements and non-functional requirements. The functional requirements define the functionality that is required of the system and it may include screen shots and report layouts. The non-functional requirements will generally include security, reliability, performance, and portability requirements, as well as usability and maintainability requirements.

2.5.3
Design

The design of the system consists of engineering activities to describe the architecture or structure of the system as well as activities to describe the algorithms and functions required to implement the system requirements. It is a creative process concerned with how the system will be implemented, and its activities include architecture design, interface design, and data structure design. There are often several possible design solutions for a particular system, and the designer will need to decide on the most appropriate solution.

The starting point is the problem domain and it is essential that the problem to be solved is clearly understood from a number of different angles. A number of potential solutions can then be identified, and each potential solution is then evaluated. This leads to the chosen solution that may, for example, be the simplest and least costly.

---

[11] Essentially, the mathematical language allows the proof of properties of the specification which is useful.

Design is an iterative process and involves describing the system at a number of different levels of abstraction. The designer starts off with an informal picture of the design that is then refined by adding more information.

The design may be specified in various ways such as graphical notations that display the relationships between the components making up the design. The notation may include flow charts or various UML diagrams such as sequence diagrams, state charts. Program description languages or pseudocode may be employed to give specifications of algorithms and data structures that are the basis for implementation. Natural language is often employed to express information that cannot be expressed formally. The design activities include

- Architecture design of system (with all sub-systems)
- Abstract specification of each sub-system
- Interface design (for each sub-system)
- Component design
- Data structure design
- Algorithm design

The design methods employed will give several views of the system:

- Data flow view (system modelled using data transformations that take place)
- Entity-relation view (describes the logical data structures being used)
- Structural view of system components and their interactions

Functional design involves starting with a high-level view of the system and refining it into a more detailed design. The system state is centralized and shared between the functions operating on that state.

Object-oriented design has become popular in recent years and is based on the concept of information hiding developed by Parnas [Par:72]. The system is viewed as a collection of objects rather than functions, with each object managing its own state information. The system state is decentralized and an object is a member of an object class. The definition of a class includes attributes and operations on class members, and these may be inherited from superclasses. Objects communicate by exchanging messages.

It is essential to verify and validate the design with respect to the system requirements, and this will be done by traceability of the design to the system requirements and design reviews.

2.5.4
Implementation

This phase involves translating the design into the target code, and it involves writing or generating the actual code. The code to be produced is typically divided among the development team, with each programmer responsible for one or more modules. The coding activities will generally include code reviews or walkthroughs to ensure that high-quality source code is produced and to verify its correctness. The code reviews will verify that the source code conforms to the coding standards and that maintainability issues are addressed. They will also verify that the code produced is a valid implementation of the software design.

Software reuse has become more important in recent times as it provides a way to speed up the development process. Components or objects that may be reused need to be identified and handled accordingly. The implemented code may use software components that have either been developed internally or purchased off-the-shelf.

The benefits of reuse include increased productivity and a faster time to market. There are inherent risks with customized-off-the shelf (COTS) software as the supplier may decide to no longer support the software or there is no guarantee that a component that has worked successfully in one domain will work correctly in a different domain. It is therefore important to consider the risks of reuse as well as the benefits to be gained from their use.

2.5.5
Testing

Testing is conducted to verify that quality has been built into the software and that the implemented software is valid with respect to the requirements. There are various types of testing that may be conducted including unit testing, integration testing, system testing, performance testing, and user acceptance testing. These are described below:

Unit Testing

Unit testing is performed by the programmer on the completed unit (or module) and prior to its integration with other modules. These tests are written by the programmer, and the objective is to show that the code satisfies the design. Each unit test case is documented and it should include a test objective and the expected result.

Code coverage and branch coverage metrics are often recorded to give an indication of how comprehensive the unit testing has been. These metrics provide visibility into the number of lines of code executed as well as on the branches covered during unit testing.

The developer executes the unit tests; records the results; and corrects any identified defects and re-tests the software. It is becoming popular in recent years to write the unit test cases before the code, and the code is written to pass the unit test cases.

Integration Test

The development team performs this type of testing on the integrated system, once all of the individual units work correctly in isolation. The objective is to verify that all of the modules and their interfaces work correctly together and to identify and resolve any issues. Units may work correctly in isolation but may fail when integrated with other units.

Sub-system Test

Large systems are composed of several sub-systems and the objective of sub-system testing is to verify that each sub-system works correctly prior to the testing of the entire system. It is generally conducted by an independent test group, and the goal is to verify the correctness of each sub-system with respect to the sub-system requirements. Any areas requiring correction will be identified, corrected, and verified.

System Test

The purpose of system testing is to verify that the implementation is valid with respect to the system requirements. It involves the specification of system test cases that are traceable to the system requirements and the execution of these test cases will verify that the system requirements have been correctly implemented. An independent test group generally conducts this type of testing.

Any system requirements that have been incorrectly implemented will be identified and defects logged and reported to the developers. The test group will verify that the corrected software is valid and regression testing will be conducted to verify system integrity. System testing may include security testing, usability testing, and performance testing.

The preparation of the test environment for a large system will require detailed planning as it may require special hardware and tools. It is essential that the test environment be set up as early as possible as the timely execution of the test cases is dependent on it.

Performance Test

The purpose of performance testing is to ensure that the performance of the system is within the bounds specified in the non-functional requirements. It may include load performance testing, where the system is subjected to heavy loads over a long period of time, and stress testing, where the system is subjected to heavy loads during a short time interval.

This testing often involves the simulation of many users using the system, and it involves measuring the response times for various activities. It may also need to determine the scalability of the system to support future growth. Test tools are essential in carrying out this type of testing as a large number of users and heavy loads need to be simulated.

User Acceptance Test

The objective of this type of testing is to verify that the product satisfies the business requirements and meets the customer expectations. It is conducted by business analysts and customer representatives, and its successful completion demonstrates that the customer requirements are satisfied and that the customer is happy to accept the product.

It is usually performed under controlled conditions at the customer site, and it matches the intended real-life behaviour of the system. The customer sees the product in operation and can judge whether the system is fit for purpose.

2.5.6
Maintenance

This phase continues after the release of the software product to the customer. Any problems that the customer notes with the software are reported as per the customer support and maintenance agreement. The support issues will generally require investigation, and the issue may be a defect in the software, an enhancement to the software product, or due to a misunderstanding. The support and maintenance team will identify the causes of any identified defects and will implement an appropriate solution to resolve. Testing is conducted to verify that the solution is correct and that the changes made have not adversely affected other parts of the system. Mature organizations will conduct post-mortems to learn lessons from the defect[12] and will take corrective action to prevent a re-occurrence.

The presence of a maintenance phase suggests an acceptance of the reality that problems with the software will be identified post-release. The role of software inspections and testing is to identify as many defects as possible prior to release and minimize the risk that serious defects will be found post-release. The goal of building a correct and reliable software product the first time is very difficult to achieve, and the customer is always likely to find some issues with the released software product.

It is accepted today that in order to have a good-quality product that quality will need to be considered and built into each step in the development process. The more effective the in-phase inspections of deliverables, the higher the quality of the resulting implementation, with a corresponding reduction in the number of defects detected by the test groups. The testing group plays a key role in verifying that the system is correct, and testing continues until there is confidence that the software is fit for purpose and the number of defects remaining in the software is minimal.

It can never be said with absolute confidence that there are no remaining defects in the software, and at best, all that may be done is to employ statistical techniques as a measure of the confidence that the software is correct.

Some computer scientists such as Dijkstra and Hoare argued that in order to produce correct software the programs ought to be derived from their specifications using mathematics, and that mathematical proof should be employed to demonstrate the correctness of the program with respect to its specification. They argued that this offers a rigorous framework to develop programs adhering to the highest quality constraints. However, in practice mathematical techniques have proved to be cumbersome to use, and to date the mathematical techniques have not gained acceptance in the software engineering community. In general, they have been useful for very small projects but have not scaled up well to large-scale industrial projects.

The safety-critical area is one domain in which mathematical techniques have been successfully applied: for example, the presence or absence of safety properties such as "when a train is in a level crossing, then the gate is closed" is essential to demonstrate in this domain. There is a need for extra rigour in the software development process used in these domains.

Many software companies may consider one defect per thousand lines of code (KLOC) to be reasonable quality. However, if the system contains 1 million lines of code this is equivalent to a 1000 post-release defects, which is unacceptable.

Some mature organizations have a quality objective of three defects per million lines of code. This goal is known as six sigma (6σ) and it was developed by Motorola. It was

---

[12]This is essential for serious defects that have caused significant inconvenience to customers. The software development organization will wish to learn lessons to determine what went wrong in its processes that prevented the defect from been identified during peer reviews and testing. Actions to prevent a re-occurrence will be identified and implemented.

originally applied to its manufacturing businesses and subsequently applied to its software organizations. The intention was to reduce the variability in manufacturing processes and to ensure that the processes performed within strict quantitative process control limits. Motorola was awarded the first Malcom Baldridge Quality award for its commitment to quality as exhibited by the six-sigma initiative.

Six sigma been applied to other manufacturing and software companies to minimize and manage the variability in software processes. There are six steps to six sigma:

- Identify the product (or service) you create.
- Identify your customer and your customer's requirements.
- Identify your needs to satisfy the customer.
- Define the process for doing the work.
- Mistake-proof the process and eliminate waste.
- Ensure continuous improvement by measuring, analysing, and controlling the improved process.

One important measure of quality is customer satisfaction with the company, and customer feedback may be obtained informally or formally. One formal approach is to define a customer satisfaction survey and to request customers to provide structured feedback. The information may be used to determine the overall level of customer satisfaction with the company. The questions in a customer survey questionnaire could include

- Quality and reliability of the product
- Usability of the product
- Testing effectiveness
- Customer support

The feedback from customer satisfaction surveys is valuable, and a mature company will develop appropriate action plans to address the key findings. The trend in customer satisfaction over a period of time is important, as companies will wish to improve to serve their customers better.

2.6
Software Inspections

Software inspections play a key role in building quality into software products and verifying that the products are of high quality. There are a number of well-known approaches such as the Fagan methodology [Fag:76]; Gilb's approach [Glb:94]; and Prince2's approach. Fagan inspections were developed by Michael Fagan of IBM. It is a seven-step process that identifies and removes errors in work products. There is a strong economic case for identifying defects early as the cost of correction increases the later that it is discovered in the software life cycle. The Fagan inspection process mandates that requirement documents, design documents, source code, and test plans are all formally inspected by experts independent of the author of the deliverable to ensure quality.

There are various *roles* defined in the inspection process including the *moderator* who chairs the inspection. The moderator is skilled in the inspection process and is responsible for ensuring that all of the participants receive the appropriate materials for the inspection and that sufficient preparation is done by all. The moderator will chair the inspection meeting and will cancel the inspection if the inspectors have done inadequate preparation. The moderator will also ensure that the inspectors chosen are appropriate and have the required background to inspect the work products. The moderator will ensure that the defects identified are recorded, and that the speed of the inspection does not exceed the recommended guidelines. The *reader's* responsibility is to read or paraphrase the particular deliverable, and the *author* is the creator of the deliverable and has a special interest in ensuring that it is correct. The *tester* role is concerned with the testing viewpoint. The seven steps in the Fagan inspection process [ORg:02] are

- Planning
- Overview
- Prepare
- Inspect
- Process improvement
- Re-work
- Follow-up

The defects identified will generally be classified into various types. A mature organization will record the inspection data, as this will enable analysis to be performed. The data will allow the organization to determine how effective it is in finding defects in the phase that they were created. A phase containment metric is maintained by some organizations, and it records the percentage of defects found by inspections versus the total number of defects found.

2.7
Software Testing

Software testing plays a key role in verifying that a software product is of high quality and matches the customers' quality expectations. It is both a constructive activity in that its role is to verify the correctness of the software and a destructive activity in that the objective is to find as many defects as possible in the software. Testing verifies that the software is fit for purpose and that the requirements have been correctly implemented, as well as identifying defects present in the software.

Various types of testing were discussed in Section 2.5.5. The testing needs to be planned and this includes identifying its scope as well as the test environment, support tools, and resources required.

The test cases are then designed for the various types of testing from the requirements and design documents. Tests are then executed, the results logged and reported, with any defects corrected and re-tested. The quality of the testing is dependent on the maturity of the test process, and a good software test process will include several of the following activities:

- Test planning and risk management
- Dedicated test environment and test tools
- Test case definition
- Test automation
- Formality in handover to test department
- Test execution
- Test result analysis
- Test reporting
- Measurements of test effectiveness
- Post-mortem and test process improvement (Fig. 2.7)

Metrics are generally maintained to provide visibility into the effectiveness of the testing process. Testing is described in more detail in [ORg:02].

2.8
Software Project Management

The timely delivery of high-quality software requires good management and engineering processes. Software projects have a history of being delivered late or over-budget, and good project management practices play a key role in the timely delivery of high-quality and reliable software. Project management includes the following activities:

- Estimation of cost, effort, and schedule for the project
- Identifying and managing risks
- Preparing the project plan
- Preparing the initial project schedule and key milestones
- Obtaining approval for the project plan and schedule
- Staffing the project
- Monitoring progress, budget, schedule, effort, risks, issues, change requests, and quality
- Taking corrective action
- Re-planning and re-scheduling
- Communicating progress to affected stakeholders
- Preparing status reports and presentations

The project plan will contain or reference several other plans such as the project quality plan; the communication plan; the configuration management plan; and the test plan.

Project estimation and scheduling are difficult as often software projects are breaking new ground and differ from previous projects. That is, previous estimates may often not be a good basis for estimation for the current project. Often, unanticipated problems can arise for technically advanced projects, and the estimates may often be optimistic. Gantt

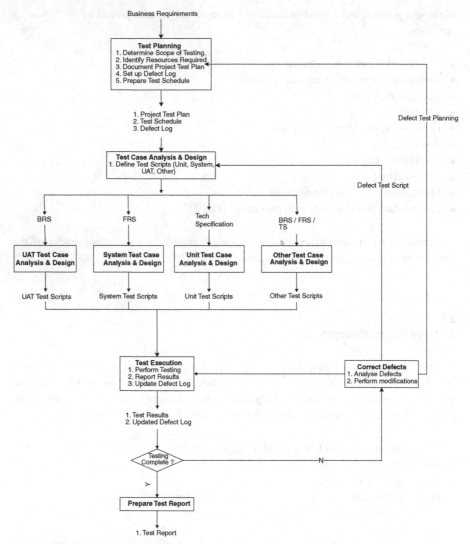

Fig. 2.7 Simplified test process

charts are often employed for project scheduling, and these show the work breakdown for the project as well as task dependencies and allocation of staff to the various tasks.

The effective management of risk during a project is essential to project success. Risks arise due to uncertainty and the risk management cycle involves[13] risk identification; risk

―――――――

[13] These are the risk management activities in the Prince2 methodology.

analysis and evaluation; identifying responses to risks; selecting and planning a response to the risk; and risk monitoring.

Once the risks have been identified they are logged (e.g. in the Risk Log). The likelihood of each risk arising and its impact is then determined. The risk is assigned an owner and an appropriate response to the risk determined.

2.9
Process Maturity Models

The CMMI is a framework to assist an organization in the implementation of best practice in software and systems engineering. It is an internationally recognized model for process improvement and assessment that is used worldwide by thousands of organizations.

The SEI and other quality experts believe that there is a close relationship between the quality of the delivered software and the quality and maturity of the processes used to create the software. Therefore, there is a need to focus on the software process as well as on the product. The SEI applied the process improvement principles used in the manufacturing field to develop process maturity models for the software field, and they developed models such as the CMM and its successor the CMMI.

The CMMI consists of five maturity levels with each maturity level consisting of a number of process areas. Each process area consists of a set of goals, and these goals are implemented by practices related to that process area.

The emphasis on level 2 of the CMMI is on maturing management practices such as project management, requirements management, configuration management. The emphasis on level 3 of the CMMI is to mature engineering and organization practices and to define standard processes for the organization. Level 4 is concerned with ensuring that key processes are performing within strict quantitative limits and adjusting processes to perform within these limits. Level 5 is concerned with continuous process improvement. Maturity levels may not be skipped in the staged implementation of the CMMI as each maturity level is the foundation for the next level.

There is also a continuous representation of the CMMI that allows the organization to focus on improvements to key processes. However, in practice it is often necessary to implement several of the level 2 process areas before serious work can be done on implementing a process at a higher maturity level. The use of metrics [Fen:95, Glb:76] becomes more important as an organization matures, as metrics allow the performance of an organization to be objectively judged.

The CMMI allows organizations to benchmark themselves against other similar organizations. This is generally done by formal SEI SCAMPI appraisals conducted by an authorized SCAMPI lead appraiser. The results of a SCAMPI appraisal are generally reported back to the SEI, and there is a strict qualification process to become an authorized lead appraiser. An appraisal is useful in verifying that an organization has improved, and it enables the organization to prioritize improvements for the next improvement cycle.

The time required to implement the CMMI in an organization depends on its size and current maturity. It generally takes 1–2 years to implement maturity level 2 and a further 1–2 years to implement level 3.

The use of the CMMI provides a solid engineering approach to the development of software. It requires high-quality processes to be in place for project management, requirements development and management, design and development, reviews and testing, independent quality audits, and so on. These include

- Developing and managing requirements
- Doing effective design
- Managing projects
- Selecting and managing subcontractors
- Building quality into the product with peer reviews
- Performing rigorous testing
- Performing independent audits

The CMMI focuses on the management and organization practices rather than on the technical engineering practices. It states what the organization needs to do to mature its processes rather than how this should be done.

2.10
Review Questions

1. What are your views on the Standish Research Reports conducted since 1994 and on the current state of IT project delivery?
2. What are the main challenges in software engineering and how can they be overcome?
3. Describe various software life cycles such as the waterfall model and the spiral model.
4. Discuss the benefits of Agile over conventional approaches. List any risks and disadvantages.
5. Describe the Fagan Inspection Methodology and the Gilb Inspection Methodology. Describe the benefits of software inspections.
6. Describe the main activities that take place in software testing.
7. Describe the main activities in project management and investigate project management methodologies such as Prince2.

2.11
Summary

The birth of software engineering was at the NATO conference held in 1968 in Germany. This conference highlighted the problems that existed in the software sector in the late 1960s, and the term "software crisis" was coined to refer to these. This led to the realization that programming is quite distinct from science and mathematics, and that software engineers need to be properly trained to enable them to build high-quality products that are safe to use.

The Standish group conducts research on the extent of problems with the delivery of projects on time and budget. Their research indicates that it remains a challenge to deliver projects on time, on budget, and with the right quality.

Programmers are like engineers in the sense that they build products. Therefore, programmers need to receive an appropriate education in engineering as part of their training. The education of traditional engineers includes training on product design and an appropriate level of mathematics.

Software engineering involves multi-person construction of multi-version programs. It is a systematic approach to the development and maintenance of the software, and it requires a precise statement of the requirements of the software product and then the design and development of a solution to meet these requirements. It includes methodologies to design, develop, implement, and test software as well as sound project management, quality management, and configuration management practices. Support and maintenance of the software is properly addressed.

Software process maturity models such as the CMMI have become popular in recent years. They place an emphasis on understanding and improving the software process to enable software engineers to be more effective in their work. The next chapter gives an introduction to the CMMI.

Capability Maturity Model Integration

3

Key Topics

> CMMI Maturity Levels
> CMMI Capability Levels
> CMMI Staged Representation
> CMMI Continuous Representation
> CMMI Process Areas
> Appraisals

3.1
Introduction

The Software Engineering Institute[1] developed the Capability Maturity Model (CMM) in the early 1990s as a framework to help software organizations improve their software process maturity. The CMMI is the successor to the older CMM, and its implementation brings best practice in software and systems engineering into the organization. The SEI and many other quality experts believe that there is a close relationship between the maturity of software processes and the quality of the delivered software product.

---

[1] The SEI was founded by the US Congress in 1984 and has worked successfully in advancing software engineering practices in the USA and worldwide. It performs research to find solutions to key software engineering problems, and its proposed solutions are validated through pilots. These solutions are then disseminated to the wider software engineering community through its training programme. The SEI's research and maturity models have played an important role in helping companies to deliver high-quality software consistently on-time and on-budget. The SEI opened a European office in Frankfurt, Germany, in 2004.

G. O'Regan, *Introduction to Software Process Improvement*, Undergraduate Topics in Computer Science, DOI 10.1007/978-0-85729-172-1_3,
© Springer-Verlag London Limited 2011

The CMM was built upon the work of quality gurus such as Deming [Dem:86], Juran [Jur:00], and Crosby [Crs:79]. These quality gurus were effective in transforming struggling manufacturing companies with quality problem to companies that could consistently produce high-quality products. Further, improvement to quality led to cost reductions and higher productivity as less time was spent in re-working defective products. Their success was due to the focus on improving the manufacturing process and in reducing variability in the process. The work of these quality experts is discussed in more detail in [ORg:02].

Similarly, software companies need to have quality software processes to deliver high-quality software to their customers. The SEI has collected empirical data to suggest that there is a close relationship between software process maturity and the quality of the delivered software. Therefore, there is a need to focus on the software process as well as on the product.

The CMM was released in 1991 and its successor, the CMMI® model, was released in 2002 [CKS:06]. The CMMI is a framework to assist an organization in the implementation of best practice in software and systems engineering. It is an internationally recognized model for process improvement and is used worldwide by thousands of organizations.

The focus of the CMMI is on improvements to the software process to ensure that they meet business needs more effectively. A *process* is a set of practices or tasks performed to achieve a given purpose. It may include tools, methods, material, and people. An organization will typically have many processes in place for doing its work, and the object of process improvement is to improve these to meet business goals more effectively.

The process is an abstraction of the way in which work is done in the organization and is seen as the glue (Fig. 3.1) that ties people, procedures, and tools together.

It may be described by a process map which details the flow of activities and tasks. The process map will include the input to each activity and the output from each activity. Often, the output from one activity will become the input to the next activity. A simple example of a process map for creating the system requirements specification is described in Fig. 3.2. The input is the business requirements and the output is the systems requirements specification.

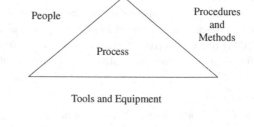

Fig. 3.1 Process as glue for people, procedures, and tools

Fig. 3.2 Sample process map

The origins of the software process improvement field go back to Walter Shewhart's work in the 1930s on statistical process control. This work was later refined by Deming and Juran, and these quality gurus argued that high-quality processes are essential to the delivery of a high-quality product, and that the quality of the end product is largely determined by the processes used to produce and support it.

The ISO/IEC 12207 standard for software processes distinguishes between several categories of software processes including the primary life cycle processes for developing and maintaining software; supporting processes to support the software development life cycle; and organization life cycle processes. These are summarized in Fig. 3.3.

Watt Humphries began applying the ideas of Deming, Juran, and Crosby to software development at IBM. His approach was published in his book *Managing the Software Process* [Hum:89], and he later moved to the SEI to work on software process maturity models with the other SEI experts. The SEI released the Capability Maturity Model in the early 1990s and this process model has proved to be effective in assisting companies in improving their software engineering practices and in achieving consistent results and high-quality software.

The CMM is a process model and it defines the characteristics or best practices of good processes. It does not prescribe how the processes should be done and allows the organization the freedom to interpret the model to suit its particular context and business needs. It also provides a roadmap for an organization to get from where it is today to a higher level of maturity. The advantage of model-based improvement is that it provides a place to start process improvements and a common language and shared vision.

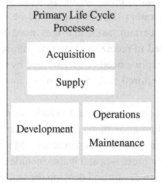
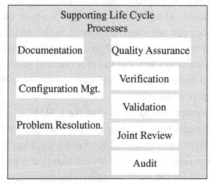
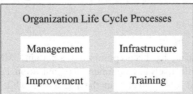

Fig. 3.3 ISO/IEC 12207 standard for software engineering processes

The CMM model consists of five maturity levels with the higher maturity levels representing advanced software engineering capability. The lowest maturity level is level 1 and the highest is level 5. The SEI developed an assessment methodology to determine the maturity of software organizations, and initially most organizations were assessed at level 1 maturity. However, over time companies embarked on improvement initiatives and matured their software processes, and many companies are now performing at the higher maturity levels.

The first company to be assessed at CMM level 5 maturity[2] was the Motorola plant in Bangalore in India. The success of the software CMM led to the development of other process maturity models such as the systems engineering capability maturity mode (CMM/SE) which is concerned with maturing systems engineering practices, and the people capability maturity model (P-CMM) which is concerned with improving the ability of the software organizations to attract, develop, and retain talented software engineering professionals.

The SEI commenced work on the CMMI® [CKS:06] in the late 1990s. This is a replacement for the older CMM model and its development included merging the software CMM and systems CMM, and ensuring that the new model was compatible with the ISO 15504 standard.[3] It is described in the next section.

3.2
The CMMI

The CMMI consists of five maturity levels with each maturity level (except level 1) consisting of a number of process areas. Each process area consists of a set of goals and these must be implemented by a set of related practices in order for the process area to be satisfied. The practices specify what is to be done rather than how it should be done. Processes are activities associated with carrying out certain tasks, and they need to be defined and documented. The users of the process need to receive appropriate training to enable them to carry out the process, and process discipline need to be enforced by independent audits. Process performance needs to be monitored and improvements made to ineffective processes.

The emphasis for level 2 of the CMMI is on maturing management practices such as project management, requirements management, configuration management. The emphasis on level 3 of the CMMI is on maturing engineering and organization practices. Maturity level 3 is concerned with defining standard organization processes and it also includes process areas for the various engineering activities needed to design and develop the software.

---

[2]Of course, the fact that a company has been appraised at a certain CMM or CMMI rating is no guarantee that it is performing effectively as a commercial organization. For example, the Motorola plant in India was appraised at CMM level 5 in the late 1990s while Motorola lost business opportunities in the GSM market.

[3]ISO 15504 (popularly known as SPICE) is an international standard for software process assessment.

Level 4 is concerned with ensuring that key processes are performing within strict quantitative limits and adjusting processes, where necessary, to perform within these limits. Level 5 is concerned with continuous process improvement. Maturity levels may not be skipped in the staged implementation of the CMMI, as each maturity level is the foundation for work on the next level.

There is also a continuous representation[4] of the CMMI that allows the organization to focus its improvements on key processes that are closely related to its business goals. This allows it the freedom to choose an approach that should result in the greatest business benefit rather than proceeding on the standard improvement roadmap. However, in practice it is often necessary to implement several of the level 2 process areas before serious work can be done on maturing a process to a higher capability level. The motivation for the implementation of the CMMI includes the following (Table 3.1 and Fig. 3.4):

Table 3.1 Motivation for CMMI implementation

Motivation for CMMI implementation
Enhances the credibility of the company
Marketing benefit of CMMI maturity level
Implementation of best practice in software and systems engineering
Logical path to improvement
It increases the capability and maturity of an organization
It increases the capability of subcontractors
It provides improved technical and management practices
It leads to higher quality of software
It leads to increased timeliness of projects
It reduces the cost of maintenance and incidence of defects
It allows the measurement of processes and products
It allows projects/products to be quantitatively managed
It allows innovative technologies to be rigorously evaluated to enhance process performance
It improves customer satisfaction
It changes the culture from fire fighting to fire prevention
It leads to a culture of improvement
It leads to higher morale in company

The CMMI model covers both the software engineering and systems engineering disciplines. Systems engineering is concerned with the development of systems that may or may not include software, whereas software engineering is concerned with the development of

---

[4]This book is focused on the implementation of the staged representation of the CMMI rather than the continuous representation. This is my preferred approach to process improvement as it provides a clearly defined roadmap and also allows benchmarking of organizations. Appraisals against the staged representation are useful since a CMMI maturity level rating is awarded to the organization, and the company may use this to publicize its software engineering capability.

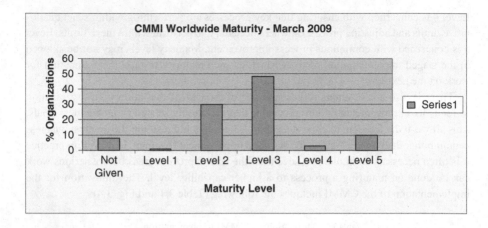

Fig. 3.4 CMMI worldwide maturity

software systems. The model contains extra information relevant to a particular discipline, and this is done by discipline amplification.[5]

The CMMI allows organizations to benchmark themselves against similar organizations. This is generally done by a formal SEI SCAMPI Class A appraisal[6] conducted by an authorized SCAMPI lead appraiser. The results will generally be reported back to the SEI, and there is a strict qualification process to become an authorized lead appraiser. The qualification process helps to ensure that the appraisals are conducted fairly and objectively and that the results are consistent. An appraisal is useful in verifying that an organization has improved, and it enables the organization to prioritize improvements for the next improvement cycle. Small organizations will often prefer a SCAMPI Class B or C appraisal as these are less expensive and time consuming.[7]

The time required to implement the CMMI in an organization depends on its size and current maturity. It generally takes 1–2 years to implement maturity level 2, and a further 2–3 years to implement level 3. The implementation of the CMMI needs to be balanced

---

[5]Discipline amplification is a specialized piece of information that is relevant to a particular discipline. It is introduced in the model by text such as "For Systems Engineering".

[6]A SCAMPI appraisal is a systematic examination of the processes in an organization to determine the maturity of the organization with respect to the CMMI. An appraisal team consists of a SCAMPI lead appraiser, one or more external appraisers, and usually one internal appraiser. It consists of interviews with senior and middle management and reviews with project managers and project teams. The appraisers will review documentation and determine the extent to which the processes defined are effective as well as the extent to which they are institutionalized in the organization. Data will be gathered and reviewed by the appraisers, ratings produced, and the findings presented to the organization.

[7]Small organizations may not have the budget for a formal SCAMPI Class A appraisal. They may be more interested in an independent SCAMPI Class B or C appraisal, which is used to provide feedback on their strengths and opportunities for improvement. Feedback allows the organization to focus its improvement efforts for the next improvement cycle.

Table 3.2   Benefits of CMMI implementation

Benefit	Actual saving
Cost	34%
Schedule	50%
Productivity	61%
Quality	48%
Customer satisfaction	14%
Return on investment	4:1

against the day-to-day needs of the organization in delivering products and services to its customers.

The SEI has gathered data from organization on the benefits gained from the implementation of the CMMI. The quantitative results in Table 3.2 are the median results reported to the SEI [SEI:09].

The processes implemented during a CMMI initiative will generally include the following:

– Developing and managing requirements
– Design and development
– Project management
– Selecting and managing subcontractors
– Managing change and configurations
– Peer reviews
– Risk management and decision analysis
– Testing
– Audits

3.3
CMMI Maturity Levels

The CMMI is divided into five maturity levels (Fig. 3.5) with each maturity level (except level 1) consisting of several process areas. The maturity level of an organization is a predictor of the results that will be obtained from following the software processes in the organization. The higher the maturity level of the organization, the more capable it is and the more predictable its results. The current maturity level acts as the foundation for the improvements to be made in the move to the next level.

The maturity levels provide a roadmap for improvements in the organization, and maturity levels are not skipped in a staged implementation. A particular maturity level is achieved only when all process areas belonging to that maturity level (and all process

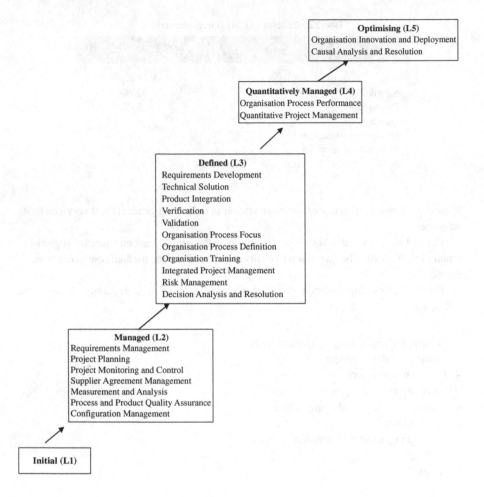

Fig. 3.5 CMMI maturity levels

areas belonging to lower maturity levels) have been successfully implemented and institutionalized[8] in the organization (Table 3.3).

The implementation of the CMMI generally starts with improvements to processes at the project level. The focus at level 2 is on improvements to managing projects and suppliers, and improving project management, supplier selection, and management practices, and so on.

---

[8] Institutionalization is a technical term and means that the process is ingrained in the way in which work is performed in the organization. An institutionalized process is defined, documented, and followed in the organization. All staff have been appropriately trained in its use and process discipline is enforced via audits. It is explained by the phrase "That's the way we do things around here".

Table 3.3   CMMI maturity levels

Maturity level	Description
Initial	Processes are often ad hoc or chaotic with performance usually unpredictable. Success in a level 1 organization is often due to the heroics of people rather than having high-quality processes in place. Level 1 organizations often abandon the defined process in times of crisis, and there is no mechanism in place to enforce the process
	These immature organizations are often unable to repeat previous success, since success is due to heroic efforts of its people rather than processes. These organizations often over-commit as they often lack an appropriate estimation process on which to base project commitments
	Fire fighting is a way of life in these organizations. High-quality software might be produced but at a cost including long hours, high level of re-work, over-budget, and schedule and unhappy customers. Projects do not perform consistently as their success is dependent on the people involved
	Among the weaknesses in the processes are poor change control, poor estimation and project planning, few procedures, and weak enforcement of standards
Managed	A level 2 organization has good project management practices in place, and planning and managing new projects is based on experience with similar previous projects
	The process is planned, performed, and controlled. A level 2 organization is disciplined in following processes, and the process is enforced with independent audits
	The status of the work products produced by the process is visible to management at major milestones, and changes to work products are controlled. The work products are placed under appropriate configuration management control
	The requirements for a project are managed and changes to the requirements are controlled. Project management practices are in place to manage the project, and an elementary set of measures are defined for budget, schedule, and effort variance. Subcontractors are managed
	Independent audits are conducted to enforce the process. The processes in a level 2 organization are defined at the project level
Defined	A maturity level 3 organization has standard processes defined that support the whole organization
	These standard processes ensure consistency in the way that projects are conducted across the organization. There are guidelines defined that allow the organization process to be tailored and applied to each project
	There are standards in place for design and development and procedures defined for effective risk management and decision analysis
	Level 3 processes are generally defined more rigorously than level 2 processes, and the definition includes the purpose of the process, inputs, entry criteria, activities, roles, measures, verification steps, output, and exit criteria. There is also an organization-wide training programme

Table 3.3 (continued)

Maturity level	Description

Quantitatively managed	A level 4 organization sets quantitative goals for the performance of key processes, and these processes are controlled using statistical techniques
	    Processes are stable and perform within narrowly defined limits. Software process and product quality goals are set and managed
	    A level 4 organization has predictable process performance, with variation in process performance identified and the causes of variation corrected

Optimizing	A level 5 organization has a continuous process improvement culture in place, and processes are improved based on a quantitative understanding of variation Defect prevention activities are an integral part of the development life cycle. New technologies are evaluated and introduced (where appropriate) into the organization. Processes may be improved incrementally or through innovative process and technology improvements

The improvements at level 3 involve a shift from the focus on projects to the organization. It involves defining standard processes for the organization, and projects may then tailor the standard process (using tailoring guidelines) to produce the project's software process. Projects are not required to do everything in the same way as the tailoring of the process allows the project's defined software process to reflect the unique characteristics of the project, i.e. a degree of variation is allowed as per the tailoring guidelines.

The implementation of level 3 requires defining procedures and standards for engineering activities such as design, coding, and testing. Procedures are defined for peer reviews, testing, risk management, and decision analysis.

The implementation of level 4 involves achieving process performance within defined quantitative limits. This involves the use of metrics and setting quantitative goals for project and process performance, and managing process performance. The implementation of level 5 is concerned with achieving a culture of continuous improvement in the company. The causes of defects are identified and resolution actions implemented to prevent a re-occurrence.

3.3.1
CMMI Representations

The CMMI is available in the staged and continuous representations. Both representations use the same process areas as well as the same specific and generic goals and practices.

The staged representation was described in Fig. 3.5 and is the approach used in this book. It follows the well-known improvement roadmap from maturity level 1 through

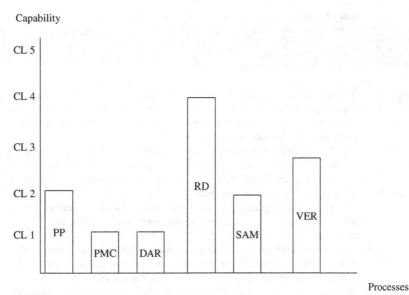

Fig. 3.6 CMMI capability levels

improvement cycles until the organization has achieved its desired level of maturity. The staged approach is concerned with organization maturity and allows statements of organization maturity to be made, whereas the continuous representation is concerned with individual process capability.

The continuous representation is illustrated in Fig. 3.6 and it has been influenced by the ISO 15504 standard for process assessment. It is concerned with improving the capability of selected processes and gives the organization the freedom to choose the order of improvements that best meet their business needs. The continuous representation allows statements of individual process capability to be made. It employs six capability levels and a process is rated at a particular capability level.

Each capability level consists of a set of specific and generic goals and practices, and the capability levels provide a path for process improvement within the process area. Process improvement is achieved by the evolution of a process from its current capability level to a higher capability level. For example, a company may wish to mature its project planning process from its current process rating of capability level 2 to a rating of capability level 3. This requires the implementation of practices to define a standard project planning process as well as collecting improvement data. The capability levels are given in Table 3.4.

An incomplete process is a process that is either not performed or only partially performed. A performed process carries out the expected practices and work products. However, such a process may not be adequately planned or enforced. A managed process is planned and executed with appropriately skilled and trained personnel to carry out the tasks and activities. The process is monitored and controlled and periodically enforced via audits.

Table 3.4 CMMI capability levels for continuous representation

Capability level	Description
Incomplete (0)	The process does not implement all of the capability level 1 generic and specific practices. The process is either not performed or partially performed
Performed (1)	A process that performs all of the specific practices and satisfies its specific goals. Performance may not be stable
Managed (2)	A process at this level has infrastructure to support the process. It is managed, i.e. planned and executed in accordance with policy, its users are trained; it is monitored and controlled and audited for adherence to its process description
Defined (3)	A process at this level has a defined process, i.e. a managed process that is tailored from the organization's set of standard processes. It contributes work products, measures, and other process improvement information to the organization's process assets
Quantitatively managed (4)	A process at this level is a quantitatively managed process, i.e. a defined process that is controlled by statistical techniques. Quantitative objectives for quality and process performance are established and used to control the process
Optimizing (5)	A process at this level is an optimizing process, i.e. a quantitatively managed process that is continually improved through incremental and innovative improvements

A defined process is a managed process that is tailored from the standard process in the organization using tailoring guidelines. A quantitatively managed process is a defined process that is controlled using quantitative techniques. An optimizing process is a quantitatively managed process that is continuously improved through incremental and innovative improvements.

The process is rated at a particular capability level provided it satisfies all of the specific and generic goals of that capability level, and it also satisfies the specific and generic goals of all lower capability levels (Fig. 3.7).

This book is concerned with the implementation of the staged representation of the CMMI. The reader is referred to [CKS:06] for further information on the continuous representation.

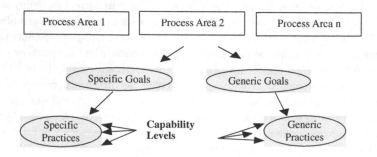

Fig. 3.7 CMMI – continuous representation

3.4
Categories of CMMI Processes

The process areas on the CMMI can be divided into four categories. These are given in Table 3.5.

Table 3.5   CMMI process categories

Maturity level	Description
Process management	The process areas in this category are concerned with activities to define, plan, implement, deploy, monitor, control, appraise, measure, and improve the processes in the organization. They include – Organization process focus – Organization process definition – Organization training – Organization process performance – Organization innovation and deployment
Project management	These process areas are concerned with activities to create and maintain a project plan, tailoring the standard process to produce the project's defined process, monitoring progress with respect to the plan, taking corrective action, the selection and management of suppliers, and the management of risk. They include – Project planning – Project monitoring and control – Risk management – Integrated project management – Supplier agreement management – Quantitative project management
Engineering	These process areas are concerned with engineering activities such as determining and managing requirements, designing and developing the software, testing, and maintenance of the product. They include – Requirements development – Requirements management – Technical solution – Product integration – Verification – Validation
Support	These process areas include activities that support product development and maintenance. They include – Configuration management – Process and product quality assurance – Measurement and analysis – Decision analysis and resolution

3.5
CMMI Process Areas

This section provides an overview of the process areas of the CMMI model. All maturity levels with the exception of level 1 contain several process areas. The process area are described in more detail in later chapters (Table 3.6).

Table 3.6 CMMI process areas

Maturity level	Process area	Description of process area
Level 2	REQM	*Requirements management* This process area is concerned with managing the requirements for the project and ensuring that the requirements, project plan(s), and work products are kept consistent
	PP	*Project planning* This process area is concerned with estimation for the project, developing and obtaining commitment to the project plan, and maintaining the plan
	PMC	*Project monitoring and control* This process area is concerned with monitoring progress with the project and taking corrective action when project performance deviates from the plan
	SAM	*Supplier agreement management* This process area is concerned with the selection of suppliers, documenting the (legal) agreement/statement of work with the supplier, and managing the supplier during the execution of the agreement
	MA	*Measurement and analysis* This process area is concerned with determining management information needs and measurement objectives. Measures are then specified to meet these objectives, and data collection and analysis procedures are defined. Data are collected and measurements analysed and communicated
	PPQA	*Process and product quality assurance* This process area is concerned with providing objective visibility to management on the extent of process compliance. Non-compliance issues are documented and resolved by the project team
	CM	*Configuration management* This process area is concerned with the management of change. It involves setting up a configuration management system; identifying the items that will be subject to change control and controlling changes to them. Configuration audits are conducted

Table 3.6 (continued)

Maturity level	Process area	Description of process area
Level 3	RD	*Requirements development* This process area is concerned with eliciting and defining customer, product, and product–component requirements and analysing and validating the requirements
	TS	*Technical solution* This process area is concerned with the design, development, and implementation of an appropriate solution to the customer requirements
	PI	*Product integration* This process area is concerned with the assembly of the product components to deliver the product, and verifying that the assembled components function correctly together
	VER	*Verification* This process area is concerned with ensuring that selected work products satisfy their specified requirements. This is achieved by peer reviews and testing
	VAL	*Validation* This process area is concerned with demonstrating that the product or product component is fit for purpose and satisfies its intended use
	OPF	*Organization process focus* This process area is concerned with planning and implementing process improvements based on a clear understanding of the current strengths and weakness of the organization's processes
	OPF	*Organization process definition* This process area is concerned with creating and maintaining a usable set of organization processes. This allows consistent process performance across the organization
	OT	*Organization training* This process area is concerned with developing the skills and knowledge of people to enable them to perform their roles effectively
	IPM	*Integrated project management* This process area is concerned with tailoring the organization set of standard processes to define the project's defined process. The project is managed according to the project's defined process
	RSKM	*Risk management* This process area is concerned with identifying risks and determining their probability of occurrence and impact should they occur. Risks are identified and managed throughout the project
	DAR	*Decision analysis and resolution* This process area is concerned with formal decision-making. It involves identifying options, specifying evaluation criteria and method, performing the evaluation, and recommending a solution

Table 3.6 (continued)

Maturity level	Process area	Description of process area
Level 4	OPP	*Organization process performance* This process area is concerned with obtaining a quantitative understanding of the performance of selected organization processes in order to quantitatively manage projects in the organization
	QPM	*Quantitative project management* This process area is concerned with quantitatively managing the project's defined process to achieve the project's quality and performance objectives
Level 5	OID	*Organization innovation and deployment* This process area is concerned with incremental and innovative process improvements
	QPM	*Causal analysis and resolution* This process area is concerned with identifying causes of defects and taking corrective action to prevent a re-occurrence in the future

3.6
Components of CMMI Process Areas

The maturity level of an organization indicates the expected results that its projects will achieve and is a predictor of future project performance. Each maturity level consists of a number of process areas, and each process area consists of specific and generic goals and specific and generic practices. Each maturity level is the foundation for improvements for the next level.

The specific goals and practices are listed first and then followed by the generic goals and practices. The specific goals and practices are unique to the process area being implemented and are concerned with what needs to be done to perform the process. The specific practices are linked to a particular specific goal, and they describe activities that when performed achieve the associated specific goal for the process area (Fig. 3.8).

The generic goals and practices are common to all process areas for that maturity level and are concerned with process institutionalization at that level. Four common features organize the generic practices and these are the following:

– Commitment to perform
– Ability to perform
– Directing implementation
– Verifying implementation

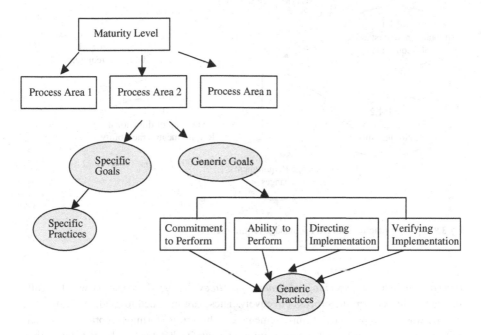

Fig. 3.8 CMMI staged model

They describe activities that when implemented achieve the associated generic goal(s) for the process area. The commitment to perform practices relate to the creation of policies and sponsorship of process improvement; the ability to perform practices are related to the provision of appropriate resources and training to perform the process; the directing implementation practices relate to activities to control and manage the process; and verifying practices relate to activities to verify adherence to the process.

The implementation of the generic practices institutionalizes the process and makes it ingrained in the way that work is done. Institutionalization means that the process is defined, documented, and understood. Process users are appropriately trained and the process is enforced by independent audits. Institutionalization helps to ensure that the process is performed consistently and is more likely to be retained during times of stress. The degree of institutionalization is reflected in the extent to which the generic goals and practices are satisfied. The generic practices ensure the sustainability of the specific practices over time.

There is one specific goal associated with the requirements management process area and it has five associated specific practices (Fig. 3.9):

The components of the CMMI model are grouped into three categories: namely, required, expected, and informative components. The *required category* is essential to achieving goals in a particular area and includes the *specific* and *generic goals* that must be implemented and institutionalized for the process area to be satisfied. The *expected*

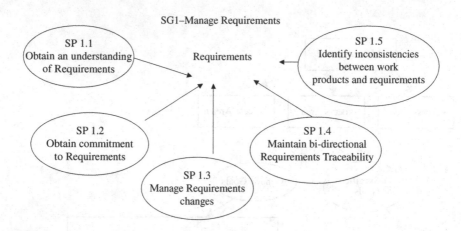

Fig. 3.9 Specific practices for SG1 – manage requirements

category includes the *specific and generic practices* that an organization will typically implement to perform the process effectively. These are intended to guide individuals or groups who are implementing improvements or who are performing appraisals to determine the current maturity of the organization. They state what needs to be done rather than how it should be done thereby giving freedom on the most appropriate implementation for the organization.

The informative category includes information to guide the implementer on how best to approach the implementation of the specific and generic goals and practices. These include *sub-practices, typical work products, discipline amplifications*. This information assists with the implementation of the process area.

The implementation and institutionalization of a process area involves the implementation of the specific and generic practices. The specific practices are concerned with process implementation and are described in detail in later chapters. The generic practices are concerned with process institutionalization and are summarized in Table 3.7.

The generic goals support an evolution of process maturity, and the implementation of each generic goal provides a foundation for further process improvements. That is, a process rated at a particular maturity level has all of the maturity of a process at the lower levels and the additional maturity of its rated level. In other words, a defined process is a managed process; a quantitatively managed process is a defined process; and so on.

Several of the CMMI process areas support the implementation of the generic goals and practices. These process areas contain one or more specific practices that when implemented may either fully implement a generic practice or generate a work product that is used in the implementation of the generic practice. The implementation of the generic practices is supported by the following process areas (Table 3.8).

Table 3.7 CMMI generic practices

Generic goal	Generic practice	Description of generic practice
GG 1 Performed process	GP 1.1	*Perform base practices* The purpose of this generic practice is to produce the work products and services associated with the process (i.e. as specified in the specific practices). These practices may be done informally without following a documented process description and success is dependent on the individuals performing the work. That is, the basic process is performed but it may be immature
GG 2 Managed process	GP 2.1	*Organization policy* The organization policy is established by senior management and sets management expectations of the organization
	GP 2.2	*Plan the process* This generic practice is concerned with preparing a plan to perform the process. The plan will assign responsibilities and document the resources needed to perform the process as well as any training requirements. The plan/schedule are revised as appropriate
	GP 2.3	*Provide resources* The purpose of this generic practice is to ensure that the resources required to perform the process (as specified in the plan) are available when required
	GP 2.4	*Assign responsibility* The purpose of this generic practice is to assign responsibility for performing the process and developing the work products
	GP 2.5	*Train people* This generic practice is concerned with ensuring that people receive the appropriate training to enable them to perform and support the process
	GP 2.6	*Manage configurations* This generic practice is concerned with identifying the work products created by the process that will be subject to configuration management control. These are documented in the plan for the process
	GP 2.7	*Identify and involve relevant stakeholders* This is concerned with ensuring that the stakeholders are identified (as described in the plan for the process) and involved appropriately during the execution of the process

Table 3.7   (continued)

Generic goal	Generic practice	Description of generic practice
	GP 2.8	*Monitor and control the process* This generic practice is concerned with monitoring process performance and taking corrective action when necessary
	GP 2.9	*Objectively evaluate adherence* This generic practice is concerned with conducting audits to verify that process execution adheres to the process description
	GP 2.10	*Review status with higher level management* This generic practice is concerned with providing higher level management with appropriate visibility into the process
GG 3 Defined process	GP 3.1	*Establish a defined process* This generic practice is concerned with tailoring the organization set of standard processes to produce the defined process
	GP 3.2	*Collect improvement information* This generic practice is concerned with collecting improvement information and work products to support future improvement of the processes
GG 4 Quantitatively managed process	GP 4.1	*Establish quantitative objectives* This is concerned with agreeing quantitative objectives (e.g. quality/performance) for the process with the stakeholders
	GP 4.2	*Stabilize sub-process performance* This generic practice is concerned with stabilizing the performance of one or more key sub-processes of the process using statistical techniques. This enables the process to achieve its objectives
GG 5 Optimizing process	GP 5.1	*Ensure continuous process improvement* This generic practice is concerned with systematically improving selected processes to meet quality and process performance targets
	GP 5.2	*Correct root cause of problems* This generic practice is concerned with analysing defects encountered to correct the root cause of these problems and to prevent re-occurrence

Table 3.8 Implementation of generic practices

Generic goal	Generic practice	Process area supporting implementation of generic practice
GG 2 Managed process	GP 2.2 Plan the process	Project planning
	GP 2.5 Train the people	Organization training Project planning
	GP 2.6 Manage configurations	Configuration management
	GP 2.7 Identify/involve relevant stakeholders	Project planning
	GP 2.8 Monitor and control the process	Project monitoring and control
	GP 2.9 Objectively evaluate adherence	Process and product quality assurance
GG 3 Defined process	GP 3.1 Establish defined process	Integrated project management Organization process definition
	GP 3.2 Improvement information	Integrated project management Organization process focus Organization process definition
GG 4 Quantitatively managed process	GP4.1 Establish quantitative objectives for process	Quantitative project management Organization process performance
	GP 4.2 Stabilize sub-process performance	Quantitative project management Organization process performance
GG 5 Optimizing process	GP 5.1 Ensure continuous process improvement	Organization innovation and deployment
	GP 5.2 Correct root cause of problems	Causal analysis and resolution

3.7
SCAMPI Appraisals

Many organizations that embark on a CMMI improvement initiative will arrange to have an appraisal conducted to better understand their current software process maturity. The appraisal is an independent examination of the processes used in the organization against the CMMI standard. Its objective is to identify strengths and weaknesses in the processes and to prioritize improvements for the next improvement cycle.

The SCAMPI methodology is the appraisal methodology used with the CMMI and it comes in three distinct flavours (SCAMPI Classes A, B, C). These classes vary in formality, the cost, effort, and timescales involved; the rating of the processes; and the reporting of results.

A large organization generally has more funding available for appraisals, and it will often be interested in a formal SCAMPI Class A appraisal. This allows it to obtain a formal CMMI rating that may be reported back to the SEI, and it may then benchmark itself against other organizations. Smaller organizations will often arrange to have a less expensive SCAMPI Class C appraisal conducted to identify strengths and weaknesses in its processes. Appraisals allow an organization to

– Understand the strengths and weaknesses in its processes
– Understand its current maturity
– Prioritize improvements for the next improvement cycle
– Benchmark itself against other organizations (SCAMPI Class A)
– Relate its strengths and weaknesses to the CMMI practices

The scope of the appraisal includes the process areas to be examined, and the projects and organization unit. It may be limited to the level 2 process areas or the level 2 and level 3 process areas, and so on. The scope depends on how active the organization has been in process improvement and the extent to which it has implemented software engineering best practice.

The appraisal will identify gaps that exist with respect to the implementation of the CMMI practices for each process area within the scope of the appraisal. The appraisal team will conduct interviews and reviews of documentation, and they will determine the extent of implementation of the practices within scope. The appraisal findings are presented and may be summarized in a written report. The findings are then used to plan and prioritize the next improvement cycle. There are three phases in an appraisal:

– Planning the appraisal
– Conducting the appraisal
– Reporting the results

Chapter 9 discusses appraisals in more detail.

3.8
Review Questions

1. Describe the CMMI model.
2. Describe the staged and continuous representations of the CMMI. What are the advantages and disadvantages of each representation?
3. Describe the CMMI maturity levels and the process areas in each level.

4. What is the purpose of the CMMI generic practices? How are they implemented?
5. What is the difference between implementation and institutionalization in the CMM?
6. What is the purpose of CMMI appraisals and how do they fit into the software process improvement cycle?

3.9
Summary

The Capability Maturity Model Integration is a framework to assist an organization in the implementation of best practice in software and systems engineering. It was developed at the Software Engineering Institute and is used by many organizations around the world.

The SEI and other quality experts believe that there is a close relationship between the quality of the delivered software and the maturity of the processes used to create the software. Therefore, there needs to be a focus on the process as well as on the product, and the CMMI contains best practice in software and systems engineering to assist in the creation of high-quality processes.

The process is seen as the glue that ties people, technology, and procedures coherently together. Processes are activities associated with carrying out certain tasks, and they need to be defined and documented. The users of the process need to receive appropriate training on their use, and process discipline needs to be enforced with independent audits. Process performance needs to be monitored and improvements made to ineffective processes.

The CMMI consists of five maturity levels with each maturity level (except level 1) consisting of several process areas. Each maturity level acts as a foundation for improvement for the next improvement level and each increase in maturity level represents more advanced software engineering capability. The higher the maturity level of the organization, the more capable it is, and the more predictable its results. The lowest level of maturity is maturity level 1 and the highest level is maturity level 5.

Each process area consists of a set of specific and generic goals, and these must be implemented by an associated set of specific and generic practices. The practices specify what is to be done rather than how it should be done, and the organization is given freedom in choosing the most appropriate implementation to meet its needs.

The SCAMPI appraisal methodology is used to determine the maturity of software organizations. This is a systematic examination of the processes used in the organization against the CMMI model, and it includes interviews and reviews of documentation. A successful SCAMPI Class A appraisal allows the organization to report its maturity rating to the SEI and to benchmark itself against other companies. Appraisals are a part of the improvement cycle, and improvement plans are prepared after the appraisal to address the findings and to prioritize improvements.

The next chapter is concerned with setting up a CMMI improvement initiative, and it explains the activities and teams involved.

Setting Up a CMMI Initiative

4

4.1
Introduction

The implementation of the CMMI is a project and as with any project it needs good planning and project management to ensure its success. Once an organization makes a decision to embark on a CMMI initiative, a project manager needs to be appointed to manage the project. The CMMI project manager will treat the implementation as a standard project, and plans are made to implement the CMMI within the approved schedule and budget. The improvement initiative will often consist of several improvement cycles, with each improvement cycle implementing one or more process areas. Small improvement cycles may be employed to implement findings from an appraisal or improvement suggestions from staff.

One of the earliest activities carried out on any improvement initiative is to determine the current maturity of the organization with respect to the CMMI model. This will usually

G. O'Regan, *Introduction to Software Process Improvement*, Undergraduate Topics
in Computer Science, DOI 10.1007/978-0-85729-172-1_4,
© Springer-Verlag London Limited 2011

involve a SCAMPI[1] Class B or C appraisal conducted by one or more experienced appraisers. The findings will indicate the current strengths and weaknesses of the processes as well as gaps with respect to the practices in the CMMI. This initial appraisal is important, as it allows management in the organization to understand its current maturity with respect to the model and to communicate where it wants to be, as well as how it plans to get there. The initial appraisal assists in prioritizing improvements for the first improvement cycle, which is usually to implement the CMMI level 2 process areas. These include

- Project planning and monitoring and control
- Requirements management
- Configuration management
- Process and product quality assurance
- Measurement and Analysis
- Selection and Management of Suppliers

The project manager will then prepare a project plan and schedule. The plan will detail the scope of the initiative, the budget, the process areas to be implemented, the teams and resources required, the initial risks identified, the key milestones, the quality and communication plan, and so on.

The project schedule will detail the deliverables to be produced, the resources required, and the associated timeline for delivery.

4.2
Approach to Continuous Improvement

The need for a process improvement initiative often arises due to the realization that the organization is weak in some areas in software engineering, and that it needs to improve to achieve its business goals more effectively. The starting point of any improvement initiative is an examination of the business needs of the organization, and these may include goals such as delivering high-quality products on time or delivering products faster to the market.

The software process improvement initiative is designed to support the organization in achieving its business goals more effectively. The steps include examining organization needs; conducting an appraisal to determine the current strengths and weaknesses; and analysing the results to formulate an improvement plan. The improvement plan is

---

[1]There are three types of SCAMPI appraisals (Class A, B, C) which may be carried out in an organization, and they vary in formality and expense. A SCAMPI Class A appraisal has strict requirements and the appraisal team consists of four to nine members. It is conducted when an organization wants its processes rated against the CMMI standard to benchmark itself against other organizations. The appraisal results including the maturity rating are reported back to the SEI. A SCAMPI Class C appraisal is the least formal and costly appraisal type and is generally sufficient at the start of an improvement initiative.

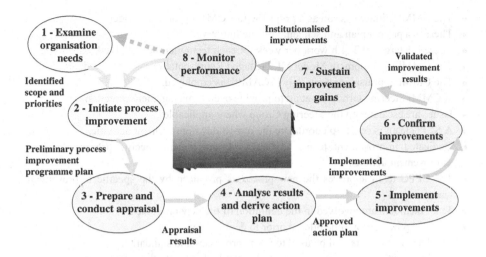

Fig. 4.1 Steps in process improvement

then implemented; the improvements monitored and confirmed as being effective; and the improvement cycle repeat. These steps are described in Fig. 4.1.

There is more than one approach to implement the CMMI. A small organization has fewer resources available, and team members will typically be working part-time. Larger organizations may be able to assign people full-time to the improvement project. The improvement cycle suggested in this book is influenced by the IDEAL model and is described in Fig. 4.2. The following is the approach to improvement suggested in this book:

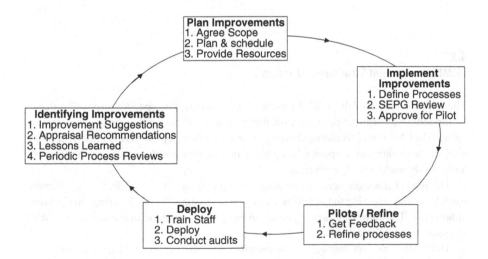

Fig. 4.2 Continuous improvement cycle

- The CMMI initiative is run as a project with a CMMI project manager.
- There is a project plan and schedule for the initiative.
- There is a target of 3–4 h work per week for each team member involved.
- The CMMI Development Model V1.2 (Staged Representation) is employed.
- The CMMI appraisal methodology (SCAMPI) is employed.
- A CMMI Steering Group is set up to provide overall management direction.
- Issues are escalated to the Steering Group where applicable.
- A SEPG team is set up to coordinate the day-to-day improvement activities.
- Dedicated improvement teams are set up to implement specific process areas or improvement actions.
- The SEPG team approves the new processes produced by the specific improvement teams.
- Team members are involved in the definition of the new processes.
- Selected processes will be piloted prior to deployment.
- Feedback from pilots will be used to refine processes and standards.
- Staff are trained on the new processes and standards prior to their deployment.
- Staff are encouraged to make improvement suggestions.
- Audits are conducted to verify that the processes are followed.
- Lessons learned will feed into improvement cycles.
- Periodic process reviews are conducted to determine which processes are working well and which need to be adjusted.
- Independent appraisals are carried out at the end of an improvement cycle.
- Feedback from appraisals (strengths and weaknesses) will be acted upon in the next improvement cycle.
- Appropriate training and consultancy are provided during the initiative.

The continuous improvement cycle is described in more detail in Table 4.1.

4.3
CMMI Improvement Structure and Teams

The implementation of the CMMI requires several teams with specific responsibilities to be formed. These teams will oversee the initiative and actively participate in its implementation. The CMMI project manager is responsible for setting up the various teams, defining a charter to explain the purpose of each team, providing orientation to the team members, and actively working with each team.

The project manager needs to be active in monitoring progress, identifying potential roadblocks and resolving them, and escalating issues to the SPEG or Steering Group where appropriate. The following is a suggested improvement structure and teams for a CMMI implementation (Table 4.2).

The CMMI project manager is responsible for running the CMMI initiative as a project. This involves tracking and managing the schedule, budget, effort, risks, and issues during the project and reporting progress to the SEPG team who will coordinate the day-to-day implementation of the CMMI. The project manager will report progress to the

Table 4.1 Continuous improvement cycle

Activity	Description
Identify improvements to be made	The improvements to be made during an improvement cycle come from several sources: – Improvement suggestions from staff – Lessons learned by projects – Periodic process reviews – Recommendations from CMMI appraisals – CMMI implementation strategy
Plan improvements	A project plan and schedule is prepared for a large improvement cycle (involving the implementation of several process areas) For a shorter improvement cycle an action plan (with owners and target completion dates) will often be sufficient
Implement improvements	The plan will detail the resources required to carry out the improvements The improvements will generally be conducted by a dedicated improvement team and approved by the SEPG The improvements will consist of new processes, standards, templates, procedures, guidelines, checklists, and tools (where appropriate) to support the process
Pilots/refine	Selected new processes and standards will often be piloted[2] prior to their deployment to ensure that they are fit for purpose The feedback from the pilot is used to refine the process prior to its general deployment
Deploy	The processes and standards are deployed using a structured approach: – Staff are trained on the new processes and standards – Staff receive support during the deployment – Audits are conducted to ensure that the new processes are followed
Do it all again	Improvement is continuous and as soon as an improvement cycle is complete its effectiveness is considered and a new improvement cycle is ready to commence

Steering Group who provide management sponsorship of the initiative and who have the management influence to remove any roadblocks that may arise.

The project manager will work closely with the specific improvement teams that are set up and resourced by the SEPG. These teams are responsible for implementing one or more CMMI process areas such as project planning and project monitoring and control; requirements management; configuration management. The teams involved in a typical implementation of CMMI level 2 are described in Fig. 4.3.

---

[2]The result from the pilot may be that the new process is not suitable to be deployed in the organization or that it needs to be significantly revised prior to deployment.

Table 4.2 CMMI improvement structure and teams

Role/Team	Members	Responsibility
CMMI Project Manager	CMMI Project Manager	Project manage the CMMI improvement project Provide leadership on process improvement Plan and coordinate CMMI improvements Ensure Steering Group, SEPG, and improvement teams receive appropriate training on the CMMI Chair the SEPG team and report progress of improvement teams to SEPG Report progress to the Steering Group Facilitate review of improvement suggestions at SEPG Facilitate the review of lessons learned at the SEPG Facilitate periodic process reviews Facilitate independent appraisals Maintain continuous improvement cycle
Steering Group (Project Board)	Senior manager(s) and CMMI project manager	Provides management sponsorship of initiative Provides resources and funding for the initiative Meets monthly, bi-monthly, or quarterly Reviews progress with initiative Uses influence to remove any roadblocks that arise with the improvement activities
SEPG team	Managers, technical, and CMMI project manager	Coordinate day-to-day improvement activities Generally meets every 2 weeks Provides direction and support to improvement teams Provides sufficient staff/resources to teams Review and approve new processes Coordinate pilots of new processes Coordinate training on new processes and standards Coordinate rollout of new processes and standards
Improvement teams	Process users and CMMI project manager	Focus on specific process area(s) Teams will usually meet weekly (or bi-weekly) Review the current process "as is" and define the new process "to be" (brainstorming/CMMI) Identify and create standards, templates, procedures, guidelines, and tools needed to support the new process Get feedback from the SEPG on the new process Conduct pilots to ensure the new process is effective Refine process as appropriate to address the feedback Obtain approval from the SEPG on the new process Provide any required training on the new process Conduct rollout of new process
Staff	All affected staff	Participate in improvement teams as directed by CMMI project manager and SEPG

Table 4.2 (continued)

Role/Team	Members	Responsibility
External Consultancy	External Consultant	Participate in pilots (as directed by CMMI project manager) Participate in training on new processes Adhere to new processes Conduct appraisal to determine initial maturity and assist in planning of first improvement cycle Provide expertise on the CMMI and software engineering Review progress made during the initiative and conduct periodic process reviews Provide training on the CMMI and software engineering disciplines Conduct appraisal at end of each improvement cycle and identify strengths and weaknesses in the organization processes

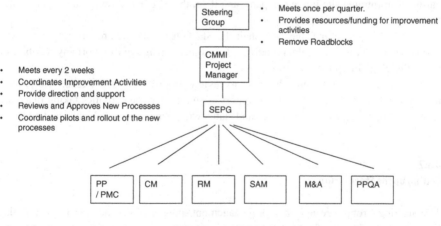

Improvement Structures / Teams

Steering Group
- Meets once per quarter.
- Provides resources/funding for improvement activities
- Remove Roadblocks

CMMI Project Manager

- Meets every 2 weeks
- Coordinates Improvement Activities
- Provide direction and support
- Reviews and Approves New Processes
- Coordinate pilots and rollout of the new processes

SEPG

PP / PMC   CM   RM   SAM   M&A   PPQA

- Teams meet weekly
- Improvement Teams focus on specific process areas
- Define New Processes & Templates
- Processes reviewed & approved by SEPG.

Fig. 4.3 CMMI improvement structure and teams

4.3.1
Setting Up the SEPG Team

The SEPG team is one of the first teams to be set up in the initiative. It is responsible for day-to-day coordination of the improvement initiative, and it provides direction and support to the improvement teams working on the implementation of specific process areas.

The members of the SEPG will include management and technical representatives, and the team members will receive appropriate training on the CMMI. The CMMI training will typically include

- Overview of software process improvement
- Overview of the CMMI and maturity levels
- Overview of CMMI process areas

The SEPG team will decide on the number of improvement teams to be initially set up as well as the members of each team. Typically, team members will need to spend a minimum of 3–4 h per week working on improvement activities as otherwise little progress will be made. This requires that an appropriate balance is kept between the normal day-to-day project and support work that team members are involved in and the software process improvement activities.

The SEPG team will review and approve the new processes and standards that are developed by the improvement sub-teams, and it will also coordinate pilots, rollout, and training on the new processes and standards. The SEPG may decide to place processes and standards on an Intranet site in the company, and if so, the SEPG will review and approve the Intranet site prior to its deployment.

The CMMI project manager will chair the SEPG team and will report progress, risks, and issues regularly during the initiative. The project manager will report any roadblocks to the Steering Group for resolution.

The SEPG team will generally meet to review progress every 2 weeks. The project manager will provide a regular status report to summarize the activities taking place, as well as listing the key risks and issues and status with respect to the schedule and budget.

4.3.2
Setting Up the Steering Group

The Steering Group is responsible for management sponsorship of the improvement initiative, and it provides the funding and resources required to enable the improvement teams to implement their assigned process areas.

The steering group is typically composed of senior and middle managers, and it has sufficient influence to remove any roadblocks that may arise during the initiative. The team will resolve any issues that have been escalated by the SEPG team.

The steering group will not be involved in the day-to-day implementation of the CMMI, and so the team members do not require detailed training on the CMMI model. They will receive high-level training on the CMMI and process improvement and the benefits that are gained from implementing the CMMI.

The steering group will ensure that a balance is kept between project work and process improvement activities. It approves the organization policy for software development, and this policy states the management expectations of the way that work will be done in the organization. All projects need to be carried out consistently with this policy.

The Steering Group is also responsible for reviewing and approving the project plan for the improvement initiative, as well as the schedule and budget. The CMMI project manager is a member of the Steering Group and will prepare regular status reports to provide visibility into progress with the improvement initiative and also the status with respect to the allocated budget, schedule, and effort, as well as documenting the key risks and issues.

The Steering Group typically meets less frequently than the SEPG and a frequency of bi-monthly or once per quarter is often sufficient. Extra meetings (in response to serious issues) may be scheduled where appropriate.

4.3.3
Setting Up Dedicated Improvement Sub-teams

The dedicated improvement teams are responsible for the implementation of one or more CMMI process areas. For example, the project management improvement team will usually implement the project planning and project monitoring and control process areas. The SEPG is responsible for setting up the improvement team; selecting team members; and providing orientation and training to the team members.

The team members will receive appropriate orientation on the CMMI model to enable them to implement their assigned process areas effectively. The CMMI project manager will conduct a kick-off session to commence work on the improvements and this includes introducing team members, communicating the objectives of the team and the planned deliverables, and the roles of the team members. The team will usually commence its work with process mapping and this involves defining and understanding the process as currently performed, i.e. the process "as is".

The team then critically examines the current process and brainstorms ways to improve it. Strengths and weaknesses in the current process are considered as well as best practice in the CMMI for the process area. The specific and generic practices in the CMMI for the process area will be considered and used to guide the definition of the new process, i.e. the process "to be". Once the new process is agreed there will be a need to identify the standards, procedures, guidelines, checklists, and templates required to support the new process.

The CMMI project manager may be a member of or may chair the specific improvement team. The project manager will facilitate the process mapping session and will apply the CMMI specific and generic practices to the process area and verify that the specific and generic goals are satisfied.

The number of improvement teams set up at any period of time will depend on the size of the organization and the amount of time that the organization can devote to software process improvement. Larger organizations have more resources available and are in a position to set up several improvement teams at the start of the initiative. Small organizations have fewer resources available and it may only be practical to set up only one or two improvement teams at any one time.

It is essential that sufficient time is available to team members to work on improvement activities, as otherwise little progress will be made in the initiative. The steering group is responsible for ensuring that the team members have 3–4 h of time available to them to work on their improvement activities.

The SEPG is responsible for reviewing and approving the new processes and standards, and it will coordinate the pilots, rollout, and training on the new processes and standards.

The improvement team will act upon any feedback that the SEPG provides, and it will participate in pilots, training, and rollout as directed by the SEPG team. The CMMI project manager will report progress and issues for all active improvement teams to the SEPG and the Steering Group.

4.3.4
Role of the CMMI Project Manager

The CMMI project manager plays a key role in managing the improvement initiative. This includes

- Setting up the various teams (SEPG, Steering Group, and specific improvement teams)
- Providing training and orientation to the various teams
- Managing the improvement initiative as a project
- Preparing the project plan and schedule
- Tracking schedule, effort, and budget
- Managing project risks and issues
- Reporting progress regularly to the Steering Group
- Chairing the SEPG team and discussing progress, risks, and issues
- Recording minutes and actions from SEPG meetings
- Providing guidance and direction to specific improvement teams
- Ensuring roadblocks are identified and resolved appropriately

The CMMI project manager is required to have a strong background in the CMMI and software process improvement. A good understanding of SCAMPI appraisals is required as well as good verbal and written communication. The CMMI project manager needs skill in influencing people to change behaviour, as a software process improvement initiative involves changing the way that work is done in the organization. The project manager will need to be highly motivated to drive the improvement project to a successful conclusion.

4.3.5
Risks to Success

Software process improvement initiatives do not always succeed, and it is important to understand some of the reasons why initiatives fail and to identify and manage risks. Senior management need to be fully behind the initiative, as this will ensure that middle managers and staff on the ground remain fully committed. Some common causes of failure include

- Lack of senior management commitment to the initiative
- Lack of buy-in from staff
- Lack of sufficient time to perform the improvement activities
- Poor project management of the initiative
- Lack of participation from staff in defining the new processes
- New processes may not meet the needs of the process users
- Lack of pilots on the new processes and standards
- Inadequate training on new processes and standards
- Lack of enforcement of new processes and standards
- Lack of sense of ownership of processes and standards
- Insufficient communication of issues to senior management

It is essential that staff participate in the definition of the new processes and standards as this will help to promote ownership and buy-in of the processes by staff. It will also help to ensure that the new processes and standards fully meet the needs of the process users.

4.4
Planning the Improvement Cycle

A major improvement cycle such as the implementation of a CMMI maturity level requires detailed planning and scheduling. However, the planning required for a small improvement cycle such as the implementation of a small number of process improvements may be as simple as an action plan. Large improvement cycles will require dedicated improvement teams to be set up to implement specific process areas, whereas improvement actions may be assigned to individuals for smaller cycles.

A CMMI project manager is assigned to manage a major improvement cycle and a project plan and schedule prepared. The project plan records the key project planning information such as the business case, the key project goals and objectives for the initiative, the scope of the initiative, as well as the process areas to be implemented. The roles and responsibilities of the various teams and individuals involved are recorded in the project plan. The project plan also documents the approved budget as well as the key project milestones and the high-level estimates for the work to be done.

The project manager will set up the risk and issue logs and will be proactive in identifying risks early in the project and managing risks throughout the project. The project manager will work with the improvement teams to ensure successful delivery of the desired improvements and will inform the SEPG of progress and any roadblocks that may impede progress.

For a shorter improvement cycle (e.g. such as the implementation of recommendations from an appraisal or the implementation of improvement suggestions from staff) it will usually be sufficient to employ an improvement action plan. Such an action plan will include target dates and owners for the various improvement actions, and the project manager and SEPG will track these to completion.

4.4.1
Appraisals

Appraisals were discussed in Section 3.7   and play a key role in software process improvement. They allow an organization to understand its current software process maturity and the strengths and weaknesses in its processes.

An initial appraisal is conducted at the start of the initiative to assist with planning. The improvements are then implemented, and an appraisal is conducted at the end of the improvement cycle to determine the progress made. The extent to which the CMMI has been implemented is determined, as well as strengths and opportunities for improvement to the processes (Fig. 4.4).

An appraisal is an independent evaluation of the practices in an organization against a model or standard. One or more experienced appraisers who are knowledgeable on the model conduct it. The SCAMPI appraisal methodology (Class A, B, or C) is used to conduct appraisals against the CMMI model. The scope of the appraisal will often be the level 2 or level 3 process areas, and the appraisal will identify strengths and weaknesses and gaps with respect to the implementation of the CMMI.

The appraisal will typically consist of interviews and reviews of documentation, and the appraisal team[3] will determine the extent to which the CMMI goals as well as the specific

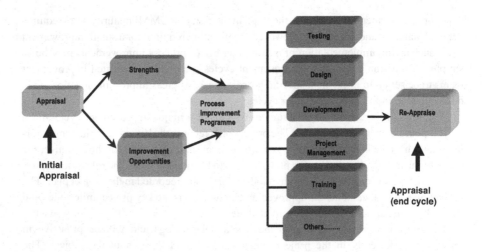

Fig. 4.4 Appraisals and process improvement

---

[3] The appraisal team could be the CMMI project manager only (if the project manager is a SCAMPI trained appraiser); alternatively, it could be an external appraiser and the project manager. For

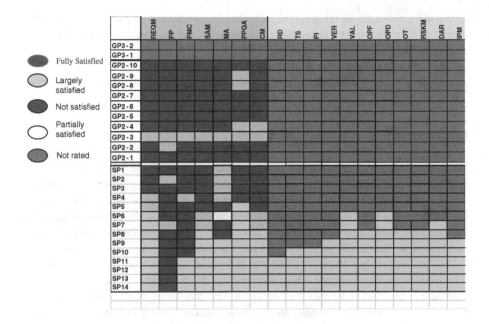

Fig. 4.5 CMMI appraisal results summary

and generic practices for each process area within the scope of the appraisal are satisfied. Sample output[4] from an L2 appraisal is presented in Fig. 4.5, and each column represents a CMMI process area with each row representing a specific or generic practice.

Colour coding is employed to indicate the extent to which the specific or generic practice has been implemented and satisfies the CMMI requirements:

– Fully satisfied
– Largely satisfied.
– Partially satisfied
– Not satisfied
– Not rated

The appraisal output will often be presented in a PowerPoint presentation by the lead appraiser and documented in the appraisal report. These summarise the appraisal findings including the strengths and weaknesses of the processes. The ratings of the process areas

---

very large organizations interested in a very formal appraisal it could be a large team of four to nine appraisers including a SCAMPI lead appraiser. There is a strict qualification process for a SCAMPI lead appraiser and it requires attending the official SEI CMMI and SCAMPI training as well as conducting two appraisals under the direction of a qualified SCAMPI lead appraiser.

[4]The output presented in Fig. 4.5 indicates the extent of implementation (e.g. fully, largely, partially) of each specific and generic practice for each process area within the scope of the appraisal. This output is produced only when ratings are part of the appraisal for a SCAMPI Class A appraisal.

within the scope of the appraisal will be recorded (where ratings are a part of the appraisal), as well as the overall CMMI rating for the organization and the gaps that exist with respect to the targeted CMMI maturity level.

The appraisal findings are valuable and will allow the CMMI project manager to plan and schedule the next improvement cycle. Appraisals are discussed in detail in Chapter 9.

4.4.2
CMMI Project Plan

The CMMI project manager will prepare the project plan for the CMMI initiative. It will include the business case for the initiative, the approved budget, and the key project milestones. It will document the approach taken, as well as the goals and objectives of the improvement initiative. The scope of the initiative including the process areas to be implemented will be defined in the plan. The stakeholders and teams involved will be documented as well as the key success factors and any assumptions, risks, and dependencies.

The project plan will include a section on estimation, and the estimation may be based on a work-breakdown structure where the estimates for the various phases of the project (and deliverables within the phase) are recorded. The knowledge, skills, and tools required to carry out the improvement project are also recorded. The initial risks to the success of the initiative are documented, and the project manager will need to be proactive in identifying and managing risks during the project.

The project plan will include sections on quality and test planning and communication planning. The quality planning covers how quality will be built into the deliverables, and communication planning covers how communication will take place during the project. The communication to the stakeholders will include project status reports and project meetings with the various stakeholders.

The plan will include a section on configuration management, and this will detail how changes will be controlled during the project. It will detail where the project deliverables will be placed, as well as defining how releases will be done. It will define how the deployment of the new processes and standards is done.

Once the project plan has been approved by the stakeholders, the project manager is in a position to prepare the project schedule. This will detail the various phases of the project life cycle and the tasks and activities to be conducted.

4.4.3
CMMI Project Schedule

The project schedule details the tasks and activities to be carried out during the improvement project; the effort and duration of each task and activity; and the resources required. The schedule shows how the project will be delivered within the key project parameters such as time and cost without compromising quality in any way (Fig. 4.6).

The project manager will manage the schedule and will take corrective action when project performance deviates from expectations. The project schedule will be updated regularly during the improvement project (usually weekly or bi-weekly).

Fig. 4.6 CMMI implementation schedule

4.4.4
CMMI Kick-Off Session

The implementation of the CMMI is a major initiative for an organization, and it is essential to raise its profile early in the initiative. This will allow senior management to state its importance and to motivate the staff involved in its implementation. A CMMI kick-off meeting is important as it sets the scene for the activities in the CMMI implementation for the years ahead.

The meeting allows the CMMI project manager to give an introduction to the CMMI, its benefits, the improvement initiative planned for the organization, and the teams and people involved. A senior manager will typically open the kick-off meeting and will introduce the CMMI project manager as well as stating the importance of the initiative to the organization, their commitment to it, and the expectation that all staff in the organization will give it full support. The project manager will give a presentation on the CMMI including

- Introduction to the CMMI and software process improvement
- Benefits of software process improvement
- Teams involved in the improvement initiative
- Approach to CMMI implementation
- People involved and team composition
- Goals and objectives of the initiatives
- The timelines
- Next steps

Senior management will commit to making resources available to support the initiative, and senior management support is essential in ensuring that middle management and staff make the initiative a priority.

4.5
Implementation of Improvements

Once the specific improvement teams have been set up and the team members appropriately trained, the teams are ready to commence work on their assigned process areas. The improvement teams will generally meet weekly, and the first task is to prepare a plan for the implementation of its assigned process areas. The CMMI project manager will work closely[5] with the team to ensure that the plan is realistic and will address the CMMI requirements. The plan will detail the activities to be carried out and the deliverables to be produced. These include

- Policy for the performance of the process (There will usually be one policy that covers all of the relevant process areas.)
- Process map to show the flow of activities for the process area
- Procedure or guidelines that describe the process in more detail
- Templates and standards to assist in the performance of the process
- Checklists to assist in the performance of the process
- Evaluation and selection of tools to support the performance of the process
- Metrics to measure the effectiveness of performance of the process
- Training materials to assist in piloting and rollout of the process

---

[5]The CMMI project manager may be a member or may chair the improvement team. It will depend on the experience of the team.

The CMMI project manager may be a member of each improvement team or may work closely with the teams to drive improvements and to determine progress on a regular basis. Any roadblocks that arise are first communicated to the SEPG, and if the SEPG is unable to resolve the issue it is escalated to the Steering Group.

The project manager will report progress regularly to the SEPG and at appropriate intervals to the CMMI Steering Group.

4.5.1
Process Mapping

The starting point for each improvement team is to understand the process as it is currently performed and to determine the extent to which it is effective. The stakeholders of the process participate in the discussion of how the process is currently performed, and the process is then sketched pictorially with activities and their inputs and outputs recorded graphically. This graphical map is a representation of the process "as is".

The approach used in this book is to represent activities in the process by rectangles (with tasks within an activity being numbered). Each activity has an input and an output and these are recorded in the process map. There may be standards to support the process (e.g. procedures and templates), and the tasks and activities are conducted by various roles. The process maps presented here are kept as simple and abstract as possible and focus on inputs, tasks, activities, and outputs.

For example, Fig. 4.7 is a simple process map that is part of supplier selection.

There are two activities listed in this process map. These are the "Issue RFP" activity that has two tasks and the "Evaluate Proposals" activity that has four tasks associated with it. A more detailed process would specify standards to support the process and the roles involved in carrying out the tasks and activities. Entry and exit criteria could be specified as well as any verification steps and measures.

Process mapping was discussed earlier in Section 1.6, and the process map is an abstraction of the way that work is done. The team critically examines the process map to determine how effective the process is, and weaknesses are identified. The CMMI specific and generic practices for the process area are considered, as they contain best practice for process performance.

This leads to modifications to the definition of the current process to yield the process "to be". Once the team has agreed to the new process the templates required to support the process become clear from an examination of the input and output to the various activities. Templates will be prepared to standardize input and output from the process. Procedures or guidelines will be required to provide detailed information on how the process is to be carried out.

The SEPG team is responsible for approving the processes and deliverables produced by the improvement team. The SEPG may approve without comments or it may require changes to the process and deliverables prior to approval.

Fig. 4.7 Sample process map

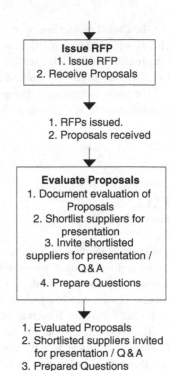

Once the deliverables for a process area have been approved by the SEPG they are ready for piloting (where required) or deployment. The SEPG will decide whether a pilot is required prior to deployment.

4.5.2
Layout of Templates

Templates are employed to support the process and it is desirable that they have a common look and feel. The first three to four pages for each template should have identical headings such as

- Title page
- This includes a unique document number, the date the current version was prepared, and the release status of the document
- It may include an abstract and an approval section
- Version history
- This includes the history of who modified the document, the reason for modification, and the date of modification
- Table of contents
- Introduction

- This includes the purpose of the document, the definition of any acronyms, and references to other documents
- Template version number
- Each template has an associated version number

There are standard templates available (e.g. the IEEE standards) for various activities in software engineering. The organization may decide to use or tailor the IEEE standards to meet its needs or it may decide to devise its own templates.

4.5.3
Layout of Procedures and Guidelines

Processes are an abstraction of the way in which work is done. They need associated procedures or guidelines to describe in detail how the process is performed. It is desirable that these have a common look and feel with common sections such as

- Title page
- Version history
- Table of contents
- Introduction
- Overview of process
- Process map
- Details
- Training and metrics
- Roles and responsibilities

4.6
Piloting the Process

The SEPG team will decide if the new processes and standards need to be piloted prior to their deployment. This involves the following:

- New process is approved for pilot by the SEPG.
- Project(s) and staff are selected for the pilot.
- Training is provided to all staff that will participate on the pilot.
- The CMMI project manager will communicate the objectives of the pilot to all participants.

The pilot then commences and the CMMI project manager will work closely with the participants to determine the effectiveness of the new process and standards.

- The participants will prepare feedback as to what went well and what went poorly during the pilot.

- The project manager and SEPG will consider the feedback and decide whether the process and standards are ready to be rolled out.
- The processes and standards are refined accordingly.
- If the pilot is unsuccessful the improvement team and the CMMI project manager will analyse the reasons why and develop an appropriate strategy for the process area.

4.7
Rolling Out Process

The SEPG team is responsible for approving the new process for rollout and for coordinating the activities for rollout. These include the following:

- New process is approved for rollout by the SEPG.
- Training material on the process is prepared by the improvement team and approved by SEPG.
- Training is provided on the new process to all affected staff.
- The Intranet site with the standards will be updated to include the new process and standards.
- The induction checklist will be updated to include induction on the new process and standards.
- The audit checklist will be updated to audit the new process and standards.

The new process and standards will be deployed on all new projects (and possibly on projects that have recently commenced). The post-rollout activities may include

- Induction to new staff on the new process
- Audits to verify that the new process is followed and effective
- Metrics on the performance of the process are periodically reviewed to ensure that its performance is effective

4.8
Review Questions

1. Discuss the approach suggested for software process improvement in this book.
2. Discuss the continuous software process improvement cycle.
3. Describe the teams involved in a typical software process improvement initiative.
4. Discuss the planning and scheduling required in a software process improvement initiative.

5. Describe the activities that take place during the kick-off session of a software
   process improvement initiative.
6. Describe the activities involved in process mapping.
7. Describe the purpose of pilots of new processes.
8. Describe how a new process may be rolled out to the staff in the organization.
9. Describe how appraisals fit into the software process improvement cycle.

4.9
Summary

This chapter was concerned with the activities and teams required to set up a CMMI
improvement initiative in an organization. It requires detailed planning and the initiative
needs to be managed as a project.

A CMMI project manager is assigned to run the initiative, and the project manager is
responsible for defining the approach to implementation and setting up the teams involved.
These include the Steering Group, the SEPG, and dedicated improvement teams. The
CMMI project manager will ensure that all team members receive appropriate training.

A CMMI improvement initiative consists of one or more improvement cycles. A major
improvement cycle will implement several process areas, whereas minor improvement
cycles may be concerned with implementing actions from an appraisal or improvement
suggestions from staff.

One of the earliest activities in an appraisal is to determine the current maturity of the
organization with respect to the CMMI model, as well as strengths and weaknesses in its
processes. The first improvement cycle has often been concerned with the implementation
of level 2 of the CMMI.

A CMMI initiative is run as a project with a project manager assigned. The CMMI
project manager will prepare the project plan and schedule, monitor and report progress,
and manage risks and issues. The project manager will work closely with the dedicated
improvement teams and will assist in process mapping and in defining improved processes.

The SEPG will approve the new processes and templates and coordinate any pilots, as
well as coordinating the rollout of the new processes and standards. A software process
improvement programme involves

– Identify improvements to be made
– Plan improvements
– Implement improvements
– Pilots and refine
– Deploy
– Do it all again

The next chapter is concerned with the implementation of CMMI level 2 in an
organization.

CMMI Level 2 Implementation

5

Key Topics

> Requirements Management
> Project Management
> Configuration Management
> Process and Product Quality Assurance
> Measurement and Analysis
> Supplier Agreement Management

5.1
Introduction

This chapter is focused on the implementation of maturity level 2 in an organization. A CMMI level 2 organization has policies for managing a project, and procedures to implement these policies have been established. Practices are in place to ensure that the process is planned, performed, and controlled, and the process is enforced with independent audits.

The status of the work products produced by the process is visible to management at major milestones, and changes to the work products are controlled. The work products are baselined and placed under appropriate configuration management control.

A level 2 organization has increased control over its projects and requirements and is in a position to repeat previous project success. Planning and managing new projects is based on experience with similar projects. Realistic project commitments are made based on the results achieved on previous projects, and historical data are available and used.

The requirements for a project are managed and any changes to the requirements are controlled. Project management practices are in place to plan and manage the project, and basic project measures are defined to judge project performance. Historical data such as

G. O'Regan, *Introduction to Software Process Improvement*, Undergraduate Topics
in Computer Science, DOI 10.1007/978-0-85729-172-1_5,
© Springer-Verlag London Limited 2011

budget, schedule and effort variance are maintained and used to improve the planning of future projects. The project works with its subcontractors to establish a strong customer–supplier relationship.

The objective in implementing level 2 of the CMMI is to institutionalize effective management practices for projects and to enable practices that were successful in earlier projects to be repeated. The process areas to be implemented[1] are

- Requirements Management
- Project Planning
- Project Monitoring and Control
- Supplier Agreement Management
- Configuration Management
- Measurement and Analysis
- Process and Product Quality Assurance

Improvement teams will be set up to implement these process areas. These could potentially lead to seven separate process improvement teams, but in practice, some teams will be responsible for more than one process area. For example, the project management improvement team is usually responsible for project planning and project monitoring and control process areas. It may also be responsible for the measurement and analysis and supplier agreement management process areas. There will usually be separate process improvement teams to implement the requirements management and configuration management process areas.

The implementation of the process and product quality assurance process area may be done by the SEPG team, as often the CMMI project manager will have a clear view on how this independent function should be implemented. In small organizations the SEPG team may be the only improvement team, and it may be responsible for implementing all level 2 process areas over a period of time.

The SEPG will decide on the number of improvement teams to be set up initially, and this will depend on the resources available for the improvement activities. The SEPG team will keep a balance between the normal day-to-day work of employees and the improvement activities.

The project plan for the improvement initiative will describe the approach to the implementation of CMMI level 2. The schedule will detail the timelines and resources required for setting up and training the various improvement teams as well as the tasks that they will complete. These will include the definition of processes and procedures, checklists, training material, tools, pilots, and rollout of the new processes and standards.

---

[1] It is mandatory to implement the supplier agreement management process when there is outsourcing of product development.

5.2
Project Management

The project management improvement team is responsible for implementing the CMMI requirements for the project planning and project monitoring and control process areas, thereby leading to good project management practices. Further improvements are made to the project management practices in later improvement cycles, as part of the implementation of process areas such as risk management, integrated project management, and quantitative project management at the higher maturity levels.

The scope of work for this team is the specific and generic goals and practices for the project planning and project monitoring and control process areas. The generic practices were discussed earlier, and they include GP 2.1–GP 2.10 for level 2. These need to be implemented and institutionalized for all of the level 2 process areas.

Table 5.1 details the specific goals and practices for the project planning process area. They essentially state that estimates for the project should be established and that the project plan should then be developed and approved by the stakeholders. The project plan will need to be maintained during the project. The specific and generic goals must be satisfied and the practices (or acceptable alternatives) need to be implemented and institutionalized.

There is a need for estimation of guidelines or a procedure to enable estimates to be produced consistently. It would be inappropriate to have an estimation procedure such as

Table 5.1 CMMI requirements for project planning process area

Specific goal	Specific practice	Description of specific goal/practice
SG 1		*Establish estimates*
	SP 1.1	Establish scope of project
	SP 1.2	Establish estimates of work products and task attributes
	SP 1.3	Define project life cycle
	SP 1.4	Establish estimates of effort and cost
SG 2		*Develop a project plan*
	SP 2.1	Establish the budget and schedule
	SP 2.2	Identify project risks
	SP 2.3	Plan for data management
	SP 2.4	Plan for project resources
	SP 2.5	Plan for needed knowledge and skills
	SP 2.6	Plan stakeholder involvement
	SP 2.7	Establish the project plan
SG 3		*Obtain commitment to the plan*
	SP 3.1	Review plans that affect the project
	SP 3.2	Reconcile work and resource levels
	SP 3.3	Obtain plan commitment

"Go ask Fred",[2] as this clearly relies on an individual and is not a repeatable process. The estimates may be based on a work-breakdown structure, function points, or another appropriate methodology. There may be several approaches to estimation in the various projects. A high-level process map for project planning is given in Fig. 5.1:

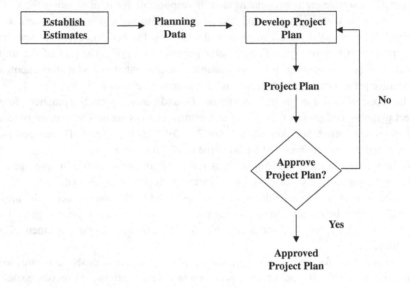

Fig. 5.1 High-level process map for project planning

Table 5.2 details the specific goals and practices for the project monitoring and control process area. They state that the progress of the project should be monitored against the plan and that corrective actions should be taken when progress deviates from expectations. This involves monitoring key project parameters such as budget, effort, and schedule as

Table 5.2 CMMI requirements for project monitoring and control

Specific goal	Specific practice	Description of specific practice/goal
SG 1		*Monitor project against plan*
	SP 1.1	Monitor project planning parameters
	SP 1.2	Monitor commitments
	SP 1.3	Monitor project risks
	SP 1.4	Monitor data management
	SP 1.5	Monitor stakeholder involvement
	SP 1.6	Conduct progress reviews
	SP 1.7	Conduct milestone reviews
SG 2		*Manage corrective action to closure*
	SP 2.1	Analyse issues
	SP 2.2	Take corrective action
	SP 2.3	Manage corrective action

---

[2] Unless Fred is the name of the estimation methodology or the estimation tool employed.

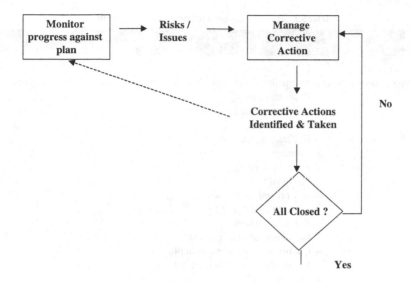

Fig. 5.2 High-level process map for project monitoring and control

well as risks and issues. The project manager will conduct progress and milestone reviews to determine progress and will communicate the status of the project regularly. All issues identified will be managed and corrective actions tracked to closure (Fig. 5.2).

Typical deliverables[3] for project management are in Table 5.3, and they include process maps, procedures or guidelines, templates, and checklists.

The process maps provide an abstract high-level summary of the activities in the process; the project management guidelines provide the detailed procedure for carrying out the process; the risk management guidelines describe how risks are identified and managed; and the estimation guidelines define how estimation is done.

Templates support the process and allow consistent input and output during the different parts of the process. Finally, checklists are employed as an aid to performing the process.

5.2.1
Project Management Processes

The starting point for improvements to any process area is to understand the process as it is currently being performed. Often, there will be some process in place, and the focus will be to understand it and to mature the process to meet the CMMI requirements. Occasionally, there will be no process in place, and in such cases it will be necessary to fully define it.

---

[3] The actual deliverables required for the project management process area will depend on its approach to implementation and its current maturity. Some organizations may have a lot of the expected deliverables in place. Further, the use of tools to support the process may reduce the need for deliverables (e.g. the risk and issue logs may be automated). Some organizations may implement some of the level 3 process areas associated with project management (e.g. risk management) at this stage. The deliverables in Fig. 5.3 are an example of what may be produced.

Table 5.3 Typical templates for project management

Template	Typical contents
Project plan	This is usually a Microsoft Word document with the following sections: – Business case – Project goals and objectives – Project scope – Key success factors – Estimation – Project life cycle – Financial budget – Key project milestones – Initial project risks – Project resources – Configuration management – Quality and communication planning – Knowledge and skills required – Stakeholders
Project schedule	This is often done in Microsoft Project and it allows the various tasks to be recorded as well as the effort and resources required
Risk log	This may be implemented in a Microsoft Excel spreadsheet with columns for – Risk number, risk type, raiser of risk, date raised, description – Likelihood of risk, impact of risk, risk category – Response type, counter measure, allocated to, status
Issue log	This may be implemented in a Microsoft Excel spreadsheet with columns for – Issue number, raiser of issue, date raised – Issue type, description, severity, urgency – Assigned to, resolution actions, due date, status
Lessons learned log	This may be implemented in a Microsoft Excel spreadsheet with columns for – Lesson number, lesson learned type, raiser, date raised, description – Comments and recommendations
Weekly report/project board report	This may be implemented in a Microsoft Word document with sections for – Completed deliverables (current week) – New risks and issues – Schedule, effort, and budget status – Quality and test status – Key risks and issues – Milestone status – Deliverables planned (next week)
End project report	This may be implemented in a Microsoft Word document with sections for – Achievement of objectives – Budget, schedule, and effort performance – Impact of change requests – Quality and milestone performance

Table 5.3 (continued)

Template	Typical contents
Lessons learned report	This may be implemented in a Microsoft Word document with sections for – Key lessons learned – Actions, owner, due date

Process maps	Procedure/guidelines
Project planning Project monitoring and control	Project management guidelines Risk management guidelines Estimation guidelines
Templates	*Checklist*
Project plan Project schedule Risk log Issue log Lessons learnedlog Weekly project report Project board report End project report Lessons learned report	Project management

Fig. 5.3 Typical deliverables for project management

Process mapping is useful as it provides an abstract view of how the work is currently performed. The CMMI project manager often facilitates the process mapping session as described in Chapter 4. The process as currently performed is documented and critically examined. It is then improved by implementing the specific and generic practices, and it is approved by the stakeholders once it meets their needs.

The process map helps in identifying the templates that will be required to support the process. The input and output from the activities in the process map are examined, and the need for supporting templates is considered. Templates allow individual work products to be produced consistently.

The project planning process may be unique to the individual project in a CMMI level 2 organization. That is, each project may have a distinct process and standards for project management. Alternatively, the CMMI project manager may decide to implement the project management process as a standard process for the organization, and this will enable project management to be performed consistently in the organization.

The process mapping for project planning will involve participation from the stakeholders including managers and project managers. It will consider the flow of activities associated with project planning and the input and output of the various activities. These activities will often include

– Project request
– High-level estimates of budget, effort, and schedule

- Project authorization
- Preparation of project plan
- Setting up the project board
- Defining project controls
- Identification of risks
- Preparation of project schedule
- Project communication
- Project implementation
- Project closure

Figure 5.4 provides an example of a project planning process map. Its purpose is to aid the discussion on process mapping for project planning, and every organization will have its own specifics for the process.

The project monitoring and control process is concerned with monitoring project execution and taking corrective action when project performance deviates from expectations. A sample project monitoring and control process map is provided in Fig. 5.5.

The process map will generally include

- Monitoring the project plan and schedule
- Monitoring key project parameters
- Conducting progress and milestone reviews
- Monitoring risks, issues, and change requests
- Monitoring resources
- Reporting the project status to management and project board
- Analysing issues and taking corrective action

5.2.2
Project Management Procedure or Guidelines

The project planning and project monitoring and control process maps show the flow of the activities in the processes. The role of the process map is to provide an abstraction of the process, and it is not intended that it will provide all of the details as to how the process is performed as this will be documented elsewhere.

The objective of the project management procedure (or guidelines) is to provide sufficient information to allow the process practitioner to carry out the process. It will include sections to describe the various activities in the process as well as the roles involved. It may include some of the following:

- How a project comes about
- How a project is authorized
- How estimation is done
- How the project plan and schedule is produced

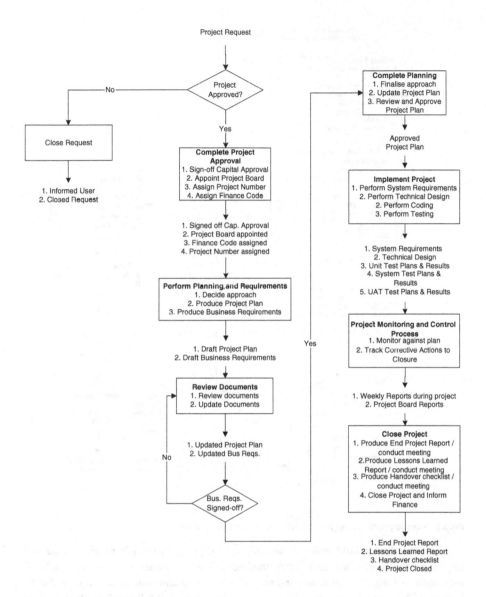

Fig. 5.4 Sample process map for project planning

- How the requirements are produced
- How suppliers are selected
- How risks are managed
- How project monitoring and control takes place
- How project implementation takes place
- How the project is closed

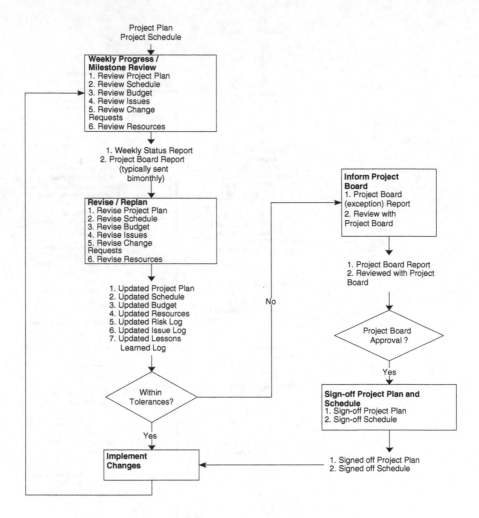

Fig. 5.5 Sample process map for project monitoring and control

The procedure should make it easy for a new project manager to understand and implement the project management methodology. The procedure will satisfy the CMMI requirements for project planning and project monitoring and control, and it may also be influenced by best practice in project management such as the Prince2 methodology or PMBOK from the Project Management Institute (PMI).

5.2.3
Project Management Templates

The definition of the process maps will identify inputs and outputs to the various activities. It may be desirable to receive input or produce output in a consistent format, and templates for input and output help to achieve this. Typical templates employed for project management are given in Table 5.3.

5.2.4
Project Management Checklist

Checklists are useful in ensuring that the tasks have been completed. The sample project management checklist checks that project planning has been appropriately performed and that controls are in place (Table 5.4).

Table 5.4 Sample project management checklist

No.	Item to check
1.	Has tailoring been completed?
2.	Is the project plan complete and approved?
3.	Are the risk log, issue log, and lessons learned log set up?
4.	Are the responses to the risks and issues appropriate?
5.	Is the Microsoft Schedule (or equivalent) set up?
6.	Is the project schedule up to date?
7.	Is the project appropriately resourced?
8.	Are estimates available for the project? Are they realistic?
9.	Has quality planning been completed for the project?
10.	Does the project have a business case?
11.	Has the change control mechanism been set up for the project?
12.	Has project communication been appropriately planned?
13.	Is the project directory set up for the project?
14.	Are the key milestones detailed in the project plan?

5.2.5
Institutionalization

The specific practices for project planning and project monitoring and control are concerned with the implementation of good project management practices. The institutionalization of project management is concerned with ingraining these practices in the way that work is done. Institutionalization helps to ensure that the process is performed consistently and retained during times of stress.

This includes practices related to the creation of policies for project management; practices related to the provision of appropriate resources and training to perform the process; practices to control and manage the process; and practices related to verifying compliance to the process. Process users are appropriately trained, and the process is enforced by independent audits.

The organization policy states management expectations of how software projects should be conducted in the organization. It will include a section on project management.

The project management process itself needs to be planned, and resources such as a project manager need to be in place as well as any tools required (e.g. estimation) for performing the process. The project manager assigns responsibilities for producing the deliverables. All involved in the process receive appropriate training. Project managers may be trained in project management methodologies such as Prince2 or PMBOK.

The deliverables produced (e.g. project plans and schedules) are placed under an appropriate level of configuration management. The stakeholders involved are identified and documented in the project plan. The project manager will keep the stakeholders involved during the project.

The project manager will monitor progress, risks, and issues during the project and corrective action taken as appropriate. These will be reported in the regular status reports sent to management and the project board, with the status reviewed with management regularly during the project.

An independent audit of the project (including project management) will be conducted during the project, with any non-compliance issues identified and assigned to the project team for resolution.

5.3
Supplier Agreement Management

The purpose of this process area is to manage the acquisition of product from suppliers where there exists a formal agreement. It is concerned with best practice for establishing and satisfying supplier agreements and includes practices to select suppliers, defining an agreement with the supplier, executing the agreement, and accepting the supplier product.

The supplier management improvement team is responsible for implementing the specific and generic goals and practices for this process area.[4] The activities associated with supplier selection typically include

- Identify candidate suppliers
- Identify evaluation team
- Define evaluation criteria
- Issue Request for Proposal (RFP)
- Receive proposals
- Shortlist suppliers for presentation
- Rate suppliers against evaluation criteria
- Make decision
- Negotiate agreement and statement of work
- Manage the supplier

The specific goals and practices for supplier agreement management are stated in Table 5.5.

A high-level process map describing the activities for establishing a supplier agreement is detailed in Fig. 5.6.

The implementation of some of the specific practices will involve other process areas as they involve project management, decision analysis, testing activities, and deployment and configuration management activities. Figure 5.7 provides a high-level process map to satisfy a supplier agreement.

---

[4] This process area is not applicable to companies that are not using a third-party supplier.

Table 5.5 CMMI requirements for supplier agreement management

Specific goal	Specific practice	Description of specific practice/goal
SG 1		*Establish supplier agreements*
	SP 1.1	Determine acquisition types
	SP 1.2	Select suppliers
	SP 1.3	Establish supplier agreements
SG 2		*Satisfy supplier agreements*
	SP 2.1	Execute the supplier agreement
	SP 2.2	Monitor selected supplier processes
	SP 2.3	Evaluate selected supplier work products
	SP 2.4	Accept the acquired product
	SP 2.5	Transition products

Fig. 5.6 High-level process map for establishing supplier agreement

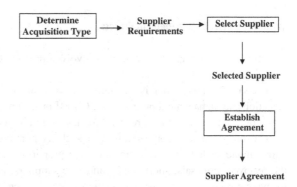

Fig. 5.7 High-level process map for satisfying supplier agreement

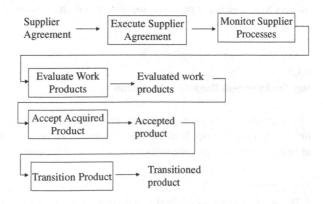

Process maps	Procedure/guidelines
Supplier selection	Supplier agreement management procedure
Templates	Checklist
Procurement plan Request for proposal (RFP) RFP evaluation Statement of work (SOW)	Supplier agreement management

Fig. 5.8 Deliverables for supplier agreement management process area

Typical deliverables[5] for the supplier agreement management process area include process maps, procedures or guidelines, templates, and checklists. The process maps provide a high-level summary of the activities in the process; the procedures or guidelines provide the details behind the process map. The templates support the process and the checklists are an aid to ensure that the process is correctly performed (Fig. 5.8).

5.3.1
Supplier Agreement Management Process

A sample process map of the activities involved in supplier selection and management is provided in Fig. 5.9.

The sample process map is intended to serve as an aid to the discussion on the supplier selection and management process. The CMMI project manager will facilitate the process mapping at a session with the relevant managers and project managers.

The process map includes activities such as purchase planning; identifying candidate suppliers; defining evaluation criteria; preparing and issuing the RFP; evaluating the received proposals; shortlisting candidate suppliers; inviting the shortlisted suppliers to make a presentation; conducting checks on reference sites; completing the evaluation and preparing an evaluation report; selecting the preferred supplier; negotiating a legal agreement with the supplier including a statement of work.

The decision and analysis process area (DAR) is a supporting process area to supplier agreement management. It includes best practice on decision analysis and enables decision makers to choose the appropriate supplier based on objective data. It is described in detail in Chapter 6.

5.3.2
Supplier Agreement Management Procedure

The supplier agreement management procedure (or guidelines) will provide the details behind the process map. It will define the procedure by which the activities in the process are carried out as well as the roles involved. It will include

---

[5] The actual deliverables required will depend on its current approach to supplier selection and management.

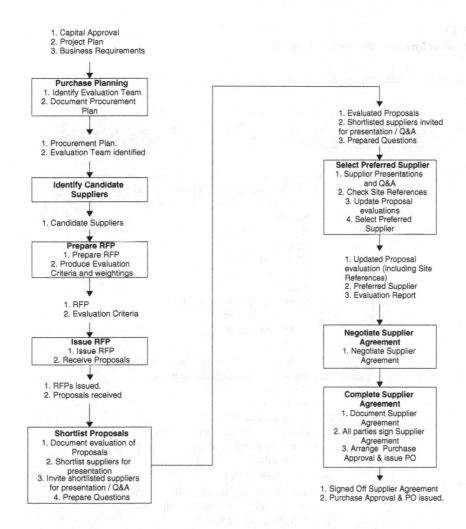

Fig. 5.9 Supplier agreement management process map

- How planning for purchasing is done
- How candidate suppliers are identified
- How requests for proposals are carried out
- How suppliers are shortlisted
- How evaluation criteria is prepared
- How formal evaluation of the shortlisted suppliers takes place
- How the decision of the preferred supplier is made
- How a formal supplier agreement (including legal and statement of work) is negotiated, agreed, and documented
- Roles and responsibilities

The procedure should make it easy for new staff and the stakeholders involved to understand the process and their role in performing it.

5.3.3
Supplier Agreement Management Templates

Typical templates employed for supplier agreement management are described in Table 5.6.

Table 5.6   Supplier agreement management templates

Template	Typical contents
Procurement plan	This is typically a Microsoft Word document. It provides an audit trail of procurement activities and includes – Background and scope of procurement – Schedule – Roles and responsibilities – Candidate suppliers – Evaluation method – Evaluation criteria – Evaluation of proposals – Supplier presentation schedule – Evaluation summary – Preferred supplier – Legal agreement
Request for proposal (RFP)	This is typically a Microsoft Word document. It details what needs to be provided in the proposal: – Background – Requirements – Company details – Company experience and competence – Summary of proposal – Closing date – Evaluation criteria
RFP evaluation	This may be implemented as an Excel spreadsheet. It records scores against the criteria for each vendor: – Weightings (per criterion) – Score per criterion – Total score
Statement of work	This is typically a Microsoft Word document. It details what the vendor will supply as well as the standards to be followed. It may include – Project objectives – List of deliverables – Budget, schedule, and milestones – Project resources – Milestone payments – Change control – Standards to be followed – Acceptance criteria – Training, warranty, and support – Incentives and penalties

5.3.4
Supplier Agreement Management Checklist

Checklists are useful as a reminder to the process user to ensure that all steps in the process have been carried out. A sample checklist for the supplier agreement management process is in Table 5.7.

Table 5.7 Supplier agreement management checklist

No.	Item to check
1.	Has the project management maturity of supplier been evaluated?
2.	Does the formal agreement include change control?
3.	Are milestone payments linked to approved and signed off project deliverables?
4.	Are reviews of project and testing deliverables part of the SOW?
5.	Does the formal agreement include the user acceptance test criteria?
6.	Does the formal agreement include the test defect classification?
7.	Is the minimum level of experience required for the key supplier resources specified?
8.	Have supplier reference sites been visited?
9.	Has the maturity and capability of the supplier been considered?
10.	Has the level of training to be provided by the supplier been defined in the supplier agreement?
11.	Is the documentation to be provided by the supplier defined in the statement of work?
12.	Does the statement of work state the deliverables to be provided at the various milestones?
13.	Has the frequency/type of status meetings been defined?

5.3.5
Institutionalization

The specific practices for this process area are concerned with the implementation of best practice for establishing and satisfying supplier agreements. The institutionalization of these practices is concerned with ingraining it in the way that work is done to ensure that the process is consistently performed and retained during times of stress.

The institutionalization includes practices related to the creation of policies for supplier agreement management; practices related to the provision of appropriate resources and training to perform the process; practices to control and manage the process; and practices related to verifying compliance to the process.

The organization policy includes a section on supplier agreement management, and this states the management expectations of how supplier selection and management should be performed.

The supplier agreement management process itself needs to be planned and resources such as a project manager need to be in place, as well as any tools required for performing the process. All involved in the process receive appropriate training (e.g. training in evaluating suppliers).

The deliverables produced are placed under an appropriate level of configuration management control. The stakeholders involved are identified and documented in the project plan. The project manager will keep the stakeholders involved during the project.

The project manager will manage the supplier as per the project plan and statement of work. This will ensure that the agreement is correctly executed; that the delivered software meets customers' expectations; and that the deployment of the software to the customer site is managed appropriately.

The project manager will monitor progress with suppliers, risks and issues during the project, and take corrective action as appropriate. These will be reported in the regular status reports sent to management and the project board, with the status reviewed with management during the project.

An independent audit of the project (including supplier agreement management) will be conducted, with any non-compliance issues identified and assigned to the project team for resolution.

5.4
Requirements Development and Management

The requirements improvement team is responsible for implementing the specific and generic goals and practices for the requirements development and requirements management process areas.

Requirements management is concerned with ensuring that the project maintains an up-to-date approved set of requirements throughout the project and ensuring that the project deliverables are kept consistent with the requirements. It is an important area to get right as all project activities are planned from the approved requirements. The requirements management process area is concerned with best practice for managing the requirements of the project and in identifying inconsistencies between the requirements and the project plans and work products. Its focus is on the activities for managing the requirements as distinct from the activities in gathering the requirements.

The requirements development process area is often implemented with the requirements management process area. This level 3 process area is concerned with best practice for defining customer and product requirements. It includes practices for eliciting customer and product requirements as well as analysing and validating the requirements.

Often, the requirements are poorly controlled for projects in immature organizations. The requirements may in many cases be incomplete, inadequately documented, or untestable. In other cases, there may be major scope creep with requirements accepted from any source. Changes to the requirements may lead to a high level of re-work or cause major delays to the schedule or major increases in project cost. In some cases, changes to the requirements may not be reflected in the project plan.

There are potential impacts on other deliverables[6] when the requirements change, and it is essential that changes to the requirements be controlled with all affected deliverables

---

[6] The deliverables potentially include plans, system requirements, design and test deliverables.

Table 5.8 CMMI requirements for requirements management

Specific goal	Specific practice	Description of specific practice/goal
SG 1		*Manage requirements*
	SP 1.1	Obtain an understanding of the requirements
	SP 1.2	Obtain commitment to requirements
	SP 1.3	Manage requirements changes
	SP 1.4	Maintain bi-directional traceability of requirements
	SP 1.5	Identify inconsistencies between work products and requirements

identified and updated accordingly. The specific goals and practices for the requirements management process area are listed in Table 5.8.

A high-level process map for the requirements management process area is provided in Fig. 5.10. The task "understanding the requirements" results in an agreed set of requirements, as well as criteria to evaluate and accept the requirements. The requirements need to be

– Uniquely numbered
– Clearly stated and unambiguous
– Complete
– Consistent
– Feasible
– Testable

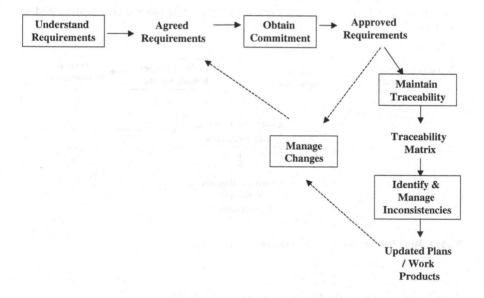

Fig. 5.10 High-level process map for requirements management

Table 5.9 CMMI requirements for requirements development

Specific goal	Specific practice	Description of specific practice/goal
SG 1		*Develop customer requirements*
	SP 1.1	Elicit needs
	SP 1.2	Develop the customer requirements
SG 2		*Develop product requirements*
	SP 2.1	Establish product and product component requirements
	SP 2.2	Allocate product component requirements
	SP 2.3	Identify interface requirements
SG3		*Analyse and validate requirements*
	SP 3.1	Establish operational concepts and scenarios
	SP 3.2	Establish a definition of required functionality
	SP 3.3	Analyse requirements
	SP 3.4	Analyse requirements to achieve balance
	SP 3.5	Validate requirements with comprehensive methods

Commitment to the requirements (including changes to the requirements) must be obtained from all stakeholders and project participants. Managing traceability is concerned with establishing traceability from the source requirement to its lower level requirements and vice versa[7] and ensuring that the traceability is updated following changes to the requirements.

The requirements development process area is concerned with best practice for defining and documenting the customer and product requirements. It is also concerned with analysing and validating the requirements.

The specific goals and practices for the requirements development process area are given in Table 5.9, and a high-level process map for this process area is described in Fig. 5.11.

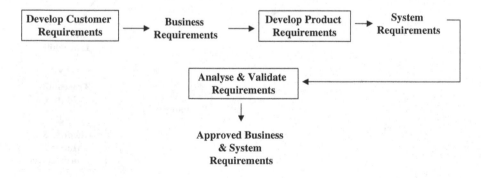

Fig. 5.11 High-level process map for requirements development

---

[7] This is typically done with a Requirements Traceability Matrix.

Often, the requirements are poorly defined for the various projects in immature organizations. They may be incomplete, inadequately documented, or un-testable leading to confusion among staff and customers. The implementation of the requirements development process area leads to best practice for defining, analysing, and validating customer and product requirements.

The customer requirements may be determined from the stakeholders by interviews or questionnaires, and the stakeholder needs and expectations are identified and consolidated. They are then converted into the customer requirements and documented in the requirements specification.[8] They are then refined and elaborated to develop the product and product component requirements. These requirements are developed in technical terms and are derived from the customer requirements. These product requirements are then allocated to product components. Internal and external interface requirements are developed.

The requirements are analysed and validated to ensure that they reflect stakeholder needs. Various operational concepts and scenarios including functionality, performance, maintenance, and support will be developed and reviewed. The requirements will be analysed to remove any conflicts and to determine whether they satisfy the objectives of higher level requirement, as well as being complete, consistent, realizable, and testable. Checklists are often employed to analyse the requirements and check the necessity of the requirement, its consistency, completeness, and feasibility.

Typical deliverables for the requirements management and requirements development process areas include process maps, guidelines, templates, and checklists. The process map provides a high-level summary of the activities involved and the guidelines provide the details behind the process map. The templates support the process and checklists act as a reminder of what needs to be done to perform the process correctly. Typical deliverables are detailed in Fig. 5.12.

Process maps	Procedure/guidelines
Requirements process map	Requirements guidelines
Change control process map	
Templates	Checklists
Business requirements	Requirements definition and
System requirements	analysis
Traceability matrix[a]	Requirements verification and
Change request form	validation
Issue log	Managing changes to requirements

Fig. 5.12 Requirements development and management deliverables ([a]There are several approaches to the implementation of requirements traceability. There may be one traceability matrix or alternatively it may be with a separate traceability matrix section in the affected project deliverable. Another approach might be to employ a requirements tracking tool rather than a traceability matrix)

---

[8] The terminology employed will vary from organization to organization. It may also be called the Business Requirements Specification (BRS).

5.4.1
Requirements Process Map

The requirements process map is an abstraction of the activities involved in defining and validating customer and product requirements. The sample process map in Fig. 5.13 includes activities for requirements elicitation and validation. It includes task to determine what the customers or business users want (i.e. the business requirements) and what the software development organization will provide (i.e. the system requirements).

The analysis and validation of the requirements may involve workshops with the stakeholders or prototyping activities to give a preliminary view of the proposed product

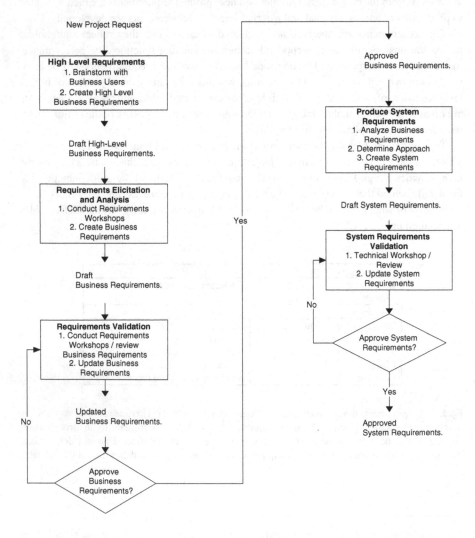

Fig. 5.13 Requirements process map

prior to its implementation. The analysis will help to ensure that the requirements are clearly stated and reflect stakeholder needs. The requirements need to be consistent and unambiguous with any dependencies and conflicts identified and addressed. They need to be complete, realizable, and testable.

The process map for managing changes to the requirements is quite distinct from the requirements development process map. It controls what the requirements development process produces and tracks requirements throughout the development life cycle.

Change control is concerned with the process of assessing the impacts of proposed changes; raising a change request and documenting the proposed change; and authorizing or rejecting the change request. The cost, schedule, and technical impacts of the proposed change will be considered, and an informed decision is then made by the stakeholders on whether to authorize or reject the proposed change. The appropriate changes are then made for approved change requests. A sample process map for managing changes to requirements is described in Fig. 5.14.

5.4.2
Requirements Procedure

The requirements procedure (or guidelines) will provide the details behind the process maps. It will define the procedure by which the requirements elicitation and definition activities are carried out, as well as the procedure by which change control is conducted. It will also detail the roles involved in the process. It will typically include sections on

- Requirements gathering and elicitation
- Requirements workshops
- Analysis and validation of requirements
- Preparation of business requirements
- Preparation of system requirements
- Traceability of requirements
- Changes to requirements
- Roles and responsibilities

Requirements elicitation goes beyond collecting requirements, as it involves identifying and documenting requirements that may not be explicitly stated by the stakeholders. The approach to elicitation may involve

- Interviews
- Surveys and questionnaires
- Prototyping
- User groups
- Observation
- Domain expert
- Use cases

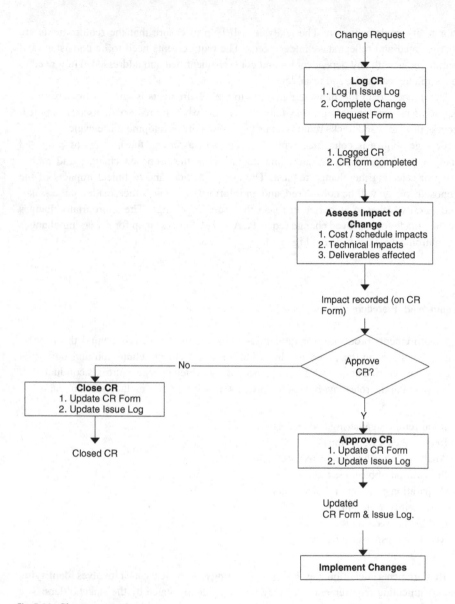

Fig. 5.14 Change control process map

Interviews are the most common method for requirements elicitation and they are effective in developing an understanding of the problem domain and in getting users to describe their work. The interviews need to be managed with open and closed questions. Questionnaires are useful in gaining feedback from a lot of people. However, they need to be well designed and the information provided needs to be validated.

Prototyping allows the users to view an early version of the system and to give feedback on the system. It is especially useful when developing a new product or using new technology where there is no prior experience. It provides early feedback on the validity of the proposed solution, and it prevents the developing organization from going too far and wasting development effort.

User groups allow several users to come together to talk about their requirements, and it allows the views of several stakeholders to be gathered at once. Observation is concerned with watching people do their work, and it helps in understanding the support that they need from the system to be implemented. A domain expert is someone with expert knowledge of a similar system or problem domain. Finally, use cases describe a user's interaction with a system and are part of the Unified Modelling Language (UML).

Requirements need to be written clearly and unambiguously. They may be supplemented by tables and diagrams, but should not contain any design or testing details except for any required design constraints. Each requirement should be given a unique number to identify it uniquely. The detail of the layout of all reports that the system is to produce should be defined.

The requirements are analysed and validated to ensure that they reflect stakeholder needs. This may involve requirements workshops with the stakeholders, and a checklist may be employed as an aid to analysis and validation. The checklists may be used to check the necessity of each requirement, its consistency, completeness, and feasibility. The objective is to ensure that the requirements are appropriately defined and accurately reflect stakeholder needs. The analysis will identify and resolve any conflicts as well as determining whether they satisfy the objectives of higher level requirement.

The requirements need to be validated[9] early in the development life cycle to ensure that the resulting product is what the customer wants. This often involves participation from customers and end users and may include prototyping, storyboards, simulation, and feedback from relevant stakeholders.

Requirements verification is concerned with ensuring that the requirements have been correctly implemented at the later stages of the development cycle. It may include informal or formal peer reviews and software testing. Software inspections are a cost-effective way to remove defects early in the software development life cycle.

The requirements management procedure should make it easy for the stakeholders involved to understand their role in carrying out the process.

5.4.3
Requirements Templates

Typical templates employed for requirements development and management are described in Table 5.10).

---

[9] Validation is often explained as "Are we building the right system?" Verification is explained as "Are we building it right?"

Table 5.10 Requirements templates

Template	Typical contents
Business requirements	This is typically a Microsoft Word document with the following sections: – Overview of business requirements (req. no, description, priority) – Detailed business requirements (req. no., sub req. no, description) – Overview of current systems – Business processes – User interface requirements
System requirements	This is typically a Microsoft Word document with the following sections: – General description – Overview of system requirements (bus. req. no, sys. req. no, description, priority, dependencies) – Detailed system requirements (description, priority, screen shot, report layout, risks and dependencies, technical and design issues) – Operational requirements – Performance requirements – Other non-functional requirements – Interface requirements
Traceability matrix	This may be done with an Excel spreadsheet that lists the requirements and shows how they map to design requirements and testing scripts Traceability sections in documents may also implement it
Change request form	This is typically a Microsoft Word document with the following sections: – Unique reference number – Description of proposed change – Impacts (technical, cost, and schedule) – Decision
Issue log	This was described earlier in Section 5.2.3

5.4.4
Requirements Checklist

There are several checklists that may be useful to employ for the requirements area. Three sample checklists are presented here including

– Requirements development and analysis
– Requirements verification and validation
– Managing changes to requirements checklist (Tables 5.11, 5.12, and 5.13)

Table 5.11 Requirements development and analysis checklist

No.	Item to check
1.	Are the requirements numbered to facilitate traceability?
2.	Is each requirement clear and unambiguous?
3.	Is each requirement testable?
4.	Does each requirement have a priority to indicate its importance?
5.	Is each requirement implementable?
6.	Have the requirements been analysed with any conflicts between the requirements resolved?
7.	Has each requirement been broken down as fully as possible?
8.	Is each requirement consistent with the project's objectives?
9.	Is each requirement necessary?
10.	Is each requirement stated as a stakeholder need?
11.	Are the requirements complete and consistent?
12.	Are the requirements correct?
13.	Are the business requirements traceable to the system requirements and vice versa?
14.	Have the technical constraints been identified?

Table 5.12 Requirements verification and validation checklist

No.	Item to check
1.	Are the business requirements/system requirements traceable to the technical design and software modules and vice versa?
2.	Are the business requirements/system requirements traceable to the system test cases and UAT test cases and vice versa?
3.	Have the business requirements specification and system requirements specification been reviewed and approved by all stakeholders?
4.	Have all sections of the templates been completed appropriately? Is there sufficient detail?
5.	Has the system testing and user acceptance testing been completed with all defects corrected?

Table 5.13 Managing changes to requirements checklist

No.	Item to check
1.	Have the impacts (cost, schedule, etc.) of changes to the requirements been considered prior to their approval?
2.	Have the affected deliverables been updated appropriately following approved changes to the requirements?

5.4.5
Institutionalization

The implementation of the specific and generic practices for requirements development and management has been described. The institutionalization of an effective requirements process is concerned with ingraining the process in the way that work is done in the organization to ensure that it is performed consistently and retained in times of stress. Institutionalization requires that there is a high-level management policy that states management expectation of how requirements will be identified, documented, and managed in the organization.

The requirements process needs to be planned and resources such as a business analyst need to be in place, as well as any tools required for performing the process. The project manager or business analyst assigns responsibilities for conducting workshops, producing the deliverables, and schedules the activities appropriately. All involved in the process receive appropriate training on the process for gathering the requirements and eliciting customer needs.

The deliverables produced (e.g. requirements specification and system requirements) are placed under an appropriate level of configuration management control. The stakeholders involved are identified and documented in the project plan and schedule. The project manager will keep the stakeholders involved during the project.

The project manager will monitor progress, risks, and issues during the project and take corrective action as appropriate. These will be reported in the regular status reports sent to management and the project board, with the status reviewed with management during the project.

An independent audit of the project (including requirements definition and management) will be conducted during the project. Any non-compliances identified will be assigned to the project team for resolution.

5.5
Configuration Management

The configuration management process area is concerned with the implementation of best practice for establishing a configuration management system; identifying work products that need to be subject to change control; controlling changes to these work products over time; controlling releases of work products; creating baselines; maintaining the integrity of baselines; providing accurate configuration data to stakeholders; recording and reporting the status of configuration items and change requests; and verifying the correctness and completeness of configuration items with configuration audits. The configuration management improvement team is responsible for implementing the CMMI requirements for this process area.

The specific goals and practices for this process area are detailed in Table 5.14 and discussed further in this section.

Table 5.14   CMMI requirements for configuration management

Specific goal	Specific practice	Description of specific practice/goal
SG 1		*Establish baselines*
	SP 1.1	Identify configuration items
	SP 1.2	Establish a configuration management system
	SP 1.3	Create or release baselines
SG 2		*Track and control changes*
	SP 2.1	Track change requests
	SP 2.2	Control configuration items
SG 3		*Establish integrity*
	SP 3.1	Establish configuration management records
	SP 3.2	Perform configuration audits

Configuration management involves the following:

- Identify what needs to be controlled
- Ensure those items are accurately defined and documented
- Ensure changes are made in a controlled manner
- Ensure that the correct version of a work product is being used
- Determine at any time the configuration status of an item
- Ensure adherence to company standards
- Plan releases

Effective configuration management allows questions such as the following to be easily answered:

- What is the correct version of the software module to be updated?
- Where can I get a copy of R4.7 of software system X?
- What version of the software system X is installed at the various customer sites?
- What changes have been introduced in the new release of software (version R4.8 from the previous release of R4.7)?
- What version of the design document corresponds to software system version R3.5?
- What customers use R3.5 of the software system?
- Are we certain that no undocumented or unapproved changes have been included in released versions of the software?

Configuration management allows the orderly development of software, and it ensures that the impacts of proposed changes are considered prior to authorization. It ensures that releases are planned and that only authorized changes to the software are made. The integrity of the system is maintained and the constituents of the software system and their version numbers are known at all times.

A change request database[10] is set up to record requests for changes during the project. The proposed change requests are documented and then considered by the change control board (CCB). The CCB is set up early in the project and its role is to consider the impacts and risks of the proposed change and decide on whether the request should be approved or rejected. A proposed change may have impacts on the schedule and budget as well as technical impacts on other work products. It is important to keep change to a minimum especially at the later stages of the project in order to reduce risks to quality. For small projects, the CCB may just consist of the project manager and the system owner.

The change request database will record the results of the review of each change request as well as the rationale for the decision. Change requests and problem reports for all configuration items are recorded and analysed, reviewed, approved, and tracked to closure.

The configuration items are the work products that are to be placed under configuration management control. These include documents and software code and they are identified and documented early in the project life cycle. They include documents such as project plans; requirements and design specifications; software code and data files; test plans; user manuals; process documents and supporting tools.

Each configuration item needs to be uniquely identified and controlled. This involves defining standards for the naming conventions for deliverables at either project or organization level and applying it consistently to the projects. A very simple approach is to employ mnemonics labels and version numbers to uniquely identify project deliverables. For example, a business requirements specification for project 005 in the Finance business area may be represented simply by

FIN_005_BRS

Configuration items will also have a version number that is incremented each time that the work product is updated. This means that standards need to be defined for version numbering for work products. For documents, a simple version numbering system v0.1, v0.2, v0.3 is often used for draft documents, with version v1.0 being the first approved version of the document. Each time a document is modified its version number is incremented, and the document history records the reasons for modification.

Source code and data files are generally maintained in a source code repository such as PVCS or VSS, and these provide an audit trail of all the changes made to the configuration items. A configuration item is often linked to other configuration items. For example, a code module may be linked to a specification or test cases.

A configuration management system is set up to store and retrieve the configuration items. This provides security and control of the configuration items as well as having procedures for

– Access controls
– Checking in/out configuration items
– Merging and branching
– Labels
– Reporting

---

[10] This may just be a simple Excel spreadsheet.

In some cases there may be one configuration management system for source code and data files and a separate system for documents. In other cases there may be one system for all configuration items.

The configuration management system allows source code or documents to be checked out of the repository, modifications to be made, and checked back into the repository. This allows the integrity of the work product to be preserved and prevents more than one person from altering the work product at the same time.

A baseline provides a stable basis for continuing evolution of the configuration items. It is a key term in configuration management and the CMMI definition of *baseline* is as follows:

DEFINITION (BASELINE)
A baseline is a set of work products that has been formally reviewed and agreed upon, that thereafter serves as the basis for future development and than can be changed only through formal change control procedures.

All changes move forward from the current baseline to create a new baseline. The CCB authorizes the release of baselines and the content of each baseline is documented. All configuration items must be approved before they are entered into controlled baselines.

The configuration management system will provide records of the configuration management activities including who modified a configuration item and when the modification took place. The records include the status of the configuration items and the status of the change requests. The revision history of the configuration items will be maintained.

Configuration management audits will be conducted during the project to verify that a proposed configuration is consistent and complete. Every project should have at least one configuration audit, and the objective is to verify the completeness and correctness of the baseline library contents. The configuration audit will check that the records correctly identify the configuration of the configuration items and will also verify compliance to the configuration management standards and procedures. Any action items from the audit are tracked to closure.

A software *configuration management plan* is prepared early in the project and is used as a basis to perform the various configuration management activities for the project. The plan will detail the various tasks to be performed including the schedule and resources, as well as the items to be placed under configuration management control. The CM plan will detail the procedure for naming configuration items, version control, and release management.[11]

Often, the role of a *software configuration manager* is employed in organizations. This may be a full- or part-time role[12] depending on the size of the organization and projects. The CM manager takes overall responsibility for configuration management in their area ensuring that configuration management activities are carried out correctly for all controlled releases. The CM manager will conduct and report the results of the CM audits.

---

[11] These procedures may be defined in the Configuration Management procedure and referenced in the CM plan.

[12] The project manager may perform the CM manager role for small organizations and projects.

Process maps	Procedure/guidelines
Change control process map Configuration management Process map	Configuration management procedure Release procedure[a] Guidelines for use of document / code Repository (e.g. VSS, PVCS)[b] Customer support procedure
Templates	Checklist
Configuration Mgt plan[c] Issue log Change request form Defect log Defect form Release note	Configuration management audit

Fig. 5.15 Configuration management deliverables ([a]This may be part of the configuration management procedure. [b]This will describe a particular repository including the checking in/checking out procedures as well as branching, merging, and labelling. [c]This may be part of the project plan)

All software releases need to be documented including the contents of the release as well as installation and rollback instructions. The release notes will detail the requirements and change requests implemented as well as the defects corrected and the version of the new release. A list of customer sites where the release has been installed will be maintained. All software releases are tested appropriately prior to their approval.

The typical deliverables for the configuration management process area include process maps, procedure and guidelines, templates, and a checklist. The process map provides an abstract summary of the activities involved; the procedure and guidelines provide the detail behind the process map. The templates support the process and the checklist helps to ensure that the process has been correctly performed. The typical deliverables are given in Fig. 5.15.

5.5.1
Configuration Management Process Map

A sample change control process map was presented in Fig. 5.14. It describes the process for raising a change request; performing an impact assessment; deciding on whether to approve or reject the change request; and proceeding with implementation (where applicable).

A sample configuration management process map is detailed in Fig. 5.16, and it shows the process for updates of configuration information following an approved change request. The deliverable is checked out of the repository; modifications are made and the changes approved; configuration information is updated and the deliverable is checked back into the repository.

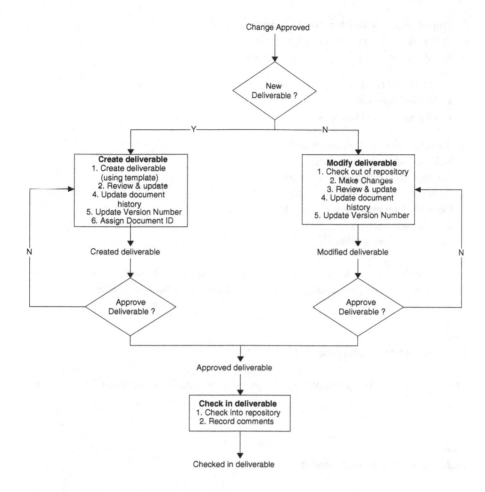

Fig. 5.16 Configuration management process map

5.5.2
Configuration Management Procedure

The configuration management procedure provides the details behind the process maps. It defines the procedure by which the activities in the process are conducted as well as the roles involved. It will include sections to describe

— The procedure for change control[13]
— The change request form
— Repository for documents and source code

---

[13] This will also describe how the change control board will function.

- Project directory structure for documents and code
- Standards for documents (standard template)
- Standards for document control management

  - Document ID (uniquely identifies document)
  - Version number
  - File naming conventions

- Source code control management
- Release and build procedures
- Configuration management planning
- Configuration management audits
- Configuration management records
- Training and metrics
- Roles and responsibilities[14]

The configuration management procedure should make it easy for a new project manager and the other stakeholders to understand and implement the process.

5.5.3
Configuration Management Templates

The following are typical templates employed in configuration management (Table 5.15).

5.5.4
Configuration Management Checklist

The configuration process area includes a specific practice (SP 3.2) to conduct a configuration management audit, and this is often conducted by the configuration manager. The configuration manager is a role assigned (or performed by the project manager) and the responsibilities include

- Establish filing structure for documents and source code
- Define how a release will be created from the repository
- Prepare releases (for independent testing or deployment)
- Record details of the release
- Verify (via configuration audits) that the constituents of the release are appropriately defined with appropriate records maintained
- Verify that the configuration management practices are consistently followed

---

[14] This may also be implemented by a test management tool for tracking defects (e.g. PV Tracker, Bugzilla).

Table 5.15 Templates for configuration management

Template	Typical contents
Configuration management plan	This may be a separate document or a section in the project plan. It details the configuration management responsibilities for the project – Roles and responsibilities – Configuration items – Naming conventions – Version control – Filing structure for project – Producing releases – CM audits
Issue log	The typical contents for the Issue Log were described in Section 5.2.3
Change request form	The typical contents for the change request form were described in Section 5.4.3
Defect log[a]	This may be a Microsoft Excel document with the following columns: – Defect number – Date raised and raiser – Description – Severity and urgency – Assigned to – Date assigned and due date – Status
Defect form	This may be a Microsoft Word document with the following sections: – Description of defect – Severity and urgency – Areas impacted (documents and software modules) – Testing to verify (unit, system, and UAT)
Release note	This may be a Microsoft Word document with the following sections: – Release ID – Content of release – CRs implemented – Defects corrected – Installation instructions – Rollback instructions

[a]The role of the CM manager is described here

Table 5.16   Sample configuration management audit checklist

No.	Item to check
1.	Is the directory structure set up for the project?
2.	Are the configuration items identified and listed?
3.	Have up-to-date versions of the templates been used for the documents?
4.	Is a unique document ID employed for each document?
5.	Is the standard version numbering system followed for the project?
6.	Are all versions of documents and software modules maintained in the document/source code repository?
7.	Is the configuration management plan up-to-date?
8.	Are the roles defined in the configuration management plan performing their assigned responsibilities?
9.	Are changes to the approved documents formally controlled?
10.	Is the version number of a document incremented appropriately following an agreed change to an approved document?
11.	Is there a change approval board set up to approve change requests?
12.	Are all releases tested prior to their approval?
13.	Is there a record of which releases are installed at the various customer sites?
14	Are all documents/software modules produced by vendors under appropriate configuration management?
15.	Have all staff been appropriately trained on the configuration management procedures and standards?

Table 5.16 presents a sample configuration management audit checklist that may be tailored to meet the needs of projects.

5.5.5
Institutionalization

The implementation of the specific goals and practices for configuration management has been discussed in this section. The institutionalization of the process requires that there is a high-level management policy that states management expectations for how configuration management should be conducted in the organization.

The configuration management process needs to be planned and resources such as a configuration manager and librarian need to be in place as well as any tools required for performing the process. The responsibilities of the configuration manager were discussed in Section 5.5.4. There may also be a librarian role to set up the filing structure for the project, or the configuration manager may perform this role.

The project manager assigns responsibilities for performing configuration management activities. All involved in the process receive appropriate training on the process.

The deliverables produced (e.g. the configuration management plan) are placed under an appropriate level of configuration management control. The stakeholders involved are identified and documented in the CM plan. The project manager will keep the stakeholders involved during the project.

The project manager will monitor progress, risks, and issues during the project and take corrective action as appropriate. These will be reported in the regular status reports sent to and reviewed with management during the project.

An independent audit of the project (including configuration management) will be conducted during the project with any non-compliance issues identified and assigned to the project team for resolution.

5.6
Process and Product Quality Assurance

The process and product quality assurance (PPQA) process area is concerned with providing visibility to management on the processes being followed and the work products being produced by the projects. It provides

- Visibility into the extent to which the defined processes are adhered to
- Visibility into the extent to which the work products conform to standards
- Visibility to management on the results of software quality assurance activities
- Tracking of corrective actions to address any identified non-compliances

This process area is concerned with the implementation of best practice to plan and conduct audits. It includes planning and conducting the audits; documenting and reporting the results to managers and affected individuals; assigning audit actions to individuals or groups to address identified non-compliances; and tracking the audit actions to completion.

Audits are planned and scheduled by the auditor. For large organizations there may be a full-time quality manager and an audit team, whereas for smaller organizations the auditor may just be a part-time role. It is essential that the auditor is independent as otherwise the audits will be ineffective.

The auditor needs to be familiar with the process and in a position to judge the extent to which the standards have been followed. It involves interviews with appropriate individuals and groups, as well as a review of documentation. The role requires good verbal and documentation skills as well as the ability to deal with any conflicts that may arise during the audit. The auditor needs to be fair and objective, and audit criteria will be employed to establish the facts in a non-judgemental manner. The audit report is then circulated to all affected individuals, groups, and managers.

Audit actions are assigned to groups and individuals, and the auditor tracks these actions to completion. In rare cases the auditor may need to escalate the audit actions to management to ensure resolution. The specific goals and practices for PPQA are given in Table 5.17.

The implementation of this process area requires an independent group (e.g. the QA group) to be set up. For small organizations this may be a part-time group of one person. It is essential that whoever is conducting the audit is fully independent of the group being

Table 5.17 CMMI requirements for process and product quality assurance

Specific goal	Specific practice	Description of specific practice/goal
SG 1		*Objectively evaluate process and work products*
	SP 1.1	Objectively evaluate processes
	SP 1.2	Objectively evaluate work products and services
SG 2		*Provide objective insight*
	SP 2.2	Communicate and ensure resolution of non-compliance issues
	SP 2.2	Establish records

Process Maps	*Procedure/guidelines*
Audit Process Map	Audit Procedure
Templates	*Checklist*
Audit Report	Audit Checklist
Audit Schedule	

Fig. 5.17 Process and product quality assurance deliverables

audited, and certainly the auditor must not be reporting to the manager whose area is being audited. The typical deliverables for this process area are shown in Fig. 5.17.

5.6.1
Audit Process

A sample process map for conducting audits is detailed in Fig. 5.18. It includes planning and scheduling audits; conducting audits and reporting results; and tracking audit actions to completion.

5.6.2
Audit Procedure

The audit procedure will provide the details behind the audit process map. It will define the procedure by which the activities in the process are carried out as well as the roles involved. It will generally include sections on

- Audit planning and scheduling
- Audit meeting
- Audit reporting
- Audit action tracking
- Escalation of actions to management
- Training

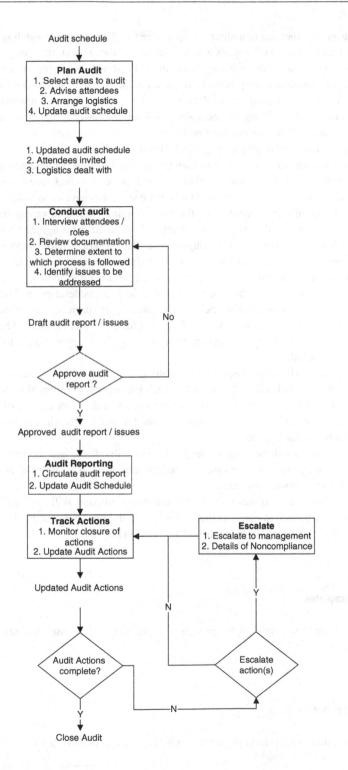

Fig. 5.18 Process and product quality assurance process map

The quality manager or auditor is responsible for planning and scheduling the audits. A representative sample of projects will be audited and the audit strategy employed depends on the culture and maturity of the organization. There will be a need for a larger number of audits to ensure that the process is ingrained in the way that work is done in the organization for organizations that are relatively new to software process improvement. Mature organizations with a strong process culture will require fewer audits. Small organizations will have fewer resources available and there may be no full auditor. Large organizations may have a full-time quality manager and a team of auditors.

It is essential that irrespective of how the quality function is implemented the auditor is independent of the area being audited. The auditor needs to be familiar with the process and in a position to judge the extent to which the standards have been followed.

The planning and scheduling of the audits requires that a representative sample of projects be sampled; the scope of the audit and proposed dates agreed with the affected groups; logistics such as room bookings organized; and audit criteria prepared.

An audit consists of interviews and document reviews. The interview is a meeting between the auditor and the process practitioners, and audit criteria will be employed to judge the extent to which the process adheres to its process description. The auditor asks the audit attendees to describe their specific role in the project, the activities that they perform, the deliverables that they produce, and the standards followed. The auditor will review appropriate documentation after the meeting, and if appropriate a follow-up audit will be conducted.

The auditor will revise notes from the audit meeting and review any required additional documents. This will allow the extent to which the process is followed to be determined. The auditor will then prepare the audit report and agree dates for closure of audit actions with the affected individuals and groups. The audit report will then be circulated to affected individuals and management.

Audit actions will be assigned to groups and individuals, and the auditor tracks the actions to completion. In rare cases the auditor may need to escalate the audit actions to management to ensure resolution.

The auditor role requires good verbal and documentation skills and auditors must be appropriately trained to carry out their roles. The individuals being audited need to receive orientation on the purpose of audits and their role in the audit.

5.6.3
Audit Templates

Typical templates employed for process and product quality assurance are described in Table 5.18.

5.6.4
Audit Checklist

A sample audit checklist to guide the auditor is provided in Table 5.19.

Table 5.18 Templates for process and product quality assurance

Template	Typical contents
Audit report	This may be a Microsoft Word with the following sections: Overview of audit 　– Area audited 　– Date of audit 　– Scope of audit 　– Auditor and attendees 　– No. of audit actions Audit findings 　– Project management 　– Requirements 　– Design 　– Coding 　– Configuration management 　– Testing and peer reviews Action plan
Audit schedule	This is typically a Microsoft Excel document that includes the following columns: 　– Area to be audited 　– Planned date of audit 　– Scope of audit 　– Auditor 　– Attendees 　– No. of audit actions 　– No. of open audit actions

5.6.5
Institutionalization

The implementation of the specific goals and practices was described in this section. The institutionalization requires that there is a high-level management policy that states management expectations of how process and product assurance should be conducted in the organization.

The quality assurance process needs to be planned and appropriate resources such as quality manager and team of auditors put in place, as well as any tools required for performing the process. The responsibilities of the auditor are to plan and schedule the audits; conduct the audits and report the results; and track the audit actions to completion.

All involved in the audit process need to receive appropriate training. This includes the participants in the audit who receive appropriate orientation; the auditor who needs to be trained in interview techniques including asking open and closed questions; effective documentation to record the results; and how to deal with any conflicts that might arise during an audit.

Table 5.19   Audit checklist

No.	Item to check
	Project management
1.	Has the project planning process been consistently followed?
2.	Has the project monitoring/control process been consistently followed?
3.	Is the project plan complete and approved?
4.	Are the risk log, issue log, and lessons learned log set up?
5.	Are the responses to the risks and issues appropriate?
6.	Is the Microsoft Schedule (or equivalent) available and up-to-date?
7.	Are the weekly reports available?
	Configuration management
1.	Has the CM plan been completed appropriately?
2.	Is the issue log employed to manage change requests?
3.	Is the change request form employed to detail the impacts of CR?
4.	Are the appropriate people involved in defining, assessing the impact, and approving the change request?
5.	Are the affected deliverables (with the CR) identified and updated?
6.	Are all documents and source code in the repository?
7.	Has a configuration management audit been conducted?
8.	Are checking in/checking out procedures followed?
9.	Are comments recorded during checking in/checking out files?
	Supplier management
1.	Is the procurement plan complete?
2.	Is the statement of work complete?
3.	Have the PM skills of the supplier been considered in the evaluation?
4.	Does the formal agreement include strict change control?
5.	Are milestone payments linked to approved project deliverables?
6.	Is the supplier agreement management process followed consistently?
	Requirements, design, and testing
1.	Are the business requirements complete and is the sign-off available?
2.	Is requirements traceability addressed?
3.	Are the system requirements complete and approved?
4.	Is the technical and database design complete and approved?
5.	Are the unit test scripts available with the results recorded?
6.	Are the system test cases available with results recorded?
7.	Are UAT test cases available with results recorded?
	Deployment and support
1.	Are the user manuals complete and available?
2.	Has all required training been provided?
3.	Is the handover to support completed for the project?
4.	Are all open problems documented?

The deliverables produced (e.g. the audit reports) are placed under an appropriate level of configuration management control. The stakeholders involved are identified and documented in the quality plan and audit schedule. The auditor will keep the stakeholders involved during the process.

The auditor will report the audit findings to affected staff and management. High-level management will be kept informed of key findings.

An independent audit (usually a third party or separate internal audit function) of the audit process will need to be conducted to ensure that the function is effective. Any non-compliance issues are identified and assigned to the auditor and quality manager for resolution.

5.7
Measurement and Analysis

This process area is concerned with the implementation of best practice for measurement to support management information needs. It involves

- Identifying management information needs
- Defining measurement objectives
- Specification of measures
- Implementation of measures
- Communicating the results
- Analysing the results

This process area supports the other level 2 process areas in objectively judging their performance. The introduction of measurement in an organization usually starts off with a small core set of measures, which is built upon later in the improvement initiative. The early focus is on measures at the project level, and this expands over time to address the information needs of the organization. The initial set of measures often includes

- Schedule estimation variance
- Effort estimation variance
- Budget estimation variance
- Size variance
- Quality status
- Total number and open number of audit actions
- Total number and open number of change requests
- Total number and open number of defects

The specific goals and practices for this process area are defined in Table 5.20.

The measurement objectives are derived from information needs of managers and projects, and measures are specified to support these needs. The measurements are defined precisely to ensure they are consistently performed and to facilitate communication.

The data collection and storage procedures specify how the data will be collected, stored, and available for future use. The data required for each specified measure will be documented, as well as the frequency and responsibilities for collection. The data collection may be a manual process or automated with tools.

Table 5.20 CMMI requirements for measurement and analysis

Specific goal	Specific practice	Description of specific practice/goal
SG 1		*Align measurement and analysis activities*
	SP 1.1	Establish measurement objectives
	SP 1.2	Specify measures
	SP 1.3	Specify data collection and storage procedures
	SP 1.4	Specify analysis procedures
SG 2		*Provide measurement results*
	SP 2.1	Collect measurement data
	SP 2.2	Analyse measurement results
	SP 2.3	Store data and results
	SP 2.4	Communicate results

Process Maps	*Procedure/Guidelines*
Measurement Process Map	Measurement Guidelines
Templates	*Checklist*
Measurement Spreadsheet Weekly Reports Project Board Reports End Project Reports	Measurement Checklist

Fig. 5.19 Measurement deliverables

The analysis procedures specify how the measurement data will be analysed and reported. It may include data analysis methods and tools such as bar charts, pie charts, histograms. The responsibilities for analysis and communication or presentation of the results need to be defined.

Once the measurement objectives, measures, data collection, storage, and analysis procedures have been specified, the projects start collecting and analysing measurement data, storing, and communicating the results.

The typical deliverables for this process area include a process map, guidelines, templates, and a checklist. The process map provides an abstract summary of the activities involved; the procedure and guidelines provide the details behind the process map. The deliverables are given in Fig. 5.19.

5.7.1
Measurement Process

A sample process map for this process area is detailed in Fig. 5.20.

The process map includes activities to identify management information needs and measurement objectives; activities to identify appropriate measures to satisfy these needs; activities to specify data collection and storage procedures; and collecting, analysing, and communicating measures.

Fig. 5.20 Sample
measurement process

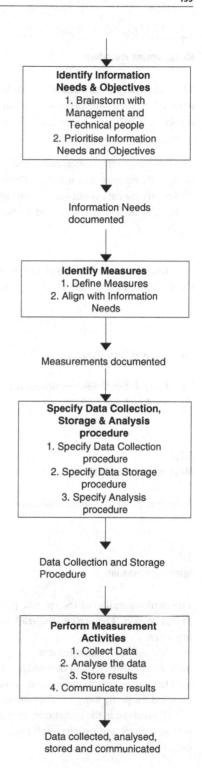

5.7.2
Measurement Procedure

The measurement procedure (or guidelines) will provide the details behind the process map. It will define the procedure by which the activities are carried out as well as the roles involved. It will include sections on

- Identifying information needs and measurement objectives
- Specifying measures to satisfy these needs
- Specifying data collection and storage procedures
- Specifying how measures are analysed and reported
- Training

Table 5.21 is a simple approach to specifying information needs, measurement objectives, measures, data collection, and reporting.

5.7.3
Measurement Templates

The typical templates employed for the measurement and analysis process areas are described in Table 5.22.

5.7.4
Measurement Checklist

A sample checklist for measurement and analysis is presented in Table 5.23.

5.7.5
Institutionalization

The implementation of the specific practices for measurement and analysis was discussed in this section. The institutionalization is addressed by the implementation of the generic practices.

The high-level management policy states management expectations for how measurement and analysis should be conducted in the organization.

The measurement and analysis process needs to be planned, and resources and tools required for performing the process need to be identified and provided.

All involved in the measurement and analysis process need to receive appropriate training on metrics and problem solving to assist them in preparing, analysing, and reporting on metrics.

Table 5.21   Implementation of measurement and analysis

Information needs	Measurement objective	Metrics	Data collection	Reporting
Timeliness of projects	Improve scheduling estimation accuracy	Schedule variance = $\dfrac{(\text{# Actual cal days} - \text{est. # cal days})*100}{\text{# Estimated calendar days}}$	MSP	Weekly and project board (PB) reports
Cost estimation accuracy	Improve budgeting estimation accuracy	Budget variance = $\dfrac{(\text{Actual spent} - \text{est. spend})*100}{\text{Estimated spend}}$	MSP/budget tracking	Weekly and PB reports
Effort estimation accuracy	Improve effort estimation accuracy	Effort variance = $\dfrac{(\text{Actual effort} - \text{est. effort})*100}{\text{Estimated effort}}$	MSP/time tracking	Weekly and PB reports
Progress of current projects	Provide visibility into progress of project	Schedule, effort, budget status; # Risks and # issues; # Open defects and severity; # Open change requests and severity	Risk/issue log/defect log	Weekly reports
Extent of adherence to the process	Improve level of compliance to processes/standards	# Non-compliances/# Audit actions	Audit reports/action tracking	QA quarterly report
Quality and reliability of software	Improve quality and reliability	# Post-release defects and severity (system); # Open defects and severity (for system); # Support calls (per system)	Support tool	Support weekly reports
Availability of systems	Improve availability of systems	# Outages per month (per system); Availability system = $\dfrac{\text{Operational time}*100}{\text{Operational time} + \text{outage time}}$	Support tool	Support weekly reports
Effectiveness of customer support	Improve efficiency of customer support	% Problems resolved within SLA goal; # Arrivals/# closures per week; # Open backlog (and severities) per week; Age of open backlog; # New problems/outages introduced	Support tool	Support weekly reports
Extent of customer satisfaction	Improve customer satisfaction	Customer satisfaction metrics	Customer survey form	Customer report

Table 5.22 Measurement and analysis templates

Template	Typical contents
Measurement spreadsheet	This may be a Microsoft Excel document with a separate sheet per project including – Planned and actual start date – Planned and actual end date – Schedule variance – Planned and actual effort – Effort variance – Planned and actual budget – Budget variance – Total CRs by severity – Open CRs by severity – Total inspection defects – Total testing defects by severity – Open testing defects by severity – Phase containment effectiveness – Total/open audit actions – Total post-release defects by severity – Open post-release defects by severity
Weekly report/project board report/end project report	These were discussed previously

Table 5.23 Measurement and analysis checklist

No.	Item to check
	Measurement and analysis
1.	Have management objectives and information needs been identified?
2.	Have measures to satisfy the information needs been identified?
3.	Have the data collection and storage procedures been specified?
4.	Have the data analysis and storage procedures been specified?
5.	Are metrics reported in the weekly reports?
6.	Are metrics reported in the project board reports?
7.	Are the metrics analysed and the results available?
8.	Have the measurement data been stored to allow future availability?

The deliverables produced are placed under an appropriate level of configuration management control. The stakeholders involved are identified and documented in the project plan and schedule.

The project manager will generally report the status of the project in weekly reports. These status reports will also include the key project metrics.

Independent project audits will be conducted, and these will consider the extent to which the measurement and analysis process is followed and effective.

5.8
Review Questions

1. Describe the implementation of project planning and project monitoring and control in an organization.
2. Describe the implementation of requirements management in an organization.
3. Describe the implementation of configuration management in an organization.
4. Describe the implementation of supplier agreement management in an organization.
5. Describe the implementation of measurement and analysis in an organization.
6. Describe the implementation of process and product quality assurance in an organization.

5.9
Summary

This chapter was concerned with the implementation of CMMI maturity level 2 in the organization. A level 2 organization has practices in place to ensure that the process is planned, performed, and controlled. There is an organization policy that states the management expectations of the way that projects will do its work, and the policy states the core values of the organization in managing projects; selecting and managing suppliers; defining requirements; configuration management; audits; and measurement and analysis.

The status of the work products produced by the process is visible to management at major milestones, and changes to the work products are controlled. The work products are placed under appropriate configuration management control, and the process is enforced via independent audits.

A level 2 organization has increased control over its projects and requirements and is in a position to repeat previous project success. Planning and managing new projects is based on experience with similar projects, and realistic commitments are made based on results achieved in previous projects.

The requirements for a project are managed and any changes to the requirements are controlled. Project management practices are in place to plan and manage the project, and basic project measures are defined to judge the performance of the project. Historical data such as budget, schedule, and effort variance are used to improve the planning of future projects. The project works with its subcontractors (if applicable) to establish a strong customer–supplier relationship.

The objective in implementing level 2 of the CMMI is to institutionalize effective management practices for projects and to allow successful practices used on earlier projects to be repeated. The level 2 process areas are

- Requirements Management
- Project Planning
- Project Monitoring and Control
- Supplier Agreement Management
- Configuration Management
- Measurement and Analysis
- Process and Product Quality Assurance

Improvement teams are set up to implement these process areas, and the SEPG team will decide on the appropriate number of teams to set up. In small organizations the SEPG may be the only improvement team. The SEPG will wish to keep a balance between the normal day-to-day work of employees and the improvement activities.

Once the organization has completed the implementation of the CMMI level 2 process areas it is ready to commence work on level 3. This is discussed in the next chapter.

CMMI Level 3 Implementation

6

6.1
Introduction

A maturity level 3 organization has standard organization-wide processes in place that are well understood and are defined in terms of procedures and standards. These standard processes ensure consistency in the way in which projects are conducted across the organization, and best practices have been generalized for use at the organization level.

It is not required that projects do things in exactly the same way in a level 3 organization, as it is clearly recognized that the projects' defined software process needs to reflect the unique characteristics of the project. It would be unreasonable to expect a small non-critical project to produce the same full suite of deliverables that a large important project would produce.

A level 3 organization builds on the foundation of project-level stability achieved by CMMI level 2 implementation. There are now organization policies in place stating management expectation for how work is to be done. The process is planned and staff receive

G. O'Regan, *Introduction to Software Process Improvement*, Undergraduate Topics
in Computer Science, DOI 10.1007/978-0-85729-172-1_6,
© Springer-Verlag London Limited 2011

appropriate training to enable them to perform the process. Work products are placed under configuration management control, and process discipline is enforced with independent process audits.

The implementation of level 3 requires a change in thinking in the organization. There is a change in thinking from what is best for individual projects to what is good for the entire organization. Further, everyone in the organization has a role to play in improving the organization.

There is an organization set of standard processes (OSSP) defined, and this describes the processes available for use in the organization. The common process supports the entire organization, and it provides a common organization-wide understanding of the activities, roles, responsibilities, and work products for each process. These are relevant for every project in the organization.

A level 3 organization has tailoring guidelines defined that allow the project to tailor the organization-wide process to yield the project's defined process. These tailoring guidelines define the level of formality and deliverables to be produced for the various categories[1] of projects in the organization. An organization-wide training program is implemented to ensure that staff have the right knowledge to carry out their roles effectively.

A level 3 organization treats its processes and procedures as assets and it has a dedicated group (Software Engineering Process Group) or SEPG in place that is responsible for the organization process assets and its software process improvement activities. The SEPG group helps to provide a strong process improvement culture as well as a structured approach to process definition, piloting, rollout, and tailoring.

Procedures and standards are defined for the various engineering activities such as design, coding, testing. There is a formal review process in place to find errors early in the life cycle, and risk management practices are formalized.

The level 3 processes are defined rigorously, and their definition includes the purpose of the process, entry criteria, inputs, activities and roles, measures, verification steps, output, and exit criteria. The process areas to be implemented for level 3 of the CMMI are as follows:

- Requirements development
- Technical solution
- Product integration
- Verification
- Validation
- Organization process focus
- Organization process definition
- Organization training
- Integrated project management
- Risk management
- Decision analysis and resolution

---

[1]It is usual to define several categories of project (e.g. large, medium, and small). Each category is defined by criteria, and the project will fall into one of the categories. Each category of project generally has an associated set of deliverables that reflect the tailoring of the process.

There are two additional generic practices (GP 3.1 and 3.2) to be implemented for processes at level 3 maturity. These two generic practices are concerned with defining a standard process and collecting improvement information to support future improvements to the process. Further, all of the processes already implemented for CMMI level 2 will need to implement GP 3.1 and 3.2.

The implementation of GP 3.1 requires that each process is defined at the organization level. It is then tailored to yield the project's defined software process (Fig. 6.1).

The implementation of GP 3.2 requires that improvement information be collected from planning and performing the processes to support future improvement of the organization's processes. The information collected is *maintained at the organization level rather than at the project level*.

The improvement information collected may include lessons learned, relevant work products, measures, and measurement results. A *central metrics repository* and an *organization process assets library* will need to be maintained to facilitate organization improvement.

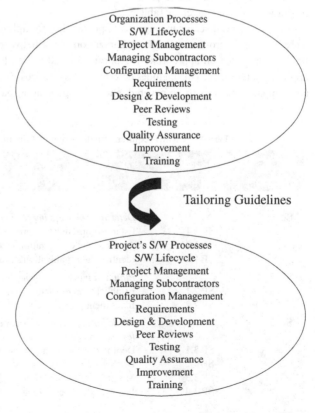

Fig. 6.1 Establishing a defined process

6.2
Organization Process Focus

The organization process focus process area is concerned with planning and implementing process improvements based on an understanding of the strengths and weaknesses of the processes and process assets in the organization. The improvements may be identified from

- Lessons learned
- Periodic process reviews
- Appraisals
- Process improvement suggestions

The organization's process needs are systematically identified by an appraisal, which is a systematic examination of the organization processes used against the CMMI standard. The appraisal may be performed to identify strengths and opportunities for process improvement or to confirm progress made in process improvement. Process improvement needs are then prioritized, and process improvement action plans prepared and implemented. New and refined processes are introduced into the organization in a controlled manner, and pilots may be conducted prior to general deployment. The CMMI requirements for this process area are given in Table 6.1.

Appraisals need senior management sponsorship to highlight the importance of software process improvement to the organization. This helps to ensure that the appraisal findings are acted on appropriately. Appraisals need to be planned and the scope of the appraisal determined. This includes determining the processes to be examined, the projects and support functions to be covered, and the organization participants. The appraisal is

Table 6.1   CMMI requirements for organization process focus

Specific goal	Specific practice	Description of specific practice/goal
SG 1		*Determine process improvement opportunities*
	SP 1.1	Establish organization process needs
	SP 1.2	Appraise the organization processes
	SP 1.3	Identify the organization's process improvements
SG 2		*Plan and implement process improvements*
	SP 2.1	Establish process action plans
	SP 2.2	Implement process action plans
SG 3		*Deploy organization process assets and incorporate lessons learned*
	SP 3.1	Deploy organization process assets
	SP 3.2	Deploy standard processes
	SP 3.3	Monitor implementation
	SP 3.4	Incorporate process-related experiences into process assets

then conducted on-site; the appraisal findings are determined; and feedback prepared and communicated to the organization.

The implementation of improvements requires buy-in across the organization. It requires participation from the process users and process owners and action plans are prepared to plan the improvements; the improvements are implemented and piloted where appropriate. Once the new processes have been approved for deployment all affected staff are trained on the new processes prior to roll out across the organization.

The implementation of improvements requires that there is an appropriate improvement structure to support these activities. It requires a steering group to oversee improvements and to provide direction, resources, and funding for improvement. The SEPG team coordinates process improvement activities, tracks progress, collects best practice, and measures improvement. Specific improvement teams need to be set up by the SEPG to carry out specific improvement actions such as defining new processes and procedures and defining training material to roll out the new processes and standards.

The deployment of new or enhanced processes in the organization needs to be planned. This involves identifying the areas of the organization affected, providing training to the process users, and supporting the users after the rollout.

It is important that process reviews be conducted periodically to get feedback on the suitability and effectiveness of the processes and to incorporate process-related experiences and lessons learned into improvement planning. Typical deliverables for the organization process focus process area included in Fig. 6.2.

Process Maps	*Procedure/Guidelines*
Improvement Process Map	Process Improvement Procedure
	Improvement Structure
Templates	*Checklist*
Improvement Suggestion Log	Appraisal Preparation
Lessons Learned Log & Report	
Appraisal Plan & Schedule	
Post Appraisal Action Plan	
Improvement Project Plan	
Improvement Schedule	
PIIDs (for Appraisal)	
Appraisal Presentations	
Training	

Fig. 6.2 Organization process focus deliverables

6.2.1
Improvement Process

A sample continuous improvement process is detailed in Fig. 6.3, and improvement is seen as a continuous activity within the organization. It involves identifying improvement to be made in the current improvement cycle; planning and implementing the improvements; piloting, refining, and deploying the new processes; checking that the improvements are effective and conducting audits to enforce the new processes. Finally, the whole cycle repeats, as improvement is continuous.

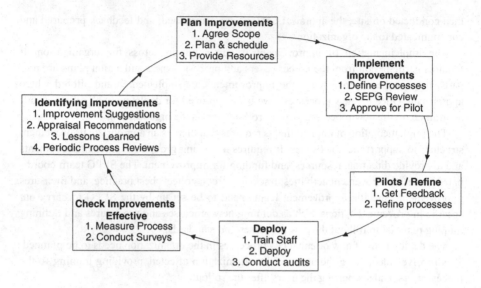

Fig. 6.3 Continuous improvement cycle

The approach to setting up an improvement initiative was described in Chapter 4. It described the continuous improvement cycle as well as describing the teams that need to be set up and their roles and responsibilities.

The continuous improvement activities are described in Table 6.2.

6.2.2
Improvement Procedure

The improvement procedure details how improvement is carried out in the organization. It will generally include sections such as

–   Approach to improvement (e.g. use of CMMI, appraisals, people, training)
–   Continuous improvement cycle (e.g. as in Fig. 6.3)
–   Improvement structure and teams (e.g. Steering Group, SEPG, improvement teams, CMMI project manager)
–   Improvement activities (as in continuous improvement cycle and Table 6.1)

Chapter 4 discusses how an organization may set up an improvement initiative and includes a discussion of the teams required as well as their roles and responsibilities. Chapter 9 discusses SCAMPI appraisals.

6.2.3
Improvement Templates

Typical templates employed for the organization process focus process area are described in Table 6.3.

Table 6.2 Continuous improvement cycle

Activity	Description
Identify improvements to be made	The improvements to be made during an improvement cycle come from several sources: – Improvement suggestions from staff – Lessons learned – Periodic process reviews – Recommendations from an independent CMMI appraisal
Plan improvements	A plan (and schedule) for the improvements is produced. For a major improvement cycle such as implementing a particular maturity level this will include producing a project plan and schedule, and so on For a shorter improvement cycle an improvement action plan (with owners and target completion dates) will be sufficient
Implement improvements	The plan will detail the resources required for to carry out the improvements The improvements will often be conducted by a specific improvement team and approved by the SEPG
Pilots/refine	New processes and standards will often be piloted prior to their deployment to ensure that they are fit for purpose Appropriate refinements are then made to the processes
Deploy	The processes and standards are deployed using a structured approach: – Train staff on the new processes and standards – Work closely and provide assistance to staff during the deployment – Conduct audits to ensure that the new standards are followed
Check improvements effective	– Check that the improvements made have been effective – This may include process reviews, surveys, and measurements of process performance
Do it all again	Improvement is continuous and as soon as an improvement cycle is complete a new improvement cycle is ready to commence

6.2.4
Improvement Checklist

Checklists may be employed as an aid to assist with planning for the appraisal (Table 6.4).

6.2.5
Institutionalization

The implementation of the specific practices for the organization process focus was discussed in this section. The institutionalization is addressed by the implementation of the generic practices.

The high-level management policy stipulates the core values for how improvement should be conducted in the organization. It may state, for example, that the policy is that

Table 6.3   Templates for organization process focus

Template	Typical contents
Improvement suggestions	This may be implemented as a Microsoft Excel spreadsheet with the following columns: – Description of suggestion – Raiser and date raised – Allocated to – Action – Status and date – Comment
Lessons learned log	This may be implemented as a Microsoft Excel spreadsheet with the following columns: – Lessons learned type – Raiser and date raised – Description – Comments and recommendations
Improvement action plan	This may be implemented as a Microsoft Excel spreadsheet with the following columns: – Issue/recommendation – Action – Owner – Due date – Status
Improvement plan and schedule	This is similar to the project plan template discussed in Chapter 4
Appraisal plan	This is typically a Microsoft Word document with the following sections – Appraisal purpose – Appraisal sponsor – Appraisal team – Appraisal team training – Mini-teams (where applicable) – Organization participants – Appraisal scope – Organization personnel and projects – CMMI model scope – Appraisal outputs – High-level schedule – Constraints – Risks – Appraisal schedule and participants at sessions

Table 6.3 Templates for organization process focus

Template	Typical contents
Appraisal schedule	This is a Microsoft Word or Excel spreadsheet that shows the sessions for each day of the appraisal
PIID (practice implementation indicator description)	This is a Microsoft Word document that lists all of the CMMI process areas within the scope of the appraisal[2] It includes the specific and generic practices for each process area and shows how they have been implemented in the organization

Table 6.4 Sample appraisal readiness checklist

No.	Item to check
1.	Is the appraisal plan complete and approved by stakeholders?
2.	Is the appraisal schedule complete and approved by stakeholders?
3.	Has appropriate training been provided to the appraisers?
4.	Have the participants been appropriately trained for appraisal?
5.	Have rooms been booked for the appraisal?
6.	Are the logistics organized for the appraisal?
7.	Have invitations been issued to the participants for the various sessions?
8.	Are the PIIDs prepared?
9.	Are the risks to the appraisal identified and managed?
10.	Has the opening presentation been prepared and approved?

periodic process reviews and appraisals will be conducted and that lessons learned will be used for improvement.

The improvement process needs to be planned, and resources such as the people and tools required need to be identified and provided. The roles involved will typically be a CMMI project manager (or coordinator), the Steering Group, the SEPG team, and the dedicated improvement teams. It will also involve the appraisal leader (and possibly appraisal team) for conducting independent appraisals.

All involved in the process will need to receive appropriate training on their roles and responsibilities. The CMMI project manager needs detailed training and knowledge of the CMMI; the SEPG team needs reasonable knowledge of the CMMI; and the appraisal team and participants need appropriate training to carry out their roles.

The deliverables produced (e.g. project plans, appraisal plans, deliverables produced by improvement teams) are placed under an appropriate level of configuration management control. The stakeholders involved are identified and documented in the project (or action) plan and schedule.

---

[2] This will need to be done for all projects within the scope of the appraisal.

The CMMI project manager will report the status of the improvement activities in regular status reports and in meetings with management.

Independent appraisals and external audits will consider the extent to which the improvement process is followed and effective.

The improvement process is implemented as a standard organization process, and it will have a documented procedure. Improvement information will typically be collected in improvement suggestions, lessons learned logs, periodic process reviews, appraisal findings, measurements, and so on.

6.3
Organization Process Definition

This process area is concerned with establishing and maintaining the organization process assets. The organization's process assets consist of the organization's measurement repository; the organization's process asset library; a description of the life cycle models employed; process tailoring guidelines and criteria; and a description of the organization set of standard processes (Fig. 6.4).

The organization set of standard processes (OSSP) consists of the standard processes employed at the organization level, and each process is decomposed into its process elements such as sub-processes, procedures, templates, forms, checklists, inputs and outputs, and entry and exit criteria.

There may be several life cycle models employed such as the waterfall model, iterative model, spiral model. These will be established and documented at the organization level, and a project will select a life cycle model based on its particular needs as well as on the needs of the organization. The life cycle selection will be based on documented criteria.

The tailoring of the organization set of standard processes to yield the project's defined software process is done in a controlled manner. Tailoring guidelines will be defined, and this generally involves defining several categories of project by criteria and stipulating the deliverables that will be produced for each category. Some deliverables will be mandatory; some will be optional; but the tailoring will be done in a controlled manner. It allows the processes employed in different projects to vary within the defined guidelines and allows the unique characteristics of the project to be appropriately addressed.

Fig. 6.4 Organization process assets

The software measurement repository supports the organization's needs for storing and analysing measurements. A common set of measures is defined for the organization set of standard processes, and these may include measures such as estimation accuracy of the size of work products; estimated and actual effort and cost; quality and test coverage. The measurement repository is used by the organization and projects.

The process asset library consists of policies, processes, procedures, life cycle models, tailoring guidelines, templates, and checklists. It may also include examples from previous projects such as quality plans, development plans, and lessons learned reports, as well as training material and best practice. The process asset library supports organization learning and process improvement, and it allows best practice and lessons learned to be shared across the organization. The specific goals and practices for this process definition process area are given in Table 6.5.

Typical deliverables for the organization process definition process area are shown in Fig. 6.5.

Table 6.5 CMMI requirements for organization process definition

Specific goal	Specific practice	Description of specific practice/goal
SG 1		*Establish organization process assets*
	SP 1.1	Establish standard processes
	SP 1.2	Establish life cycle model descriptions
	SP 1.3	Establish tailoring criteria and guidelines
	SP 1.4	Establish organization's measurement repository
	SP 1.5	Establish the organization's process asset library
	SP 1.6	Establish work environment standards

Process Maps	Procedure/Guidelines
Lifecycle Models	Tailoring Guidelines (& criteria)
Process Maps for all processes	Lifecycle Model Descriptions
	All organization processes, procedures, templates & checklists
Templates	*Checklist*
Measurement Repository Tailoring	OPD Checklist

Fig. 6.5 Organization process definition deliverables

6.3.1
Standard Process

A key feature of a CMMI level 3 organization is that processes are defined at the organization level. They may then be tailored (as in Fig. 6.1) to yield the project's defined software process. This allows projects to be performed as consistently as possible apart from differences allowed by tailoring.

Fig. 6.6 Waterfall life cycle model

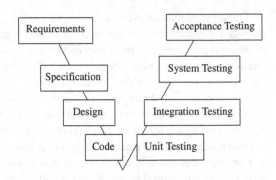

An organization may employ several software life cycles such as the waterfall model (Fig. 6.6) and the spiral model (Fig. 6.7). The starting point for the waterfall life cycle is requirements gathering and definition. It is then followed by the functional specification; the design and implementation of the software; and comprehensive testing. The testing generally includes unit, system, and user acceptance testing. The model is typically employed for projects where the requirements may be identified early in the project life cycle.

The spiral model is useful where the requirements are not fully known at project initiation. The requirements evolve during the development life cycle as an understanding of the system to be developed grows. The development proceeds in a number of spirals, with each spiral typically involving updates to the requirements, design, code, testing, and a user review of the particular iteration or spiral. This leads to a better understanding of the requirements of the system, and this then feeds into the next development cycle in the spiral. The process repeats until the requirements and product are complete.

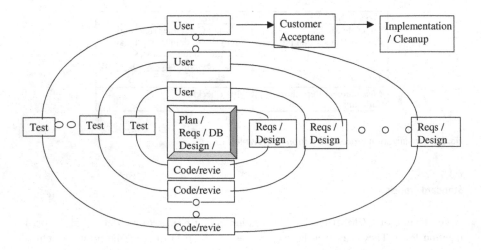

Fig. 6.7 Spiral life cycle model

6.3.2
Procedure and Guidelines

The tailoring procedure (or guidelines) details how the standard organization process may be tailored to yield the project's defined software process. One implementation of tailoring is to define several categories of project (e.g. large, medium, and small)[3] and to stipulate the deliverables that will be produced for each category of project. Another approach is to define the tailoring for each process in its detailed procedure.

Tailoring is important in ensuring that the process for the project reflects its needs. It would clearly be inappropriate to employ the same level of formality for a small low priority project as that employed for a large business critical project. Table 6.6 provides a simple example of tailoring based on two categories of project (A and B). Each category is defined in terms of criteria, and each category has an associated set of deliverables.

The organization will document the life cycle employed including the circumstances in which the life cycle is employed.

An intranet site may be defined for processes, procedures, and templates. This allows project managers and the team to obtain the relevant standards and template and to obtain up-to-date information on processes and procedures. The intranet site for the process assets will typically include

– Organization policy
– Process maps
– Procedures and guidelines
– Checklists
– Templates (project management, engineering, testing)

Table 6.6 Tailoring

Factor/type	Category A	Category B
Complexity	Low	High
Cost	< $50 k	> $50 k
Duration	<3 months	>3 months
Effort	<30 days	>30 days
Deliverables	Small task plan (combined plan/reqs/design/test document)	Project plan Project schedule Business reqs System reqs Design Test plan and scripts End project report

[3]The names of the project category may vary and the size of the project is only one factor in the category.

- Life cycle models
- Improvement suggestion mechanism
- Best practice library
- Training materials
- Central measurement repository

6.3.3
Templates

Typical templates employed for organization process definition are described in Table 6.7.

Table 6.7 Templates for organization process definition

Template	Typical contents
Measurement repository	This is typically a Microsoft Excel document with a separate sheet per project. Each sheet will typically include – Planned and actual start date – Planned and actual end date – Schedule variance – Planned and actual effort – Effort variance – Planned and actual budget – Budget variance – Total CRs by severity – Open CRs by severity – Total inspection defects – Total testing defects by severity – Open testing defects by severity – Phase containment effectiveness – Total/open audit actions – Total post-release defects by severity – Open post-release defects by severity

6.3.4
Checklist

A sample checklist for organization process definition is defined in Table 6.8.

6.3.5
Institutionalization

The implementation of the specific practices for organization process definition was described in this section. The institutionalization requires the implementation of the generic practices.

Table 6.8 Sample organization process definition checklist

No.	Item to check
1.	Are standard processes defined for all processes?
2.	Have tailoring guidelines been defined?
3.	Have the various categories of projects been defined?
4.	Have the various life cycles employed in the organization been defined?
5.	Has the measurement repository been set up?
6.	Has a best practice library been set up?
7.	Has an intranet site (or equivalent) for the processes, procedures, and templates been set up and communicated?

The high-level management policy states management expectations for how organization process definition should be conducted. It will mention the organization set of standard processes and tailoring of the process to yield the project's defined process.

The process needs to be planned, and resources such as any tools required for performing the process need to be identified and provided. All involved in the process receive appropriate training. For example, project managers will need to be trained on tailoring the organization set of standard processes.

The deliverables produced are placed under an appropriate level of configuration management control. This includes the process assets and measurement repository. The stakeholders involved are identified and documented.

Independent project audits will be conducted, and these will also consider the extent to which the organization process definition process is followed and effective. Improvement information will be collected to improve the process.

6.4
Organization Training

Training plays a key role in improving the capability of an organization and the purpose of this process area is to develop the skills and knowledge of people to enable them to perform their roles efficiently and effectively. This process area is concerned with identifying and fulfilling the training needs of the organization and is not concerned with identifying and fulfilling the training needs of projects. An organization training program involves

- Establishing the training needs of the organization
- Providing training to fulfil these needs
- Establishing and maintaining training capability
- Establishing and maintaining training records
- Assessing training effectiveness

The organization training needs will need to support the business goals of the organization and training needs that are common across projects. The process training needs are based on the skills required to perform the organization's set of standard processes.

Training may be provided in various ways including classroom-based training; informal mentoring programmes; guided self-study; web-based training; and virtual training sessions.

The organization training plan will document the training required by the organization. It will detail the training to be provided; the means by which it will be provided; and the training schedule. The training plan will be revised periodically to reflect the changing business needs of the organization. The specific goals and practices for the training process area are given in Table 6.9.

The training plan reflects the current training needs and needs to be updated regularly (e.g. monthly, bi-monthly, or quarterly) to ensure that it continues to meet the needs of the organization. The training process will typically include the following activities:

- Identify strategic training needs of the organization
- Identify individual training needs
- Identify project and support training needs
- Identify training that is common among individuals and projects
- Prepare a training schedule (annual or for quarter)
- Maintain the training schedule
- Ensure that the training is delivered (as per the schedule)
- Ensure feedback on each training course is provided
- Provide metrics on the effectiveness of the training
- Maintain training records
- Build a repository of training materials
- Provide induction training to new staff
- Assign a mentor as part of the induction process

Table 6.9   CMMI requirements for organization training

Specific goal	Specific practice	Description of specific practice/goal
SG 1		*Establish an organization training capability*
	SP 1.1	Establish strategic training needs
	SP 1.2	Determine which training needs are the responsibility of the organization
	SP 1.3	Establish the organization training tactical plan
	SP 1.4	Establish training capability
SG 2		*Provide necessary training*
	SP 2.1	Deliver training
	SP 2.2	Establish training records
	SP 2.3	Assess training effectiveness

Fig. 6.8 Organization training deliverables

Process Maps	Procedure/Guidelines
Training	Training Procedure

Templates	Checklist
Training Schedule Course Feedback	Induction

The training manager[4] (or training coordinator) will manage training in the organization. This involves identifying the training needs and determining how best to satisfy these needs. The training plan is documented and the training is executed as per the plan. The training manager will select appropriate training providers and will arrange logistics for the training courses.

The training will then be provided, and feedback on the effectiveness of training course provided and training records maintained. The training needs may be fulfilled in several ways:

– Informal training by mentor
– Induction training
– Internal training workshops
– Self-directed learning
– Off-site training classes
– Conferences
– Support for external degree courses

Typical deliverables for the organization training process area are shown in Fig. 6.8

6.4.1
Organization Training Process

A sample process map for commencing the discussion on the organization training process is detailed in Fig. 6.9. It includes activities to identify training needs; planning training to satisfy these needs; delivering training; and building training materials in the organization.

6.4.2
Training Procedure

The training procedure provides the details by which training is conducted in the organization. It will typically include sections on

---

[4]This may be a part-time role in the organization.

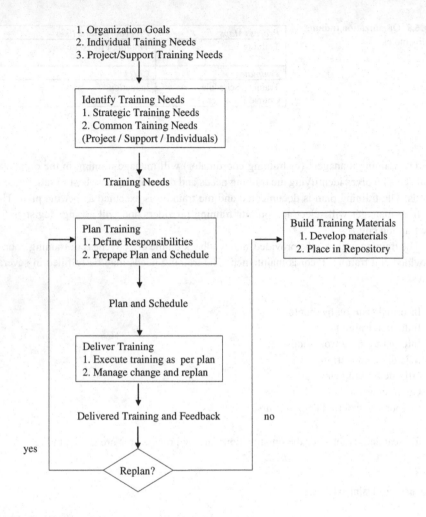

Fig. 6.9 Training process map

- Training needs and responsibilities
- Plan training
- Provide training
- Assess effectiveness of training
- Establish training materials
- Training records
- Training metrics

6.4.3
Training Templates

Typical templates employed for the organization training process area are described in Table 6.10.

Table 6.10 Templates for organization training

Template	Typical contents
Training schedule (sample schedule in Fig. 6.10)	This is typically a Microsoft Excel spreadsheet with the following columns: – Course – Cost – Date – Planned attendees – Actual attendees – Waived – Absent – Instructor – Company/internal – Venue – Feedback
Training feedback form (sample feedback in Fig. 6.11)	This may be a Microsoft Word document with the following sections: – Overall satisfaction – Quality of training materials – Suitability of course venue – Satisfaction with instructor – Applicability of course – Additional comments

Annual Organisation Training Schedule

Month	Course	Cost	Date	Planned Attendees	Actual Attendees	Waived Attendees	Absent	Instructor	Company / Internal	Venue	Course Feedback
January	Process Training (PM)	Internal	15/01/2009	UOC, FM	UOC,FM						Excellent
February	Process Training (SAM)	Internal	09/02/2009								Good
March	Rational Unified Process	External									Excellent
	Process Training (PPQA)	Internal	20/03/2009								Good
April											
May	Prince 2	External									Good
	Process Training (Reqs)	Internal	10/05/2009								Excellent
Jun											

Fig. 6.10 Annual training schedule

A sample organization training schedule to aid the discussion is described in Fig. 6.10. Figure 6.11 provides a sample training feedback form[5] that may be tailored accordingly.

6.4.4
Training Checklist

Induction plays a key role in building up the knowledge of new staff. The sample induction checklist in Table 6.11 may be used as an aid during the induction session:

---

[5]The feedback may be provided by a tool.

Training Course	
Employee Name	
Date of Course	
Item to Check	Rating (1 - 5) *
Overall Satisfaction with Course	
Satisfaction with Course Materials	
Satisfaction with Course Venue	
Satisfaction with Instructor	
Applicability of Course to Employee's Job	
* Rating (1 = V. Poor, 2 = Poor, 3 = Average, 4 = Good, 5 = Excellent)	
Additional Comments	

Fig. 6.11 Course feedback form

6.4.5
Institutionalization

The implementation of the specific practices for organization training achieves the implementation of this process area. The institutionalization is addressed by the implementation of the generic practices.

The high-level management policy states management expectations for how training will be conducted in the organization.

The training process needs to be planned, and appropriate resources provided. These include a training manager or training coordinator as well as any tools required for performing the process. All involved in the training process need to receive appropriate training.

The deliverables (e.g. the training plan) produced need to be placed under an appropriate level of configuration management control. The stakeholders involved are identified and documented in the training plan for the organization.

Independent project audits will be conducted, and these will also consider the extent to which the training process is followed and effective. Improvement information (e.g. training metrics) will be collected and used to improve the training process.

6.5
Requirements, Design, and Development

Requirements development is a level 3 process area and its implementation was discussed with the requirements management process area in Chapter 5. Requirements development

Table 6.11   Induction training checklist

Area	Item to check	Y/N
Project management	– Process for project planning – Process for monitoring/control – Project management guidelines – Estimation guideline – Risk management guidelines – Tailoring – Project plan and schedule – Risk, issue and lessons learned log – Weekly reports and project board reports – End project report – Handover to support	
Configuration management	– Configuration management and change control process – Configuration management procedure – Directory structure – File naming convention – Version numbering – Change request form – Issue and defect log – Configuration management audit checklist – Configuration management plan	
Supplier agreement management	– Supplier selection/management process – Supplier selection and management procedure – Evaluation method and criteria – Statement of work	
Process and product quality assurance	– QA procedure – QA checklist – QA report – QA schedule	
Measurement and analysis	– Metrics procedure – Measurement objectives	
Requirements analysis	– Business requirements – System requirements – Requirements checklist – Requirements guidelines – Traceability matrix	
Peer reviews	– Peer review guidelines – Planning reviews – Preparation – Conducting peer reviews	
Testing	– Testing guidelines – Project test plan – Unit, system, and UAT test plan – Test scripts – Defect log and defect form – Project test report	

Table 6.11   (continued)

Area	Item to check	Y/N
Design and development	– Design guidelines – Design specification – Design checklist – Coding standards	
Continuous improvement	– Improvement procedure – Lessons learned – Improvement suggestions	

(and all of the level 2 process areas) needs to be revisited as part of the implementation of the level 3 generic practices. These require the definition of a standard organization process and the collection of improvement information to support the process.

The technical solution process area is concerned with processes to design, develop, and implement software to meet the customer requirements. This involves identifying possible design approaches and considering their advantages and disadvantages; selecting the appropriate design solution from the available alternatives; developing the detailed design to satisfy the requirements; and implementing the design to produce a product or product component.

There may be several candidate design solutions[6] and the merits of each solution are considered prior to selection. Each potential solution has associated costs, development effort and schedule, risks, and technical performance. Screening criteria are employed to evaluate each potential solution.

Operational concepts and scenarios[7] document the interaction of product components with the environment, users, and other product components. The operational environments (e.g. operating, support and deployment) are also documented. The product component solutions that best satisfy the criteria are then selected.

The chosen design solution is documented in the design document. The design document is reviewed to ensure that it is valid with respect to the requirements. Any issues identified will need to be resolved prior to the implementation of the design.

The developers carry out the implementation of the design in a programming language. The programmers will adhere to the applicable coding language standards and the coding method employed may be

– Object-oriented programming
– Structured programming
– Automatic code generation
– Software code re-use

---

[6]This may include a customized-off-the-shelf (COTS) solution.

[7]This may be done with use cases.

The technical solution process area is also concerned with developing product support documentation, and these include user and admin guides and training documentation. These documents need to be reviewed to ensure that they are fit for purpose. The specific goals and practices for the technical solution process area are given in Table 6.12).

The decision analysis and resolution (DAR) process area supports the technical solution process area in identifying alternative solutions and selecting the most appropriate solution. This process area is discussed in detail later in this chapter.

The design document ensures that all stakeholders have a mutual understanding of the design, and it includes the software architecture, internal and external interfaces, as well as the software product component architecture. It consists of technical data packages with allocated requirements, technical drawings, specifications, design descriptions, and design databases. The design document is updated during the development life cycle to ensure that it accurately reflects changes to the design. An organization may use several design methods including

– Prototyping
– Object-oriented design
– Entity relationship models

The product integration process area is usually implemented with the technical solution process area. The implementation of the customer requirements involves the development of product components, and the product integration process area is concerned with the integration of the product components and to ensure that the integrated product functions correctly. The integration needs to be carefully managed to ensure compatibility of the internal and external interfaces.

The integration of the product components could potentially take place at the end of the software development. However, in practice it is best to reduce risk with early integration and to integrate incrementally during the development life cycle. An iterative process

Table 6.12   CMMI requirements for technical solution

Specific goal	Specific practice	Description of specific practice/goal
SG 1		*Select product component solutions*
	SP 1.1	Develop alternative solutions and selection criteria
	SP 1.2	Select product component solutions
SG 2		*Develop the design*
	SP 2.1	Design the product or product component
	SP 2.2	Establish a technical data package
	SP 2.3	Design interfaces using criteria
	SP 2.4	Perform make, buy, or re-use analysis
SG 3		*Implement the product design*
	SP 3.1	Implement the design
	SP 3.2	Develop product support documentation

Table 6.13 CMMI requirements for product integration

Specific goal	Specific practice	Description of specific practice/goal
SG 1		*Prepare for product integration*
	SP 1.1	Determine integration sequence
	SP 1.2	Establish the product integration environment
	SP 1.3	Establish product integration procedures/criteria
SG 2		*Ensure interface compatibility*
	SP 2.1	Review interface descriptions for completeness
	SP 2.2	Manage interfaces
SG 3		*Assemble product components and deliver product*
	SP 3.1	Confirm readiness of product components for integration
	SP 3.2	Assemble product components
	SP 3.3	Evaluate assembled product components
	SP 3.4	Package and deliver the product or product component

of assembling product components, evaluating them, and then assembling more product components is typically employed during the development life cycle.

The specific goals and practices for the product integration process area are detailed in Table 6.13.

Typical deliverables for the technical specification and product integration process areas are detailed in Fig. 6.12.

Process Maps	*Procedure/Guidelines*
Design and Development Process Map	Design and Development Guidelines Coding Standards (per language)
Templates	*Checklist*
Technical Design	Design Coding Standards Checklists

Fig. 6.12 Technical solution and product integration deliverables

6.5.1
Design Process

A sample process map for the design process is described in Fig. 6.13. It includes activities to document and validate the design as well as activities to perform coding and unit testing and integrating the various units.

6.5.2
Design and Development Procedure

The design and development procedure will provide the detailed procedure by which the activities in the process are carried out as well as the roles involved. It will generally include sections on

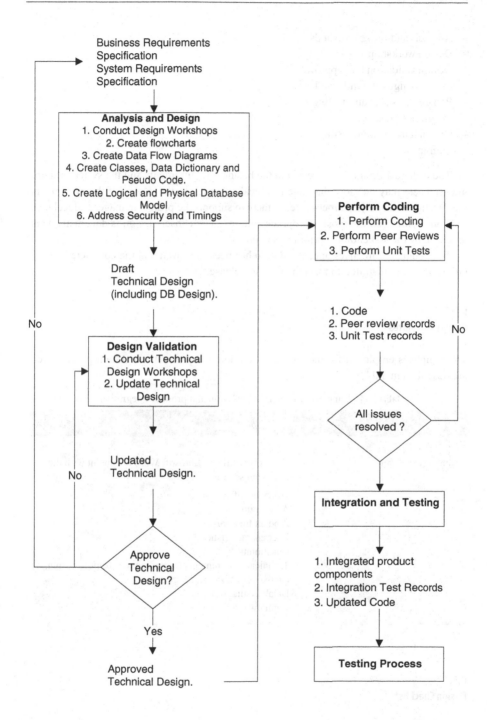

Fig. 6.13 Design and development process map

- Analysis and design methods
- Design workshops
- Design validation and approval
- Coding languages and standards
- Peer reviews and unit testing
- Integration of units
- Unit and integration testing
- Training

The technical design is created from the business requirements and the system requirements. There may be more than one technical approach to the design of the system, and the decision and analysis process area is there to support the project manager and technical staff on deciding on the most appropriate solution. The chosen design is documented and reviewed by the stakeholders prior to its approval.

The coding commences once the design has been approved and the completed code is unit tested and integrated to form the product release.

6.5.3
Design Templates

The templates employed for the technical solution and product integration process areas are described in Table 6.14.

Table 6.14   Templates for technical solution and product integration

Template	Typical contents
Technical design	This is typically a Microsoft Word document with the following sections:
	Overview of system
	Assumptions
	Product functions
	User characteristics
	Constraints
	Technical requirements (including description, design, database, user interface, class)
	Database diagram
	Dataflow diagram

6.5.4
Design Checklist

The design checklist is useful as a tool to support reviewing the content of the design document to verify its correctness. A sample design checklist is presented in Table 6.15.

Table 6.15 Sample design checklist

No.	Item to check
1.	Are the technical requirements numbered to facilitate traceability?
2.	Is each technical requirement clear and unambiguous?
3.	Is each technical requirement testable?
4.	Does each technical requirement have a priority to indicate its importance?
5.	Is each technical requirement implementable?
6.	Have the technical requirements been analysed with any conflicts resolved?
7.	Is each technical requirement defined with sufficient detail?
8.	Are the technical requirements traceable to the system requirements?
9.	Is each technical requirement necessary?
10.	Are the technical requirements complete and consistent?
11.	Does the design implement all of the business requirements?
12.	Does each technical requirement include a description, technical and design issues, the technical and database design, the user interface, class and business objects?
13.	Is there a diagram of the database schemas and tables?
14.	Is there a data flow diagram of the system?
15	Have all other technical requirements been appropriately defined?
16.	Are the technical requirements traceable to the unit test cases?
17.	Has the design been reviewed and approved by all stakeholders?

The implementation of the design involves coding; possibly sourcing COTS products; performing peer reviews to verify that the defined coding standards have been followed and that the product components are a valid implementation of the technical requirements; performing unit testing to verify and validate the individual product components; and performing integration testing to verify and validate the integrated product components.

There will usually be separate environments for developer unit testing on product components, integration testing, and system testing of the integrated product components. The verification and validation process area provides best practice on peer reviews and software testing.

6.5.5
Institutionalization

The implementation of the specific practices for technical solution and product integration was described in this section. The institutionalization is achieved with the implementation of the generic practices.

The decision analysis and resolution process area supports the technical solution process area in identifying and deciding between alternative design solutions. It may also be employed in deciding on the appropriate integration sequence for the product components.

The high-level management policy states management expectations for how design and development will be conducted in the organization.

The design and development process needs to be planned, and resources such as any people and tools required identified and provided. The roles involved will typically include analysts, developers, and testers. The tools may include design specification tools; prototyping tools; and scenario definition and management tools. The plan for design and development will typically be a separate plan from the overall project plan.

All involved in the design and development process need to receive appropriate training on carrying out design and development. This includes training on the design methods employed, the coding standards employed, and the unit testing techniques employed.

The deliverables produced are placed under an appropriate level of configuration management control. This includes the design document, the user and admin guides, the source code. The stakeholders involved are identified and documented in the plan and schedule.

The project manager will generally report the status of the project in weekly reports. These status reports will also include the status of design and development activities.

Independent project audits will be conducted, and these will also consider the extent to which the design and development process is followed and effective.

The design and development process will be tailored from the standard organization design and development process to yield the project's defined process for design and development. Improvement information will typically be collected in lessons learned logs and a central metrics repository will also be used to improve the process.

6.6
Verification and Validation

The verification and validation process areas are concerned with ensuring that the system satisfies the requirements, is fit for purpose, and is what the user wants. Verification is concerned with ensuring that the work products reflect the specified requirements, whereas validation is concerned that the product will fulfil its intended use. That is, verification ensures that "You build it right", whereas validation ensures that "You built the right thing". The implementation of these process areas involves the implementation of processes for peer reviews and testing.

The purpose of the verification process area is to ensure that selected work products meet their specified requirements. The activities in this process area include preparation for verification; performing verification; identifying corrective action; and implementing the actions. Verification helps to ensure that the product will meet the customer and product requirements and is fit for purpose.

Peer reviews play a key role in verification and assist in identifying defects early in the software development life cycle. They involve a rigorous examination of the work products by peers of the author, and the goal is to find defects as early as possible.[8] There are several

---

[8] There is a strong economic case for finding defects as early as possible, as the cost of correction increases the later the defect is found.

types of peer reviews that may be carried out including software inspections and structured walkthroughs.

The specific goals and practices of the verification process area are given in Table 6.16.

The preparation for verification includes identifying the work products to be verified and the verification methods to be employed. The methods may include various types of testing as well as peer reviews. A verification environment needs to be set up.[9]

Verification criteria are established to verify that the work products meet their specified requirements. The test cases will detail the test procedure to perform the verification and the expected results. Checklists are employed for verification in peer reviews.

Peer reviews play a key role in identifying defects early in the software development life cycle and in building quality into the software product. The preparation for peer reviews involves identifying appropriate reviewers for each work product and scheduling the reviews. Checklists are employed to ensure that the inspections are consistently performed. There are entry criteria that need to be satisfied prior to the review, i.e. the material to be inspected should be fit to be reviewed. There are several roles involved in an inspection meeting including a review leader or moderator; a reader role who is responsible for paraphrasing the work product; the author and the scribe. All involved in the peer review need to be trained appropriately.

The review leader will need to ensure that the reviewers have done adequate preparation as otherwise the review will be ineffective. The leader will chair the review meeting and deal with any conflicts that arise. The results are recorded with corrective actions assigned to the author. The review leader will verify that the actions have been implemented correctly and a follow-up review is scheduled where appropriate.

Table 6.16 CMMI requirements for verification

Specific goal	Specific practice	Description of specific practice/goal
SG 1		*Prepare for verification*
	SP 1.1	Select products for verification
	SP 1.2	Establish the verification environment
	SP 1.3	Establish verification procedures and criteria
SG 2		*Perform peer reviews*
	SP 2.1	Prepare for peer reviews
	SP 2.2	Conduct peer reviews
	SP 2.3	Analyse peer review data
SG 3		*Verify selected work products*
	SP 3.1	Perform verification
	SP 3.2	Analyse verification results

---

[9]For example, the verification environment required for peer reviews may be simply the inspection material, reviewers, and a room. A testing environment may require dedicated test tools and simulators.

Table 6.17 CMMI requirements for validation

Specific goal	Specific practice	Description of specific practice/goal
SG 1		*Prepare for validation*
	SP 1.1	Select products for validation
	SP 1.2	Establish the validation environment
	SP 1.3	Establish validation procedures and criteria
SG 2		*Ensure interface compatibility*
	SP 2.1	Perform validation
	SP 2.2	Analyse validation results

The verification activities are performed on the selected work products and the results recorded and analyzed; and corrective actions identified and implemented appropriately.

The purpose of the validation process area is to demonstrate that a product or product components fulfils its intended use. The specific goals and practices for this process area are given in Table 6.17).

Validation activities are applied to work products as well as products or product components and will demonstrate that the product or work product fulfils its intended use. The validation activities are similar to the verification process and include analysis, testing, and inspections. The validation environment should resemble the intended operating environment, and the validation activities may include participation from the end users. The key objective is to ensure that the right system is being built, as distinct from the verification activities, which confirm that the system is being built right.

The preparation for validation includes identifying the work products to be validated, the validation methods to be employed, and setting up an environment appropriate to the validation methods.

Validation criteria are established to verify that the product fulfils its intended use in its operating environment and is fit for purpose. This will include acceptance test cases that need to be satisfied.

Process Maps	*Procedure/Guidelines*
Testing Process Map	Testing Guidelines
Peer Review Process Map	Peer Review Guidelines
Templates	*Checklist*
Peer Review Form	Code Review Checklists
Project Test Plan	Document Checklists
Unit, System & UAT Test Plans	
Project Test Report	
Defect Log	
Defect Form	
Test Script	

Fig. 6.14 Verification and validation deliverables

The validation activities are performed on the selected work products and the results recorded; the results analyzed; corrective actions identified; assigned to staff for resolution; and implemented appropriately. Typical deliverables for the verification and validation process areas are shown in Fig. 6.14.

6.6.1
Testing and Peer Review Processes

A sample process map for testing is detailed in Fig. 6.15. It includes test planning and scheduling; test case analysis and design; test execution; correction of defects; and test reporting.

A sample process map for peer reviews is described in Fig. 6.16. This example includes two types of peer reviews, namely formal reviews and pass-around reviews.

A formal peer review is more rigorous than a pass-around review. It requires that the reviewers have prepared for the review by reading through the material to be reviewed with checklists, and noting comments, questions, and errors. A review leader chairs the meeting and all identified issues are logged. A review outcome is agreed and the author of the deliverable will make the agreed changes to the deliverable. The changes are verified by the review leader and a follow-up review meeting may be conducted.

A pass-around review does not have the same level of control and rigour as a formal review. The author sends the deliverable to the reviewers and requests comments by a certain date. The author modifies the deliverable to address the comments from the reviewers.

6.6.2
Testing and Peer Review Procedures

The testing guidelines will provide the details behind the test process map. It will define the procedure by which the testing activities are carried out and the roles involved. It will generally include sections on

- Description of types of testing
- Test planning and scheduling
- Test case analysis and design
- Guidelines on unit testing
- Guidelines on system, performance, and usability testing
- Guidelines on UAT testing
- Guidelines on regression testing
- Test execution
- Defect logging and resolution
- Test results and reporting
- Test completion criteria

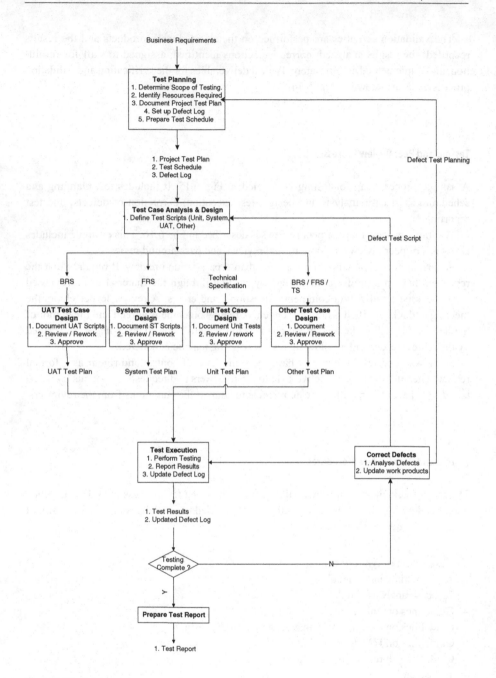

Fig. 6.15 Testing process map

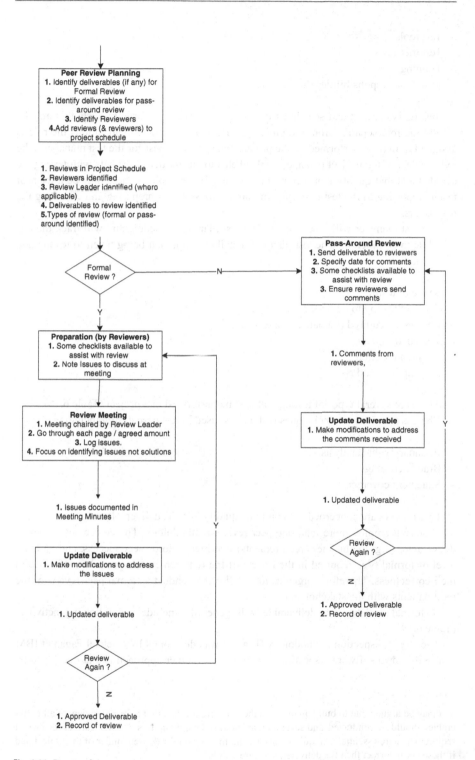

Fig. 6.16 Peer review process map

- Test tools
- Test metrics
- Training
- Roles and responsibilities

Testing is planned and scheduled by the test manager. For large projects this may be a full-time role separate from the project manager. For smaller organizations the role is assigned or may be performed by the project manager. It is best for the test manager to be independent of the project manager, as this helps to ensure that short cuts with testing are avoided and that quality is not compromised. For larger projects there may be a team of testers reporting to the test manager who are responsible for preparing and executing the test scripts.

The test manager will create the project test plan and schedule and will track the test schedule to completion. The test plan will detail the approach being taken to testing and will include

- Scope of testing
- Types of testing to be performed
- Resources required (human and hardware)
- Test environment
- Training required
- Assumptions and risks

There are several types of testing that may be performed in a project (Table 6.18). There are various test techniques that may be used in test case design including

- Boundary value analysis
- Branch coverage
- Statement coverage

Peer reviews are concerned with building quality into the deliverable and often an organization will employ more than one peer review methodology. The correctness of some deliverables (e.g. the business requirements) is critical[10] to project success, and an extra level of formality is required in the review of the requirements to provide confidence in their correctness. Therefore, organizations will often conduct a formal peer review of the requirements with the stakeholders.

A formal review of a deliverable will generally include the following activities (Table 6.19).

The Fagan inspection methodology [Fag:76] was developed by Michael Fagan at IBM is a well-known software inspection methodology. Another approach is that developed by

---

[10]It may be argued that to build quality into the software product that a formal review of all deliverables should be conducted, and several organizations actually do this. Clearly, formal reviews of requirements are essential as requirements are the foundation for the remainder of the project and if these are incorrect then the delivered software will be incorrect.

Table 6.18 Types of testing

Test type	Description	Based on	Created by
Unit testing	Unit testing is concerning with verifying the correctness of individual units of code against the design document	Design document	Developer
Unit integration testing	Unit integration testing is concerned with verifying that the integrated units/modules work correctly together	Design document	Developer
System testing	System testing is concerned with verifying that the system satisfies the functional and non-functional requirements	System requirements	Tester
System integration testing	System integration testing is concerned with verifying that the system functions correctly when it is integrated with other systems and that all of the required interfaces are working correctly	System requirements/interfaces	System tester
User acceptance testing	User acceptance testing refers to testing carried out by the users of the system to verify that the business requirements are fully satisfied by the system and that the system is fit for purpose
It may include parallel running of the system where experience-based testing is conducted by the users	Business requirements	Business analyst
Non-functional testing	This includes load/performance testing, usability, security, and maintainability testing
Load/performance testing is concerned with verifying that the system meets its performance requirements under heavy loads and stress
Usability testing is concerned with ensuring that the system satisfies the usability requirements
Security testing is concerned with ensuring that the security requirements are addressed
Maintainability testing is concerned with ensuring that the system will be easy to maintain	Business requirements/system requirements	System tester
Regression testing	This testing is employed to verify that the integrity of the system is maintained following changes or corrections of defects
They are typically a subset of the unit, system, and UAT test scripts	Business requirements/system requirements/design document	Developer/system tester/business analyst

Table 6.19   Formal review

Test type	Description
Review planning	The deliverables to be reviewed will be listed (e.g. in the project quality plan) and reviews will be included as tasks on the project schedule The review leader (or project manager) will identify the reviewers for each deliverable The review leader will handle logistics for the review (e.g. sending the deliverable to the reviewers; booking a room for the review; and sending a checklist to assist with reviewing). There may be several roles involved, e.g. leader, scribe, reader, and author
Preparation	The reviewers are required to prepare for the review by reading though the deliverable (and any other relevant material) and noting comments, questions, and concerns. Checklists are generally available to assist with the preparation
Review meeting (and review outcome)	The review leader will chair the review meeting The review will go through each page of the deliverable (or go through the source code) The items noted by reviewers on each page will be discussed and the defects logged in the peer review form (or meeting minutes) The review leader will decide (in consultation with the other reviewers) whether a second review[11] is required or whether it is sufficient for the review leader to verify that the author has made the appropriate changes
Update deliverables	The author will modify the deliverable accordingly to correct the defects noted in the review meeting form
Confirm corrections OK	The review leader will confirm that the corrections made by the author are appropriate

Tom Gilb and Dorothy Graham [Glb:94]. The Prince 2 project management methodology [OGC:04] has a methodology to conduct reviews. Software inspections are described in more detail in [ORg:02, ORg:06].

An informal approach is often adopted for the review of non-critical deliverables. A pass-around review involves the author asking the reviewer(s) to provide comments on the particular deliverable by a particular date, and the deliverable is then passed around to the reviewers. The author analyses the comments sent by the reviewers, and if there are conflicts in the review feedback a meeting is scheduled to discuss. Otherwise, the author makes the required changes and circulates the document for approval (Table 6.20).

---

[11] The decision on whether another review is required is based on the number and severity of the issues noted.

Table 6.20 Pass-around review

Test type	Description
Peer review planning	The deliverables to be reviewed will be listed in the project quality plan and schedule – Select and send deliverables to reviewers (generally by e-mail from author) – Specify dates for comments
Reviewing	The reviewers use available checklists to identify issues or comments
Receive/collate comments	Author ensures that the reviewers send comments by the due date Give extension (where appropriate) to reviewers Collate the comments Schedule meeting if conflict between comments
Update deliverable	The author will modify the deliverable accordingly to correct the comments received from the reviewers
Confirm corrections OK	The author will send the updated deliverable around to the reviewers for final comments Once the final comments have been acted upon the author circulates the deliverable for sign-off

6.6.3
Testing and Peer Review Templates

Typical templates employed for verification and validation process areas are described in Table 6.21.

6.6.4
Testing and Peer Review Checklists

There are various checklists that may be employed to improve the consistency and effectiveness of peer reviews. These checklists are often specific to particular deliverables such as the business requirements, system requirements. They include specific questions to assist the reviewers in their analysis and allow them to identify issues with the deliverable and to verify its correctness.

Checklists pose questions that are fundamental to the correctness of a document or work product and are a useful way to assist the reviewers in carrying out a thorough review. Typical checklists that may be employed include

– Checklist for requirements
– Checklist for design
– Coding standard checklists
– Checklists for project planning
– Checklists for testing

Table 6.21 Templates for testing and peer reviews

Template	Typical contents
Project test plan	This is typically a Microsoft Word document with the following sections: – Scope of testing – Types of testing to be performed – Resources required (human and hardware) – Test environment – Test deliverables – Test execution and defect tracking – Test reporting – Test acceptance criteria – Training required – Assumptions and risks
System test plan	This is typically a Microsoft Word document with the following sections: – Approach – Scope of testing – Resources and responsibilities – Preparation dates and testing dates – Testing and defect tracking – Test environment and test tools – Entry and exit criteria – Traceability – Risks and assumptions – Reporting
UAT test plan	This is typically a Microsoft Word document with the following sections: – Approach – Scope of testing – Resources and responsibilities – Preparation dates and testing dates – Testing and defect tracking – Test environment and test tools – Entry and exit criteria – Traceability – Risks and assumptions – Reporting
Test script	This is typically a Microsoft Word document with the following sections: – Test id and test type – Traceability – Objective of test and test procedure – Expected results and actual results – Tested by – Reviewed by – Pass/fail – Date – Defect no.

Table 6.21 (continued)

Template	Typical contents
Project test report	This is typically a Microsoft Word document with the following sections: – Scope of testing – Test summary – Quality status – Change request status – Open risks and issues – Test milestones – Test acceptance criteria – Test recommendation
Defect log	This was described in Section 5.5
Defect form	This was described in Section 5.5
Peer review form	This is usually a Microsoft Word document that allows the findings from the review to be recorded. It generally includes – Review item and version – Meeting date and meeting duration – Preparation time – Author – Review leader and reviewers – List of findings
Weekly report	This was discussed in Chapter 5. It will have a section on the testing conducted and the quality and change request status
Project schedule	The project schedule may include the deliverables to be reviewed, the date of the review, and the names of the reviewers

6.6.5
Institutionalization

The implementation of the specific goals and practices for verification and validation was discussed in this section. The institutionalization is addressed by the implementation of the generic goals and practices.

The high-level management policy states the organization policy for how testing and peer reviews should be conducted in the organization. Projects need to implement the organization policy.

The testing and peer review processes need to be planned, and resources such as any people and testing tools required to perform the process identified and provided. The roles involved will typically include test managers, test analysts, review leaders, and reviewers. The plan for testing will usually be a separate plan from the overall project plan. The plan for peer reviews is often recorded in the quality plan section of the project plan and on the project schedule.

There may be several test tools employed in testing such as test management tools, defect tracking tools, performance testing tools. All involved in the process need to receive appropriate training on carrying out testing, peer reviews, and on the tools.

There may be special training provided for review leaders, as this role requires the ability to deal with conflicts that might arise during the review. The leader may need to cancel the meeting if reviewers have inadequately prepared for the review. Testers need to be trained on the preparation of test cases that are derived from the business and system requirements and will also need to be trained on the test tools.

The deliverables produced (e.g. test plans and test reports) are placed under an appropriate level of configuration management control. The stakeholders involved are identified and documented in the project or test plan and schedule.

The project manager will generally report the status of the project in weekly reports. These status reports will also include the status of testing and peer review activities.

Independent project audits will be conducted, and these will also consider the extent to which the testing and peer review process are followed and effective.

The testing and peer review process will be tailored from the standard organization's process to yield the project's defined process for testing and peer reviews. Improvement information will typically be collected in lessons learned logs and a central metrics repository will also be used to improve the process.

6.7
Integrated Project Management

The purpose of the integrated project management process area is to manage the project according to an integrated process that is tailored from the organization's set of standard processes. This process area involves

- Establishing the project's defined process by tailoring the organization set of standard processes
- Managing the project using the project's defined software process
- Using and contributing to the organizational process assets
- Ensuring relevant stakeholders are actively involved in the development

The tailoring of the organization's set of standard processes to yield the project's defined software process allows the project's software process to reflect the unique characteristics of the project. That is, projects are not required to do things in exactly the same way in a level 3 organization, and the processes used by the projects may vary subject to what is allowed by the tailoring. The project is managed using the project's defined software process.

The tailoring guidelines define how the tailoring is done and it provides the procedure for tailoring from the organization down to the individual projects. It will guide the

Table 6.22 CMMI requirements for integrated project management

Specific goal	Specific practice	Description of specific practice/goal
SG 1		*Use the project's defined process*
	SP 1.1	Establish the project's defined process
	SP 1.2	Use organization process assets for planning project activities
	SP 1.3	Establish the project's work environment
	SP 1.4	Integrate plans
	SP 1.5	Manage the project using the integrated plans
	SP 1.6	Contribute to the organization process assets
SG 2		*Coordinate and collaborate with relevant stakeholders*
	SP 2.1	Manage stakeholder involvement
	SP 2.2	Manage dependencies
	SP 2.3	Resolve coordination issues

selection of a life cycle model from those available at the organization level, as well as selecting processes and standards from the organization set of standard processes according to the criteria to yield the project's defined software process.

The specific goals and practices for the integrated project management process area are given in Table 6.22.

The organization process assets are used for planning project activities. The project plan and other plans that affect the project are integrated to describe the project's defined process. The project is managed using the integrated plans and the project's defined software process. The project will contribute to the organizational process assets with measurements, improvement proposals, best practice in processes used, lessons learned, training materials, and so on.

The involvement of stakeholders is managed and the project manager works closely with relevant stakeholders to identify, negotiate, and track critical dependencies. The project manager will resolve any coordination issues with relevant stakeholders.

Typical deliverables for the integrated project management process area are shown in Fig. 6.17.

Process Maps	*Procedure/Guidelines*
Tailoring Process	Tailoring
Templates	*Checklist*
Tailoring	Tailoring

Fig. 6.17 Integrated project management deliverables

Fig. 6.18 Tailoring process

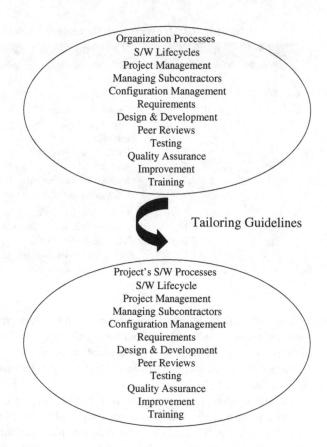

Tailoring Guidelines

6.7.1
Tailoring Process

A sample process map for tailoring is in Fig. 6.18.

6.7.2
Tailoring Procedure

The tailoring guidelines will define the procedure by which the tailoring is done. Projects vary by size and complexity, and tailoring allows the organization set of standard processes to reflect the unique characteristics of the project. Tailoring was discussed previously in Section 6.3 with the implementation of OPD. Three categories of projects are defined in the example below, and the project category is determined from factors such as complexity, cost, duration, and effort (Table 6.23).

Table 6.23 Tailoring project categories

Factor/type	Change request	Small project	Large project
Complexity	No multiple changes in functionality across modules or application areas	Multiple changes in functionality across modules or application areas	Multiple changes in functionality across applications or business areas
Cost	<25k € (including vendor and internal costs)	= 25k € and <150 k € (including vendor and internal costs)	= 150k € (including vendor and internal costs)
Duration	< 1.5 months	= 1.5 months and <4 months	= 4 months
Effort	< 15 days IS effort	= 15 days and <100 days IS effort	= 100 days IS effort

6.7.3
Tailoring Templates

The tailoring template allows the actual tailoring performed by the project to be documented. It shows how the project's processes and standards are selected from the organization set of standard processes. The example in Table 6.24 includes mandatory and optional deliverables for each category.

Table 6.24 Tailoring template

Templates	Change request	Small project	Large project
Project plan	O	O	M
Small project plan	O	M	–
Combined plan task	M	–	–
Business requirements	O	M	M
System requirements	O	M	M
Design	O	M	M
Issue log	O	O	M
Risk log	O	O	M
Lessons learned log	O	O	M
Test plans	O	M	M
Test scripts	O	M	M
Test reports	O	M	M

6.7.4
Tailoring Checklist

The tailoring checklist may be employed in the project to check that the project category has been determined and that the appropriate deliverables will be produced during the project.

6.7.5
Institutionalization

The implementation of the specific goals and practices for integrated project management was discussed in this section. The institutionalization is addressed by the implementation of the generic goals and practices.

The high-level management policy management expectations for how integrated project management should be conducted in the organization.

The integrated project management process needs to be planned, and resources such as any tools required for performing the process need to be identified and provided.

All involved in the integrated project management process receive appropriate training on tailoring the organization set of standard processes to yield the project's defined software process.

The deliverables produced are placed under an appropriate level of configuration management control. The stakeholders involved are identified and documented in the project plan and schedule.

The project manager will generally report the status of the project in weekly reports. These status reports will also include the project metrics.

Independent project audits will be conducted, and these will also consider the extent to which the integrated project management process is followed and effective.

6.8
Risk Management

The purpose of risk management is to identify potential risks as early as possible to enable risk handling and mitigation activities to be planned and invoked as needed. Risks arise due to uncertainty and risk management is concerned with managing uncertainty, and especially any associated unwanted events. Risk management is a continuous forward-looking process, and it addresses issues that could potentially have a negative impact on the project achieving its objectives. Risks need to be identified, analysed, and controlled in order for the project to be successful.

Risk management involves defining a risk management strategy; identifying and analysing risks; and handling identified risks. It may include the preparation of risk mitigation plans where appropriate.

The risk management strategy details how risks are identified, analysed, and mitigated. It discusses the sources of risks as well as the types of risk that may occur. This provides a mechanism for collecting and organizing risks, and additional sources of risk may be identified as the project progresses. The parameters associated with the risks are defined, and these include the likelihood of each risk occurring and its impact if it does occur. Risk tolerances or thresholds will define when action will be taken to mitigate the risk.

Risk identification commences early in the project and continues throughout the project life cycle. Historical data from previous projects may be examined to consider risks and issues that arose in the past and to determine whether any of these are relevant to the current project. The project manager may also identify risks from discussions with other stakeholders and the project team. Risks may be broadly classified into the following types:

- Business (e.g. collapse of subcontractors)
- Legal and regulatory (e.g. new regulations).
- Organizational (e.g. availability and skill of resources and management).
- Technical (e.g. scope creep, architecture, design)
- Environmental (e.g. flooding or fires)

The risks are identified and analysed by the project manager and other relevant stake-holders to determine the likelihood of their occurrence and impact should they materialize. The importance or criticality of the risks may then be determined and appropriate mitigation plans defined. The likelihood and impact parameters defined below may be classified as low, medium, or high[12] (Table 6.25):

Table 6.25   Risk parameters

Likelihood	Probability	Impact	Description
Low	<20%	Low	Negligible impact on project tolerances
Medium	21–50%	Medium	Puts project tolerances at risk
High	51–100%	High	Places project outside tolerances

The risk category (or criticality) may be determined from the likelihood and impact parameters. For example, one approach to defining the risk category is given in Table 6.26.

The project manager and other relevant stakeholders will devise an appropriate response to a risk in line with its criticality. The response may be to reduce the probability of occurrence of the risk and/or its impact should it occur. The following are possible responses to a risk:

- Prevention which aims to prevent the risk from materializing.
- Reduction aim to reduce the probability of occurrence or impact should it occur.
- Transfer aims to transfer the risk to a third party.
- Acceptance is when nothing can be done about the risk.
- Contingency are actions that are carried out should the risk materialize.

---

[12]Other approaches might be to determine the impact in terms of a monetary value.

Table 6.26   Risk category

Risk category	Likelihood	Impact
1	High	High
2	High	Medium
2	Medium	High
3	Medium	Medium
3	High	Low
3	Low	High
4	Medium	Low
4	Low	Medium
5	Low	Low

Table 6.27   CMMI requirements for risk management

Specific goal	Specific practice	Description of specific practice/goal
SG 1		*Prepare for risk management*
	SP 1.1	Determine risk sources and categories
	SP 1.2	Define risk parameters
	SP 1.3	Establish a risk management strategy
SG 2		*Identify and analyse risks*
	SP 2.1	Identify risks
	SP 2.2	Evaluate, categorize, and prioritize risks
SG 3		*Mitigate risks*
	SP 3.1	Develop risk mitigation plans
	SP 3.2	Implement risk mitigation plans

The response to a risk may require risk mitigation planning as well as resources. The specific goals and practices for the risk management process area are given in Table 6.27.

The organization will typically employ a risk log or tool to record the identified risks and the associated parameters. Detailed risk mitigation plans will be prepared as appropriate. The typical deliverables for the risk management process area are shown in Fig. 6.19.

Process Maps	*Procedure/Guidelines*
Risk Management Process Map	Risk Management Guidelines
Templates	*Checklist*
Risk Log	Risk Management

Fig. 6.19   Risk management deliverables

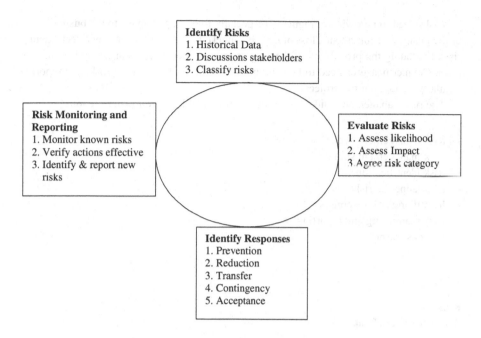

Fig. 6.20 Risk management cycle

6.8.1
Risk Management Process

A sample process map for risk management is presented in Fig. 6.20. It shows risk management as a continuous process throughout the life cycle and it includes activities for identifying risks; evaluating risks; identifying the appropriate responses to a risk; and risk monitoring and reporting.

6.8.2
Risk Management Guidelines

The risk management guidelines provide the details for how risks are identified and managed during the project. Risks need to be identified, analysed, and controlled throughout the life cycle in order for the project to be successful.

Once the initial set of risks to the project has been identified, they are analysed individually to determine their likelihood of occurrence and their impact (e.g. on cost, schedule, or quality). Countermeasures to reduce their likelihood and impact then need to be identified. Additional risks may become evident during the project, and the project manager needs to be proactive in their identification and management.

Risks need to be reviewed regularly (especially following changes to the business case or the business requirements, loss of key personnel). Events that occur may affect existing risks (including the probability of their occurrence or their impact) and may lead to new risks. Countermeasures need to be kept up to date during the project. Risks are reported regularly throughout the project.

The risk management guidelines will generally include the following sections:

– Risk management cycle
– Risk management strategy
– Risk identification
– Evaluating the risks
– Identifying risk responses
– Risk monitoring and reporting
– Lessons learned

6.8.3
Risk Management Templates

Typical templates for risk management are described in Table 6.28.

Table 6.28 Templates for risk management

Template	Typical contents
Risk log	This is typically a Microsoft Excel spreadsheet with the following columns (for each risk): Risk no. and raiser of risk Risk type Date raised and description Likelihood of risk Impact of risk Risk category Response type Counter measure Allocated to Status

6.8.4
Risk Management Checklist

The risk management checklist may be used as an aid to ensure that risk management is appropriately done during the projects (Table 6.29).

Table 6.29 Sample risk management checklist

No.	Item to check
1.	Has the initial risk analysis been performed?
2.	Is the likelihood of each risk identified?
3.	Is the impact of each risk identified?
4.	Is the risk category for each risk (based on likelihood and impact) identified?
5.	Has an appropriate response (and response type) for each risk been identified?
6.	Is the response/countermeasure for each risk effective?
7.	Is a risk owner assigned for each risk?
8.	Is the status of each risk recorded?
9.	Are risks regularly monitored and managed during the project?
10.	Are new risks identified and managed during the project?

6.8.5
Institutionalization

The implementation of the specific goals and practices was described in this section. The institutionalization is addressed by the implementation of the generic goals and practices.

The high-level management policy stipulates the core values for how risk management should be conducted. The implementation of risk management in projects needs to be consistent with this policy.

The risk management process needs to be planned, and resources and tools required identified and provided. All involved in the risk management process need to receive appropriate training.

The deliverables produced are placed under an appropriate level of configuration management control. This includes the risk log and risk mitigation plans. The stakeholders involved are identified and documented in the project plan and schedule.

The project manager will include the status of the key risks in the weekly status reports. Independent project audits will be conducted to determine the extent to which the risk management process is followed and effective. Improvement information will be collected and used to improve the risk management process.

6.9
Decision Analysis and Resolution

The decision analysis and resolution process area is concerned with supporting decision-making in the organization. The need for structured decision-making arises naturally during a project, and decision-making guidelines need to be established. These guidelines will determine which issues should be subject to a formal decision-making process, and formal evaluation is employed in making the decision.

For example, at project initiation there is a need to decide on the appropriate approach to take for the project, and this may involve a consideration of whether the project should be developed internally; outsourced to a third party software supplier; or whether customised-off-the-shelf software should be purchased. The technical developers of a new system will need to decide between alternative technical approaches to determine the most appropriate approach to implementation. The need for formal decision-making arises when

- An important decision needs to be made
- There are risks associated with the decision and these need to be identified and minimized
- Each decision has impacts on cost, effort, and schedule

The decision-making guidelines will detail criteria for which issues will be subject to formal evaluations. It will describe the decision-making process including how candidate options are identified; the evaluation method; the evaluation of the options against evaluation criteria; the recommended solution; and the chosen solution. The specific goals and practices for the decision analysis and resolution process area are detailed in Table 6.30.

Table 6.30   CMMI requirements for decision analysis and resolution

Specific goal	Specific practice	Description of specific practice/goal
SG 1		*Evaluate alternatives*
	SP 1.1	Establish guidelines for decision analysis
	SP 1.2	Establish evaluation criteria
	SP 1.3	Identify alternative solutions
	SP 1.4	Select evaluation methods
	SP 1.5	Evaluate alternatives
	SP 1.6	Selection solutions

Candidate solution options may be identified in various ways. For example, they may be identified by research (e.g. over the Internet), industry knowledge, or recommendations from colleagues. It is usually best to identify three to five alternative solutions.

Evaluation criteria will be defined for the particular evaluation. These criteria form the basis for evaluating the alternative options. They may include some of the following:

- Key tasks
- Resources needed
- Estimated effort
- Estimated duration
- Estimated cost
- Business benefit
- Advantages and disadvantages
- Risks, issues, and dependencies
- Additional specific criteria

Table 6.31   Summary of evaluation

Evaluation criteria	Option 1	Option 2	Option 2
Resources needed			
Estimated effort			
Estimated duration			
Estimated costs			
# Benefits			
# Disadvantages			
# Dependencies			
# Issues			
# Risks			
Additional criteria			

The evaluation method defines how the evaluation will be carried out and is specific to the decision being made. It typically includes

- The evaluation team
- The final decision maker
- The timescale for the evaluation
- Key assumptions
- How the facts will be gathered and the data will be evaluated

The evaluation of the various options is performed and summarized. Spreadsheets (with weightings) may be employed to perform the evaluation. A concise way to summarize the evaluation results is provided in Table 6.31.

The typical deliverables of the decision analysis and resolution process area are shown in Fig. 6.21.

6.9.1
Decision-Making Process

A sample process map for decision-making is described in Fig. 6.22.

Process Maps	Procedure/Guidelines
Decision Making Process Map	Decision Making Guidelines
Templates	Checklist
Decision Making Template	Decision Making Checklist

Fig. 6.21 CMMI deliverables for decision analysis and resolution

Fig. 6.22 Decision-making
process map

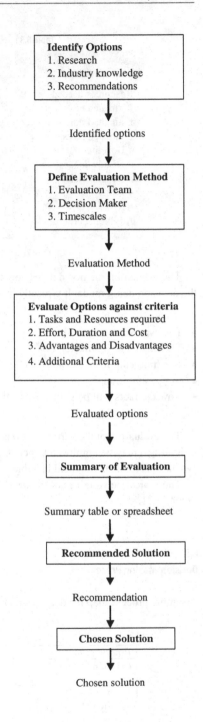

6.9.2
Decision-Making Guidelines

The decision-making guidelines will include criteria for when formal decision-making takes place and provides the detailed procedure behind the decision-making process. It will generally include sections on

- Identifying options
- Defining evaluation method
- Evaluating options
- Summary of evaluation
- Recommended solution
- Chosen solution

The candidate options may be identified by research or industry knowledge as well as recommendations from colleagues. The evaluation method will define the members of the evaluation team as well as their roles and responsibilities. It will also detail how the evaluation is performed as well as the associated timeframes. Each option is then evaluated and the results summarized.

The evaluation recommends a particular option and the decision maker makes the final decision.

6.9.3
Decision-Making Templates

Typical templates employed for the decision analysis and resolution process area are described in Table 6.32.

Table 6.32 Templates for decision-making

Template	Typical contents
Decision-making	This is typically a Microsoft Word document that generally includes the following sections: – Identification of options – Evaluation method and team – Evaluation criteria – Evaluation of options – Summary of evaluation – Recommendation – Chosen solution

6.9.4
Checklist

A sample checklist to guide decision-making is provided in Table 6.33.

6.9.5
Institutionalization

The implementation of the specific goals and practices for decision analysis was discussed in this section. The institutionalization is addressed by the implementation of the generic goals and practices.

The high-level management policy stipulates the core values for how decision-making should be conducted in the organization. Decision-making performed in projects will be consistent with the policy.

The decision-making process needs to be planned, and resources such as any tools required identified and provided. All involved in the decision-making process need to receive appropriate training.

The deliverables produced are placed under an appropriate level of configuration management control. The stakeholders involved are identified and documented in the project plan and schedule.

The project manager will generally report the status of the project in weekly reports. These status reports will also include the results of any formal decision-making.

Independent project audits will be conducted, and these will also consider the extent to which the decision-making process is followed and effective. The decision-making process will be defined as a standard organization process, and improvement information collected to improve the process.

Table 6.33   Sample decision-making checklist

No.	Item to check
1.	Is there a need to make a decision formally?
2.	Are the candidate options identified?
3.	Has the evaluation team been identified and advised of their roles?
4.	Have the timescales for the evaluation been agreed?
5.	Has the methodology for the evaluation been defined?
6.	Has the evaluation criteria been defined?
7.	Has each option been formally evaluated against the criteria?
8.	Has a summary of the evaluation been prepared?
9.	Is the recommended option and rationale detailed?
10.	Is the chosen option and rationale detailed?

6.10
Review Questions

1. Describe the process asset library in an organization?
2. Describe the software measurement repository in an organization?
3. What is the purpose of peer reviews? How does it differ from software testing?
4. What is the difference between an organization standard process and the project's defined software process?
5. Explain the difference between verification and validation.
6. Describe how the standard process may be tailored to yield the project's defined process.

6.11
Summary

A maturity level 3 organization has standard organization-wide processes in place that are well understood and are defined in terms of procedures and standards. These standard processes ensure consistency in the way in which projects are conducted across the organization, and best practices have been generalized for use at the organization level.

It is not required that projects do things in exactly the same way in a level 3 organization, as it is clearly recognized that the project's defined software process needs to reflect the unique characteristics of the project. A level 3 organization builds on the foundation of project-level stability achieved by CMMI level 2 implementation.

The implementation of level 3 requires a change in thinking in the organization from that of thinking of what is best for individual projects to what is good for the entire organization. A level 3 organization has an organization set of standard processes (OSSP) defined. These describe the processes available for use in the organization and show the activities and work products for each process that are relevant for every project. The focus is on understanding and defining a common process to support the entire organization, and this provides a common organization-wide understanding of the activities, roles, and responsibilities in the defined process.

A level 3 organization has tailoring guidelines defined that allow the project to tailor the process to yield the project's defined process. These tailoring guidelines define the level of formality and deliverables to be produced for the various projects in the organization. An organization-wide training program is implemented to ensure that staff have the right knowledge to carry out their roles effectively.

A level 3 organization treats its processes and procedures as assets and it has a dedicated SEPG group that is responsible for the organization process assets and its software process improvement activities. The SEPG group helps to provide a strong process improvement culture as well as good process definition, piloting, rollout, and tailoring approach.

Procedures and standards are defined for the various engineering activities such as design, coding, testing. There is a formal review process in place to find errors early in the life cycle, and risk management practices are formalized.

The level 3 processes are defined rigorously, and their definition includes the purpose of the process, entry criteria, inputs, activities and roles, measures, verification steps, output and exit criteria. The process areas to be implemented in CMMI maturity level 3 are

- Requirements development
- Technical solution
- Product integration
- Verification
- Validation
- Organization process focus
- Organization process definition
- Organization training
- Integrated project management
- Risk management
- Decision analysis and resolution

There are two additional generic practices (GP 3.1 and 3.2) to be implemented for processes at level 3 maturity. These two generic practices are concerned with defining a standard process and collecting improvement information to support future improvements to the process. Further, the process areas that have already been implemented for CMMI level 2 will need to implement the GP 3.1 and 3.2 generic practices.

The next chapter provides an overview of the process areas for CMMI levels 4 and 5.

CMMI Level 4 and 5 Implementation

7

7.1
Introduction

A level 4 organization sets quantitative goals for the performance of key processes, and the processes are controlled using statistical techniques to meet the needs of the stakeholders. Software process and product quality goals are set and managed, and processes are stable and perform within narrowly defined limits. A level 4 organization has predictable process performance, with variation in performance identified and the causes determined and corrected.

There are two process areas that need to be implemented for CMMI level 4. These are

- Organization process performance
- Quantitative project management

A level 5 organization builds upon the level 4 foundation and has a continuous process improvement culture in place. Processes are improved based on a quantitative understanding of variation, and defect prevention activities are an integral part of the development life cycle. The causes of defects are systematically determined and corrected,

G. O'Regan, *Introduction to Software Process Improvement*, Undergraduate Topics
in Computer Science, DOI 10.1007/978-0-85729-172-1_7,
© Springer-Verlag London Limited 2011

and new technologies are evaluated to improve process performance. New technology is introduced in a controlled manner into the organization after successful evaluations. Processes may be improved incrementally or through innovative process and technology improvements.

There are two process areas that need to be implemented for CMMI level 5. These are

- Organization innovation and deployment
- Causal analysis and resolution

7.2
Organization Process Performance

This process area is concerned with obtaining a quantitative understanding of the performance of selected processes in order to quantitatively manage projects in the organization. It involves establishing and maintaining a quantitative understanding of the organization's set of standard processes in order to support the organization in quality and process improvement. This allows the organization to baseline its process performance and to compare it with actual project performance. This information is then used to quantitatively manage its projects, and each quantitatively managed project provides performance results that become part of the baseline data for the organization process assets.

Process performance is a measure of the actual results achieved by following the process for a particular project. It includes process measures such as effort and schedule variance, and product measures such as quality, reliability, and defect density. The specific goals and practices for this process area are given in Table 7.1.

This will enable the organization to

- Determine whether the processes are behaving consistently (i.e. predictable)
- Identify processes with unpredictable behaviour
- Establish criteria for identifying whether a process or process element should be statistically managed and determine measures
- Identify processes that can be improved

Table 7.1 CMMI requirements for organization process performance

Specific goal	Specific practice	Description of specific practice/goal
SG 1		*Establish performance baselines/models*
	SP 1.1	Select processes
	SP 1.2	Establish process performance measures
	SP 1.3	Establish quality and process performance objectives
	SP 1.4	Establish process performance baselines
	SP 1.5	Establish process performance models

The first step is to determine which processes will be measured. Next the quality and process performance objectives for those processes are determined and appropriate measures chosen to give insight into quality and process performance.

One useful approach to selecting measures is Goal, Question, Metric (GQM) developed by Basili and Rombach [Bas:88]. This is a rigorous approach to measurement in which goals and measures are closely linked. The business goals are first determined. This leads to questions that relate to the extent of achievement of the business goal. Metrics are then chosen to give an objective answer to these questions:

- Define *Goals* specific to needs
- Refine the goals into *Questions*
- Deduce the *Metrics* and data to be collected to answer the questions

GQM is discussed in more detail in [ORg:02]. Process performance baselines are established and maintained of the organization set of standard processes. This involves collecting measurements from the organization's projects. Process performance models for the organization set of standard processes are established and maintained. They are used to represent past and current process performance and to predict future process performance. These performance models may be used to

- Estimate potential return on investment for process improvement activities
- Estimate and predict process performance for the project's defined software processes

7.3
Quantitative Project Management

This process area is concerned with quantitatively managing the project's defined process to achieve the project's quality and performance objectives. It involves

- Establishing and maintaining the project's quality and process performance objectives
- Selecting subprocesses in the project's defined software process to be statistically managed
- Monitoring the project to determine whether quality and process objectives are being achieved and taking corrective action
- Monitoring the performance of the selected subprocesses and taking corrective action
- Recording statistical data in the organization's measurement repository

The project's quality and process performance objectives will need to be realistic and based on an understanding of current process performance for the organization set of standard processes.[1] Quality objectives for quality attributes such as the mean time to

---

[1]The project's defined software process is derived from the organization set of standard processes by tailoring, and so its capability will be closely related to the capability of the organization's set of standard processes.

Table 7.2 CMMI requirements for quantitative project management

Specific goal	Specific practice	Description of specific practice/goal
SG 1		*Quantitatively manage the project*
	SP 1.1	Establish the project's objectives
	SP 1.2	Compose the defined process
	SP 1.3	Select the subprocesses that will be statistically managed
	SP 1.4	Manage project performance
SG 2		*Statistically manage subprocess performance*
	SP 2.1	Select measures and analytic techniques
	SP 2.2	Apply statistical techniques to understand variation
	SP 2.3	Monitor performance of selected subprocesses
	SP 2.4	Record statistical management data

failure and the number and severity of defects in the released product may be set. Process performance objectives for attributes such as percentage of defects found in software inspections and peer review activities may be set. Process performance models[2] may be employed to predict the number of defects in the released software based on the defects identified during the peer reviews and testing activities.

The specific goals and practices for the quantitative project management process area are given in Table 7.2.

Subprocesses are components of a larger defined process. The subprocesses may be further decomposed into other subprocesses and process elements. The subprocesses that will be statistically managed are chosen based on the project's needs for predictable performance.

The statistical techniques employed may include trend charts, histograms, bar charts, control charts, confidence intervals, and tests of hypotheses.

The collection and analysis of process and product measures allows special causes of variation to be identified and addressed. A special cause of process variation is characterized by an unexpected change in process performance. These causes can be investigated, analysed, and addressed to prevent future occurrence. Statistical techniques are applied to identify and understand variation in process performance.

The project will be monitored to determine whether its objectives for quality and process performance will be satisfied. Statistical techniques help the project predict whether it will be able to achieve its quality and process performance objectives, and corrective action is taken where appropriate.

---

[2]It is essential that these models be validated to ensure that they are sound. The models should be based on good empirical data and rigorously tested to ensure their validity. There is a well-known saying "All models are wrong: some are useful".

Statistical and quality management data are recorded in the organization's measurement repository.

7.4
Organization Innovation and Deployment

The purpose of this process area is to select and deploy incremental and innovative improvements that measurably improve the organization's processes and technologies. The improvements support the organization's quality and process performance objectives as derived from the organization's business objectives.

It enables the organization to select and deploy improvements to enhance its ability to meet its quality and process performance objectives. The successful implementation of this process area leads to an innovative organization that actively encourages its staff to propose potential improvements to its processes.

Improvement proposals will be collected and analysed. The improvement proposals may come from various sources including process appraisals; benchmarking; analysis of data on causes of defects; quality and process performance objectives; and improvement suggestions from staff. The analysis of the improvement proposals will consider the return on investment (ROI) from the implementation of the improvement versus the cost involved.

This process area is also concerned with identifying and searching for innovative proposals to improve processes and technology. The organization's set of standard processes are analysed to determine areas where innovative improvements would be most helpful. These are identified in various ways such as proposals from projects and the organization; examining innovations in other organizations; considering innovations documented in research literature; and maintaining awareness of technology trends.

The selected improvements are piloted prior to their deployment. This will ensure their fitness for purpose in the organization as well as any barriers and risks to their deployment.

Table 7.3 CMMI requirements for organization innovation and deployment

Specific goal	Specific practice	Description of specific practice/goal
SG 1		*Select improvements*
	SP 1.1	Collect and analyse improvement proposals
	SP 1.2	Identify and analyse innovations
	SP 1.3	Pilot improvements
	SP 1.4	Select improvements for deployment
SG 2		*Deploy improvements*
	SP 2.1	Plan the deployment
	SP 2.2	Manage the deployment
	SP 2.3	Measure the improvement effects

The actual improvements to be deployed are then selected and the improvements incorporated into the organization set of standard processes. The deployment is planned and appropriate changes made to process definitions, procedures, and standards. All affected staff are trained on the new processes and standards.

Finally, the actual return on investment is determined. This involves determining the cost of deploying the new or enhanced processes versus the monetary business benefit gained from the deployment. The specific goals and practices for organization innovation and deployment are given in Table 7.3.

7.5
Causal Analysis and Resolution

The purpose of the causal analysis and resolution process area is to identify causes of defects and to take corrective action to prevent future re-occurrence. It may include the examination of defects identified during peer reviews and testing activities as well as defects identified by the customer.

The successful implementation of causal analysis and resolution helps to improve quality and productivity, and it helps to prevent the introduction of defects into a product. It is much more cost effective to prevent defects from being introduced than to detect and correct defects later in the software development life cycle.

Several methods such as Pareto analysis, histograms, and process capability analysis are used to select defects to be analysed. Causal analysis of the selected defects is then performed with people who have an understanding of the defects. The types of defects found are analysed to identify any trends, and the root causes of the defects determined. The actions required to address the root causes are identified. There are various tools to assist in finding root causes such as cause and effect (fishbone) diagrams. Actions to address the root causes are identified and implemented.

The impact of the changes made to prevent defects is reviewed to ensure its effectiveness. The specific goals and practices for the causal analysis and resolution process area are given in Table 7.4.

Table 7.4   CMMI requirements for causal analysis and resolution

Specific goal	Specific practice	Description of specific practice/goal
SG 1		*Determine causes of defect*
	SP 1.1	Select defect data for analysis
	SP 1.2	Analyse causes
SG 2		*Address causes of defects*
	SP 2.1	Implement the action proposals
	SP 2.2	Evaluate the effect of change
	SP 2.3	Record data

7.6
Review Questions

1. Describe the Goal, Question, Metric approach developed by Basili.
2. Discuss process performance models and how they may be used for prediction. Describe how they may be validated.
3. Describe various problem tools such as Pareto analysis, trend graphs, bar charts, and histograms and describe how they may be used in problem solving
4. Describe the level 4 process areas.
5. Describe the level 5 process areas.

7.7
Summary

A level 4 organization sets quantitative goals for the performance of key processes, and the processes are controlled using quantitative techniques to meet the needs of the various stakeholders. A level 4 organization has predictable process performance with variation in process performance identified and the causes of variation determined and corrected. Software process and product quality goals are set and managed, and the processes are stable and performing within narrowly defined limits.

A level 5 organization has a continuous process improvement culture in place, and processes are improved based on a quantitative understanding of variation. Defect prevention activities are an integral part of the development life cycle. New technologies are evaluated and if successful are introduced into the organization. Processes may be improved incrementally or through innovative process and technology improvements.

Software Engineering Tools

8

8.1 Introduction

The goal of this chapter is to give a flavour of a selection of tools[1] that can support the organization in various software engineering activities. The tools considered are for project management, configuration management, design and development, testing, and so on. The organization will generally choose tools to support the process rather than choosing a process to support the tool.[2]

Mature organizations will employ a structured approach to the introduction of new tools. First, the requirements for a new tool are specified and the available options to

---

[1] The list of tools discussed in this chapter is intended to give a flavour of what tools are available, and the inclusion of a particular tool is not intended as a recommendation of that tool. Similarly, the omission of a particular tool should not be interpreted as disapproval of that tool.

[2] That is, the process comes first and then the tool rather than the other way around.

G. O'Regan, *Introduction to Software Process Improvement*, Undergraduate Topics
in Computer Science, DOI 10.1007/978-0-85729-172-1_8,
© Springer-Verlag London Limited 2011

satisfy the requirements are considered. These options may include developing a tool internally; outsourcing the development of a tool to a third party supplier; or purchasing a tool off-the-shelf from a vendor.

Several candidate tools will be considered prior to selection, and each candidate tool will be evaluated to determine the extent to which it satisfies the specified requirements. An informed decision is then made and the proposed tool will be piloted in the organization prior to its deployment. The pilot provides feedback on its suitability and will be considered prior to a decision on full deployment and whether any customization is required prior to rollout.

Finally, the users are trained on the tool, and the tool is rolled out throughout the organization. Support is provided as required for a period post-deployment. The first area for which we consider tools is project management.

8.2
Tools for Project Management

There are several tools to support project management activities such as estimation and cost prediction, planning and scheduling, monitoring risks and issues, and managing a portfolio of projects. These include tools such as Microsoft Project which is a powerful project management scheduling tool widely used by project managers throughout the world. Small projects may employ a simpler tool such as Microsoft Excel for their project scheduling activities.

The Constructive Cost Model (Cocomo) is a cost prediction model originally developed by Barry Boehm [Boe:81] to estimate effort, schedule, and cost for small and medium projects. It is based on an effort estimation equation that calculates the software development effort in person-months from the estimated project size. The estimated effort for requirements and maintenance is then derived from this.

The effort estimation calculation is based on the estimate of a project's size in thousands of source lines of code (SLOC[3]). The accuracy of the tool is limited as there is a great deal of variation among teams due to differences in the expertise and experience of the personnel in the project team.

There are several commercial variants of the tool including the Cocomo basic, intermediate, and advanced models. The intermediate model includes several cost drivers to model the project environment, and each cost driver is rated. There are over 15 cost drivers used and these include product complexity, reliability, and experience of personnel as well as programming language experience. The Cocomo parameters need to be calibrated to reflect the actual project development environment. The effort equation used in Cocomo is given by

$$\text{Effort} = 2.94 * \text{EAF} * (\text{KSLOC})^E \qquad (8.1)$$

---

[3] SLOC includes delivered source lines of code created by project staff (excluding automated code generated and also code comments).

Fig. 8.1 Microsoft Project schedule

In this equation, EAF refers to the effort adjustment factor that is derived from the cost drivers, and E is the exponent that is derived from the five scale drivers.[4] Costar tool is a commercial tool that implements the Cocomo model and may be used on small or large projects. It needs to be calibrated to reflect the particular software engineering environment, and this will enable more accurate estimates to be produced.

Microsoft Project is a project management tool that is used for planning, scheduling, and charting project information. It enables a realistic project plan to be created, and the plan will be revised regularly during the project to reflect actual progress, and the project is re-planned as appropriate (Fig. 8.1).

---

[4] The five scale drivers are factors contributing to duration and cost and they determine the exponent used in the Effort equation. Examples include team cohesion and process maturity.

A project is defined as a series of steps or tasks to achieve a specific goal. The amount of time that it takes to complete a task is termed its duration and tasks are performed in a sequence determined by the nature of the project. Resources such as people and equipment are required to perform a task. A project will typically consist of several phases such as creating the plan, tracking and managing the project, and closing the project.

The project schedule details the tasks and activities to be carried out during the project; the effort and duration of each task and activity; the percentage completed of each task, and the resources needed to carry out the various tasks. The schedule shows how the project will be delivered within the key project parameters such as time, cost, and functionality without compromising quality in any way.

The project manager is responsible for managing the schedule and will take corrective action when project performance deviates from expectations. The project schedule will be updated regularly to reflect actual progress made and the project re-planned appropriately.

Project portfolio management (PPM) treats a set of projects as a portfolio and is an effective way to manage a group of current or proposed projects. It allows the organization to choose the optimal mix and sequencing of its projects to yield the greatest business benefit to the organization.

Table 8.1 Key capabilities of Planview Enterprise

Capability	Description
Strategic planning	Define mission, objectives, and strategies
	Allocate funding/staffing for chosen strategy
	Automate and manage strategic process
Investment analysis	Devise strategic long-term plans
	Identify key criteria to evaluate initiatives
	Optimize strategic and project investments to maximize business benefit
Capacity management	Balance resources with business demands
	Ensure capacity supports business strategy
	Align top-down and bottom-up planning
	Forecast resource capacity
Demand management	Request work and check status
	Review life cycles
Project management	Scope, schedule, and execution of work
	Track/report time worked against projects
	Track and manage risks and issues
	Track/display performance and trend analysis
Financial management	Collaborate to better forecast cost
	Monitor spending
Resource management	Balance portfolios/assign people efficiently
	Improve forecasting
	Keep staff productive
Change management	Determine impact of change on schedule/cost
	Effectively manage change

It analyses the project's total expected cost, the resources required, the schedule, the benefits that will be realized as well as interdependencies with other projects in the portfolio. This allows project investment decisions to be made methodically to deliver the greatest benefit to the organization. This is a shift from the normal once off analysis of an individual project proposal, to the analysis of a portfolio of projects. PPM tools aim to manage the continuous flow of projects from concept all the way to completion.

There are several commercial portfolio management tools available from various vendors. These include Clarity PPM from Computer Associates, ChangePoint from Compuware, RPM from IBM Rational, PPM Center from HP, and Planview Enterprise from Planview. It is not possible to discuss all of these portfolio management tools, and the discussion in this section is limited to the Planview Enterprise tool.

Planview allows organizations to manage projects and resources across the enterprise and to align their initiatives for maximum business benefit. It provides visibility into and control of strategic and project portfolios and allows the organization to prioritize and manage its projects and resources. This allows it to make better investment decisions and to balance its business strategy against its available resources. Planview Enterprise Portfolio Management helps an organization to optimize its business through eight key capabilities (Table 8.1).

Planview provides dashboard views that allow key project performance indicators to be closely tracked. This includes dashboard views of variances of cost, effort, and schedule as described in Fig. 8.2.

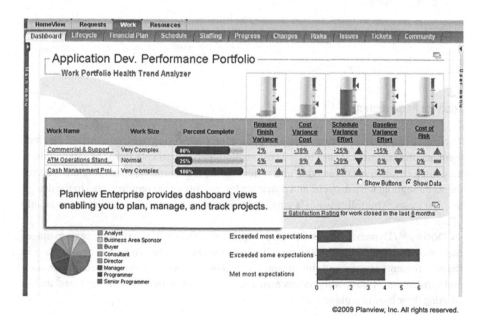

Fig. 8.2 Dashboard views in Planview Enterprise (Courtesy of Planview)

Fig. 8.3 Planview Process
Builder (Courtesy of
Planview)

Planview includes Process Builder (Fig. 8.3), which allows modelling and management
of enterprise-wide processes. It provides improved tracking, control, and audit capabilities
in key process areas such as requirements management and product development, as well
as satisfying key regulatory requirements.

The organization may define and model its process in Process Builder, and this includes
process adoption, compliance, and continuous improvement. The functionality includes

- Process design
- Process automation
- Process measurement
- Process auditing

Next, we will consider tools to support requirements development and management.

8.3
Tools for Requirements

There are many tools available to assist organizations in carrying out requirements development and management. These tools assist in eliciting requirements from the stakeholders;
modelling requirements; verifying and validating the requirements; managing the requirements throughout the life cycle; and providing traceability of the requirements to the design
and test cases. The following is a small selection of some of the tools that are available
(Table 8.2).

DOORS® (Dynamic Object-Oriented Requirements System) is a requirements management tool developed by IBM Rational. It allows the stakeholders to actively participate in
the requirements process and aims to optimize requirements communication, collaboration,
and verification. High-quality requirements help the organization in reducing costs[5] and in
meeting their business objectives.

---

[5] A good requirements process will enable high-quality requirements to be produced, and the cost of
poor quality is reduced as wastage and re-work is minimized. The requirements are the foundation

Table 8.2 Tools for requirements development and management

Tool	Description
DOORS (IBM Rational)	This is a requirements management tool developed by Telelogic (which is part of IBM Rational)
Requisite Pro (IBM Rational)	This is a requirements management and use case management tool developed by IBM Rational
Enterprise Architect (Sparx Systems)	This is a UML analysis and design tool that covers requirements gathering, through to analysis and design, to testing and maintenance. It is developed by Sparx Systems and integrates requirements management with the other software development activities
CORE (Vitech)	This is a requirements tool developed by Vitech and may be used for modelling and simulation
MKS integrity	This tool was developed by MKS and enables organizations to capture and validate software requirements and to link them to downstream development and testing activities

The tool can capture, link, trace, analyse, and manage changes to the requirements. It enhances communication and collaboration to ensure that the project conforms to the customer requirements, as well as compliance to regulations and standards.

Requirements are documented in a way that is easy to interpret and navigate. It is easy to locate information within the database, and the user requirements are recorded in a document style showing each individual requirement. It provides views of the list with assigned identifiers and also an Explorer-like navigation tree.

The DOORS tool employs links to support traceability of the requirements. Links are traversed with a simple click of the mouse to the corresponding object. The links are easy to create by dragging and dropping, e.g. a new link from the user requirements to the system requirements is created in this way. The tool provides dynamic reporting on traceability and filters may be employed to ensure that traceability is complete. Traceability is essential in demonstrating conformance to the requirements.

The management of change is an important part of the requirements process. The DOORS tool supports changes to requirements and allows an impact analysis of the proposed changes to be performed. It allows changes that could impact other requirements or design items and test cases to be tagged (Fig. 8.4).

The IBM Rational DOORS® tool

- Provides a comprehensive requirements management environment
- Provides web browser access to the requirements database
- Manages changes to requirements
- Provides scaleable solution for managing project scope and cost

---

of the system and if they are incorrect then irrespective of how good design and development are the delivered system will not be fit for purpose.

IBM Rational Doors

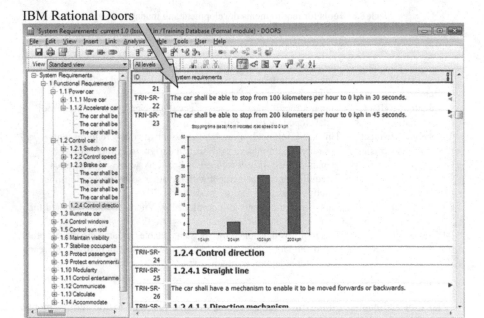

Fig. 8.4 IBM Rational DOORS tool (Courtesy of IBM)

- Provides traceability to design items, test plans, and test cases
- Provides active engagement from stakeholders
- Integrates with other IBM Rational tools

There are several other IBM Rational tools that may be integrated with DOORS®. These include System Architect, Requirements Composer, Rhapsody, and Quality Manager.

IBM Rational RequisitePro is a requirements management tool that allows requirements to be documented with familiar document-based methods as well as providing database-enabled capabilities such as requirements traceability and impact analysis. Requirements may be managed throughout the life cycle and changes to the requirements controlled.

The CORE product suite is developed by Vitech and has functionality for requirements management, modelling and simulation, and verification and validation. It supports UML activity and sequence diagrams, which enables the desired behaviour and flow of control to be captured and analysed. The tool provides

- Comprehensive end-to-end system traceability
- Change impact analysis
- Multiple modelling notations with integrated graphical views
- System simulation based on behavioural models
- Generation of documentation from the database

The Integrity tool was developed by MKS and it enables organizations to capture and validate software requirements. It enables them to link the requirements to downstream development and testing activities and to manage changes to the requirements. Next, we will consider tools to support software design and development

8.4
Tools for Design and Development

Once the system and software requirements have been specified the designers are in a position to devise an appropriate technical solution to satisfy them. This section describes tools available to support design and software development activities. The software design includes the high-level architecture of the system, as well as the lower level design and algorithms. There are various tools to support designers (Table 8.3).

IBM Rational Software Modeler® (RSM) is a UML-based visual modelling and design tool. It promotes communication and collaboration during design and development and allows information about development projects to be specified and communicated from several perspectives. It is used for model-driven development and aligns the business needs with the product.

It gives the organization control over the evolving architecture and provides an integrated analysis and design platform. Abstract UML specifications may be built with traceability and impact analysis shown.

It has an intuitive user interface and a diagram editor to create expressive and interactive diagrams. The tool may be integrated with other IBM Rational tools such as Clearcase, Clearquest, and Requisite Pro (Fig. 8.5).

Table 8.3 Tools for software design

Tool	Description
Microsoft Visio	This tool allows many types of drawings such as flow charts, work flow diagrams, and network diagrams to be created
IBM Rational Software Modeler	This is a UML-based visual modelling and software design tool
IBM Rational Rhapsody	This modelling environment tool is based on UML and provides a visual development environment for software engineers. It uses graphical models and generates code in C, C++, and Java
IBM Rational Software Architect	This modelling and development tool uses UML for designing architecture for C++ and Java applications
Enterprise Architect (Sparx Systems)	This UML analysis and design tool is used for modelling business and IT systems with traceability from requirements to analysis and design, testing and deployment. It supports code generation

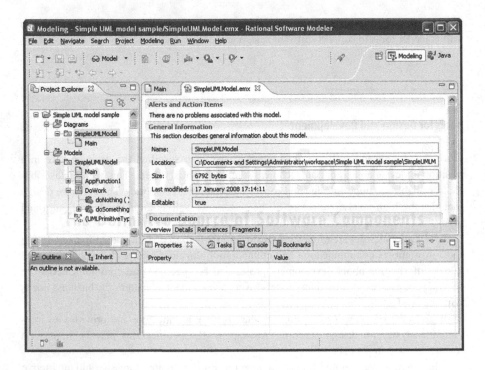

Fig. 8.5 IBM Rational Software Modeler (Courtesy of IBM)

BM® Rational® Rhapsody® is a visual development environment used in real-time or embedded systems. It helps teams collaborate to understand and elaborate requirements; abstract complexity using modelling languages such as UML; validate functionality early in development; and automate code generation to speed up the development process.

Enterprise Architect is developed by Sparx Systems and is a UML analysis and design tool used for modelling business and IT systems. It covers the full product development life cycle, including business modelling, requirements management, software design, code generation, testing. It supports automated document generation, code generation, and reverse engineering of source code. Its reverse engineering feature allows a visual representation of the software application to be provided (Fig. 8.6).

It is a multi-user graphical tool with built-in reporting and documentation. It can model, manage, and trace requirements to design, testing, and deployment, and it can trace the implementation of system requirements to model elements. It can search and report on requirements and perform an impact analysis on proposed changes to the requirements.

The tool allows deployment scripts to be built, debugged, tested, and executed from within its development environment. UML and modelling are integrated into the development process and debugging capabilities are provided. This includes run-time examination of the executing code for several programming languages, and NUnit and JUnit test classes may be generated and integrated directly into the test process.

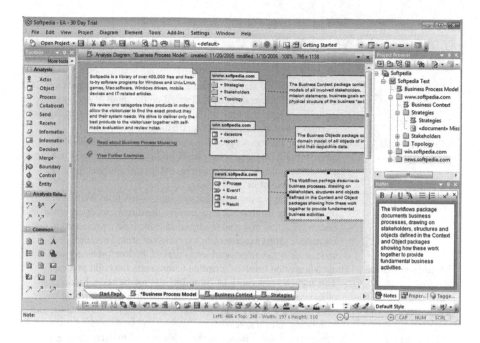

Fig. 8.6 Sparx Enterprise Architect (Courtesy of Sparx Systems)

An integrated development environment (IDE) is a software application that provides comprehensive support facilities to software developers. It includes specialized text editors; a compiler; build automation; and debugging capabilities. The features of an IDE are described in Table 8.4.

IDEs help to improve programmer productivity. They are usually dedicated to a specific programming language, although there are some multi-language tools such as Eclipse and the latest versions of Microsoft Visual Studio.

There are many IDEs available such as Microsoft Visual Studio for C and C++, JBuilder and JCreator for Java, Free Pascal for Pascal. The next section is concerned with tools to support configuration management.

8.5
Tools for Configuration Management and Change Control

Configuration management is concerned with identifying the work products that are subject to change control and controlling changes to and releases of these work products. It involves creating baselines and maintaining the integrity of baselines by providing accurate configuration data to stakeholders. It records and reports the status of configuration items and change requests and verifies the correctness and completeness of configuration items with configuration audits.

Table 8.4 Integrated development environment

Item	Description
Source code editor	This is a specialized text editor designed for editing the source code. It includes features to simplify and speed up the input of source code, including syntax checking of the code while the programmer types. Examples include Microsoft Visual Studio
Compiler or interpreter	A compiler is a computer program that translates the high-level programming language source code into object code to produce the executable code. A compiler carries out lexical analysis, parsing, and code generation An interpreter is a program that executes instructions written in a programming language. It may involve the direct execution of the code; translation of the code into an intermediate representation and immediate direct execution; or execution of stored precompiled code made by a compiler which is part of the Interpreter System
Build automation tools	Build automation involves scripting to automate the build process. This includes tasks such as compiling the source code; linking the object code and building the executable software; performing automated tests and reporting results; reporting the build status; and generating release notes
Debugger	A debugger is a software application that is used to debug and test other software programs. Debuggers offer step-by-step execution of the code or execution to breakpoints in the code. Examples include IBM Rational Purify and Microsoft Visual Studio Debugger

Visual Source Safe (VSS) is a version control management system for source code and binary files. It is developed by the Microsoft Corporation and is used mainly by small software development organizations. It allows multiple users to place their source code and work products under version control management. It is fairly easy to use and may be integrated with the Microsoft Visual Studio tool. Microsoft plans to replace VSS with its Team Systems tool.

Polytron Version Control System (PVCS) is a version control system for software code and binary files. It is developed by Serena Software Inc. and is suitable for use by large or small teams. It allows multiple users to place their source code and project deliverables under version control management, and it allows files to be checked in and checked out; baselines to be controlled; rollback of code; and tracking of check-ins. It includes functionality for branching, merging, and labelling. It includes the PV Tracker tool for tracking defects and the PV Builder tool for performing builds and releases.

The PV Tracker tool automates the capture and communication of issues and change requests. This is done throughout the software development life cycle for project teams, and the tool allows the developers to link the affected source code files with issues and changes. It allows managers to determine and report on team progress and to prioritize tasks. PV Builder maintains an audit trail of the files included in the build as well as their versions.

The IBM® Rational® Clearcase and Clearquest tools have a rich feature set, and they are among the most popular configuration management tools. Clearcase allows software code and other software deliverables to be placed under version control management, and it may be employed in large or medium projects. It can handle a large number of files and supports standard configuration management tasks such as checking in and checking out of the software assets as well as labelling and branching. Objects are stored in repositories called VOBs.

Clearquest may be linked to Clearcase as well as to other IBM Rational tools. It allows the defects in a project to be tracked, and it allows the versions of source code modules that were changed to be linked to a defect number in Clearquest.

8.6
Tools for Code Analysis and Code Inspections

Static code analysis is the analysis of software code without executing the code. It is usually performed with automated tools and the analysis conducted depends on the sophistication of the tools. Some tools may analyse individual statements or declarations, whereas others may analyse the whole source code. The objective of the analysis is to highlight potential coding errors early in the development life cycle.

The LDRA Testbed Tool automatically determines the complexity of the source code, and it provides metrics that give an indication of the maintainability of the code. A useful feature of LDRA is that it gives a visual picture of system complexity, and it has a refactoring tool to assist with reducing complexity. It automatically generates code assessment reports listing all of the files examined and providing metrics of the clarity, maintainability, and testability of the code (Fig. 8.7).

Compliance to coding standards is important in producing readable code and in preventing error-prone coding styles. There are several tools available to check conformance to coding standards including the LDRA TBvision tool which has reporting capabilities to show code quality as well as fault detection and avoidance measures. It provides users with functionality to view the results presented intuitively in various graphs and reports.

Some static code analysis tools (e.g. tools for formal methods) aim to prove properties about a particular program. This may include reasoning about program correctness or that of a program meeting its specification. These tools often provide support for assertions, and a precondition is the assertion placed before the code fragment, and this predicate is true before execution of the code. The post-condition is the assertion placed after the code fragment, and this predicate is true after the execution of the code.

There are several open-source tools available for static code analysis, and these include the RATS tools which provide multi-language support for C, C++, Perl, and PHP and the PMD tool for Java. There are several commercial tools available, and these include those that provide multi-programming language support and those that support a specific language. The LDRA Testbed tool provides support for C, C++, and Java; the Fortify tool helps developers to identify security vulnerabilities in C, C++, and Java; and the Parasoft tool helps developers to identify coding issues that lead to security, reliability, performance, and maintainability issues later.

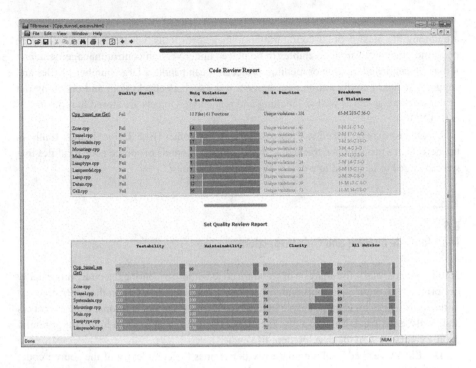

Fig. 8.7 LDRA Testbed – quality review report (Courtesy of LDRA Systems)

8.7
Tools for Testing

Testing plays a key role in verifying that the software system satisfies the requirements and is fit for purpose. There are various tools to support testing such as test planning and management tools; defect tracking tools; regression test automation tools; performance tools. The tools considered in this section include

- Test Director and Quality Center
- Winrunner
- Load Runner

Test Director is a web-based test management tool developed by Mercury[6] It provides a consistent repeatable process for gathering requirements; planning and scheduling tests; analysing results; and managing defects. It consists of four modules namely

---

[6]Mercury is now part of HP.

- Requirements
- Test Plan
- Test Lab
- Defect Management

The Requirements module supports requirements management and traceability of test cases to the requirements. The Test Plan module supports the creation and update of test cases. The Test Lab module supports execution of the test cases defined in the Test Plan module. The Defect Management module supports the logging of defects and these defects can be linked back to the test cases that failed.

Test Director supports a high level of collaboration and communication between the stakeholders. It allows the business analysts to define the application requirements and testing objectives. The test managers and testers may then design test plans, test cases, and automated scripts. The testers then run the manual and automated tests, report results, and log the defects. The developers review and correct the logged defects. Project and test managers can create status reports and manage test resources. Test and product managers decide objectively whether the application is ready to be released.

The Test Director tool is now a part of Quality Center^{TM} (Fig. 8.8) developed by HP. This tool standardizes and manages the entire test and quality process and is a web-based system for automated software quality management and testing. It employs dashboard technology to give visibility into the process.

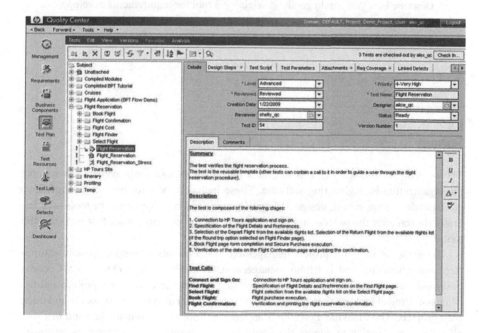

Fig. 8.8 HP Quality Center (Courtesy of HP)

Mercury developed the Winrunner tool which automatically captures, verifies, and replays user interactions. It enables defects in applications to be easily identified, and it is mainly used to automate regression testing. This helps to improve test quality productivity and allows regression testing to be performed in a timely manner. This provides confidence that enhancements to the software have had no negative impact on the integrity of the system. The Winrunner tool has been replaced by HP Unified Functional Testing software which includes HP Quick Test Professional and HP Service Test.

Mercury developed the LoadRunner testing tool, and this tools allows the software application to be tested with hundreds or thousands of concurrent users to determine its performance under heavy loads. It allows the scalability of the software system to be determined to check if its performance can support future predicted growth.

8.8
Review Questions

1. Why are tools used in software engineering?
2. How should a tool be identified for an organization and how should it be deployed?
3. What is the relationship between the process and the tool? Which comes first?
4. What tools would you recommend for project management?
5. Describe how you would go about selecting a tool for requirements development.
6. Describe various tools that are available for design and development and which are your preferred tools?

8.9
Summary

The objective of this chapter was to give a flavour of various tools available to support the organization in engineering software. These included tools for project management, configuration management, design and development, test management. The tools are generally chosen after the process has been defined, i.e. the process comes first and then the tools.

The focus on tools for project management was on tools to support project estimation and scheduling and portfolio management. The discussion included the Cocoma cost model which may be employed to estimate the cost and effort for a project and the Microsoft Project tool which is used extensively by project managers to schedule and track their projects. The Planview Portfolio Management Tool was also discussed and this tool allows an organization to choose the optimal mix of projects to maximize its return on investment.

The discussion on tools to support requirements development and management included tools such as IBM Rational DOORS, Requisite Pro, and CORE. The DOORS tool allows all stakeholders to actively participate in the requirements process and aims to optimize requirements communication, collaboration, and verification throughout the organization.

The discussion on tools to support design on development included the IBM Rational Software Modeler tool, the Sparx Enterprise Architect tool, and Integrated Developer Environments to support software developers. The Rational Software Modeler® (RSM) is a UML-based visual modelling and design tool. Enterprise Architect is a UML analysis and design tool used for modelling business and IT systems. It provides traceability from requirements to analysis and design, testing and deployment, and supports code generation. The discussion on tools to support configuration management included PVCS and Clearcase.

The discussion on tools to support testing included the Test Director, Winrunner, and Loadrunner tools. Test Director is a test management tool with modules for requirements management, test planning, test lab, and defect management. Test Director is now a part of Quality Center™, and this tool standardizes and manages the entire test and quality process.

Tool selection is done in a controlled manner. First, the organization needs to determine its requirements for the tool. Next, it will need to decide on whether an in-house solution will be developed or whether to purchase a tool from a vendor. Various candidate tools are evaluated and a decision on the proposed tool is made. Next, the tool is piloted to ensure that it meets the needs of the organization, and feedback from the pilot may lead to changes or customizations of the tool. Finally, the end users are trained on the use of the tool and it is rolled out throughout the organization.

SCAMPI Appraisals

9

Key Topics

> Appraisal Plan
> Conducting an Appraisal
> Objective Evidence
> SCAMPI (Class A, B, C) Appraisals
> Reporting the Results

9.1
Introduction

Appraisals play an essential role in the software process improvement programme. They allow an organization to understand its current software process maturity, including the strengths and weaknesses in its processes. An initial appraisal is conducted at the start of the initiative to allow the organization understand its current process maturity and to plan and prioritize improvements for the first improvement cycle. Improvements are then implemented, and an appraisal is typically conducted at the end of the cycle to confirm progress (Fig. 9.1).

An appraisal is an independent examination of the software engineering and management practices in the organization and is conducted using the SCAMPI[1] appraisal methodology [SCA:06]. The appraisal will identify strengths and weaknesses in the processes and any gaps that exist with respect to the CMMI practices.

---

[1] There are three classes of SCAMPI appraisals and these are termed Class A, B, C. They differ in the level of formality, the cost and duration, and the reporting of the appraisal results.

G. O'Regan, *Introduction to Software Process Improvement*, Undergraduate Topics in Computer Science, DOI 10.1007/978-0-85729-172-1_9,
© Springer-Verlag London Limited 2011

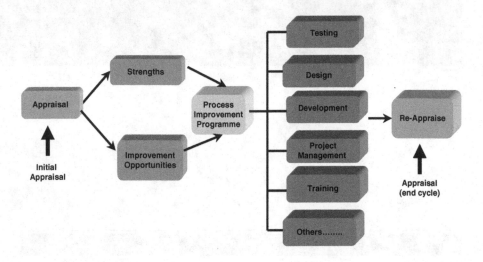

Fig. 9.1 Appraisals and process improvement

The appraisal leader kicks off the appraisal with an opening presentation. This allows the appraisal leader to introduce the appraisal team[2] and to summarize the activities that will be carried out in the days ahead. These will include presentations, interviews, reviews of project documentation, and detailed analysis to determine the extent to which the specific and generic practices have been implemented and whether the specific and generic goals for each process area within the scope of the appraisal are satisfied.

Sample output[3] from a SCAMPI Class A CMMI level 3 appraisal is presented in Fig. 9.2. Each column represents a CMMI process area and each row represents a specific or generic practice. Colour coding is employed to indicate the extent to which the specific or generic practices have been implemented. The extent of implementation may be

– Fully satisfied
– Largely satisfied
– Partially satisfied

---

[2] The appraisal team could be the CMMI project manager only (if the project manager is a SCAMPI trained appraiser); alternatively, it could be an external appraiser and the CMMI project manager. A SCAMPI Class A appraisal could involve a large team of four to nine appraisers (including a SCAMPI lead appraiser) for a large organization. There is a strict qualification process to become a SCAMPI lead appraiser, and it requires attending the official SEI CMMI and SCAMPI training and conducting two appraisals under the direction of a qualified SCAMPI lead appraiser.

[3] The type of output to be provided is agreed in discussions between the appraisal sponsor and the appraisal leader. The output may just be the strengths and improvement opportunities identified. In other cases, the ratings may just be of the specific and generic goals rather than of the practices.

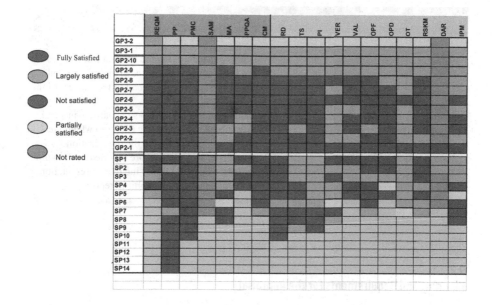

Fig. 9.2 CMMI L3 rating of practices

– Not satisfied
– Not rated

The appraisal leader will present the appraisal findings, and the appraisal output may include a presentation and an appraisal report. The appraisal output summarizes the identified strengths and opportunities for improvement. Ratings of the process areas will be provided when ratings are part of the scope of the appraisal. The ratings will indicate the current maturity of the organization's processes and any gaps that exist with respect to the targeted CMMI maturity level.

The appraisal findings allow the CMMI project manager to plan and schedule the next improvement cycle and to continue with the CMMI improvement programme. Appraisals allow an organization to

– Understand its current maturity (including strengths and weaknesses of its processes)
– Relate its strengths and weaknesses to the CMMI specific and generic practices
– Prioritize its improvements for the next improvement cycle
– Benchmark itself against other organizations (SCAMPI Class A)

There are three phases in an appraisal (Table 9.1).

Table 9.1   Phases in a CMMI appraisal

Phase	Description
Planning and preparation	This involves identifying the sponsor's objectives and the requirements for the appraisal. A good appraisal plan is fundamental to the success of the appraisal
Conducting the appraisal	The appraisal team interviews the participants and examines data to judge the extent to which the CMMI is implemented in the organization
Reporting the results	The results of the appraisal are reported back to the sponsor. This will usually include a presentation of the findings and an appraisal report

9.2
Planning and Requirements for the Appraisal

Good planning is essential to the success of the appraisal. The appraisal leader[4] will determine the appraisal objectives in discussions with the sponsor. The type of appraisal to be conducted is determined, and an appraisal plan is developed to meet the sponsor's requirements. The appraisal leader then forms a team to conduct the appraisal.

There are three classes of SCAMPI appraisals [ARC:06] that may be conducted, and they vary in formality; the appraisal findings to be generated; and the output, duration, and cost. The three classes of SCAMPI appraisals (Class A, B, and C) are defined in Fig. 9.3.

Requirements	Class A	Class B	Class C
Type of objective evidence	Documents and interviews	Documents and interviews	Documents or interviews
Ratings generated	Goal ratings required	Not allowed	Not allowed
Organizational unit coverage	Required	Not required	Not required
Minimum team size	4	2	1
Appraisal team leader requirements	Lead appraiser	Person trained and experienced	Person trained and experienced

Fig. 9.3   SCAMPI (classes of appraisals)

---

[4]For a formal SCAMPI Class A appraisal the appraisal team leader will need to be a qualified SEI SCAMPI lead appraiser.

The initial evidence provided by the organization will often consist of questionnaires and Practice Implementation Indicator Descriptions (PIIDs[5]). The appraisal leader will analyse the initial evidence to get a preliminary understanding of the organization's processes and maturity.

9.2.1
Analyse Requirements

The appraisal leader will determine the goals and objectives of the appraisal in discussions with the sponsor. The appraisal leader may give an overview of the CMMI and appraisals to the sponsor and relevant members of the organization. This is to ensure that the purpose of appraisals, the various types of appraisals that may be conducted, and the output that may be produced are understood. This is essential when the organization is relatively new to software process improvement.

It will be explained where appraisals fit into software process improvement and how the output from the appraisal is used in the next improvement cycle. The objectives of the appraisal should be realistic and constraints such as cost, schedule, and effort determined.

The business goals of the software process improvement initiative may influence the scope and type of appraisal to be conducted. The business goals may include

- Reducing costs of software development
- Delivery software consistently on time
- Delivering high-quality software
- Delivering software fast to market ahead of competitors
- Marketing benefit of CMMI maturity level as a differentiator to its competitors

A software process improvement initiative will generally focus on improvements to those processes in the organization that will lead to the greatest business benefit. The appraisal is an objective way to determine if these processes have actually improved, as well as determining their actual maturity. Some companies may be interested in the marketing benefit of a CMMI maturity level rating and may wish to benchmark themselves against other companies. They will generally be interested in a formal SCAMPI Class A appraisal.

The scope of the appraisal determines the CMMI process areas that will be appraised; the parts of the organization to be examined; the participants; and the projects and support functions involved.

The sponsor will decide on the appraisal outputs to be produced, and this may include strengths and weaknesses in the processes; ratings of the process areas appraised; a final

---

[5]The PIID is a mapping between the specific and generic practices in the CMMI model and the processes employed in the organization. It shows how the organization has implemented the CMMI. It is produced prior to the appraisal.

findings presentation with recommendations; and an appraisal report. The appraisal input gathered from the discussions will include

- Identity of appraisal sponsor
- Appraisal leader and team
- Participants in appraisal
- Objectives of appraisal
- Scope of appraisal
- Selected projects
- Constraints
- Confidentiality requirements
- Appraisal outputs

The sponsor and appraisal leader verbally agree the appraisal input which is then documented in the appraisal plan.

9.2.2
Develop Appraisal Plan

The appraisal plan is prepared by the appraisal leader, and it describes the scope of the appraisal and how it will be conducted. It will include input gathered in discussions with the appraisal sponsor and the plan documents

- Identity of appraisal sponsor
- Appraisal leader and team
- Scope of the appraisal
- Objectives and constraints
- Projects to be examined
- Participants
- Appraisal schedule
- Risks to success
- Appraisal outputs

The plan will detail the effort required, cost involved, and the schedule for the appraisal. It will also document how the appraisal will be conducted as well as the resources required. The key personnel involved will include the appraisal leader, the appraisal team, the on-site coordinator, and the participants.

The logistics requirements for the appraisal need to be determined and documented in the appraisal plan. These may include accommodation and meals, transportation, and access to rooms and equipment. The appraisal plan will describe how data are collected and validated. A sample appraisal schedule for a SCAMPI Class C appraisal is given in Fig. 9.4.

The risks to the success of the appraisal need to be identified and managed. Finally, once the appraisal plan is complete it is reviewed and approved by the appraisal sponsor.

TIME	Day 1	Day 2	Day 3
9:00	Site Briefing (Kick Off)	Team Planning	Consolidate Feedback
		Interview Project	Produce
10:00	Interview Project	Manager 3	(Informal Ratings)
	Manager 1	Consolidate Notes	Prepare Feedback
11:00	Consolidate Notes	Interview Project	Presentation
	Interview Project	Team 3	
12:00	Team 1	Consolidate Notes	Feedback
	Consolidate Notes / Lunch		
		Lunch	Presentation
13:00			
	Interview Project	Demo VSS / Intranet	
14:00	Manager 2		
	Consolidate Note	Consolidate Notes	
15:00	Interview Project	Interview QA/SEPG	
	Team 2	Consolidate Notes	
16:00	Interview Support Team	Conduct Extra	
	Team	Interviews	
17:00	Consolidate Notes	Consolidate Notes	

Fig. 9.4 Sample schedule for SCAMPI Class C appraisal

9.2.3
Select and Prepare Team

The appraisal leader is responsible for ensuring that the appraisal is conducted in accordance with the appraisal methodology. The leader will determine the size[6] and composition of the team and will select team members who are appropriately qualified and have sufficient knowledge and experience to conduct the appraisal effectively. Any knowledge and skill gaps will need to be identified and addressed by training[7] prior to the appraisal.

---

[6]The minimum acceptable team size for a SCAMPI Class A appraisal (as in Fig. 9.3) is four and the maximum is nine. The minimum team size for Class A is one and for Class B is two.

[7]The appraisers need to have received appropriate training on the CMMI reference model and on the SCAMPI appraisal methodology.

The methodology requires that the team has sufficient software engineering and management experience. Team members also need good verbal and written communication skills to enable them to carry out their roles effectively.

The appraisal leader will introduce the team members to one another and will give the team an overview of the goals of the appraisal; its scope; the appraisal plan; and the approach to the appraisal. This orientation will enable the appraisal team to carry out their assigned roles effectively.

The initial information provided by the organization (e.g. completed questionnaires and PIIDs) will be analysed and the data collection and validation methods and tools to be employed during the appraisal discussed. There are confidentiality requirements to be preserved during an appraisal. For example, everything that is said by individuals during the interviews is treated in the strictest confidence, and appraisal findings are not attributed to individuals.

There are several roles involved in the appraisal including the *on-site coordinator*[8] who takes care of the logistics to support the appraisal team leader; the *librarian* who manages the inventory of appraisal documents; *mini-teams* who are responsible for data collection for their assigned process areas; *facilitators* who conduct the interviews; and *timekeeper* who keeps the interview on time.

9.2.4
Obtain and Analyse Initial Evidence

The organization will provide initial information to the appraisal leader prior to the appraisal to show how it has implemented the CMMI. This helps the appraisal team to understand how the organization has implemented the various practices in the CMMI model and assists the team in preparing a data collection plan to verify the implementation. The initial evidence may include completed questionnaires, relevant presentations, and a PIID mapping between the CMMI specific and generic practices and the process assets of the organization.

This initial evidence is analysed by the team to enable them to understand the objective evidence available for the specific and generic practices. An inventory of the evidence available for the various CMMI practices is prepared, and the adequacy and completeness of the information provided is determined. This may result in the need for additional data which are then input into the data collection plan.

There is a need for objective evidence to substantiate implementation of every practice within the scope of the appraisal and for every project instance of that practice. The extent to which the practice has been implemented is judged by practice implementation indicators. These are given in Table 9.2.

It is important to collect as much objective evidence as possible prior to the appraisal, as this will reduce the time required for discovery activities during the appraisal. The

---

[8]The CMMI project manager is responsible for project managing the CMMI implementation and may carry out the role of on-site coordinator.

Table 9.2 Indicators of practice implementation

Indicator	Description
Direct artefact	Tangible output of the practice (e.g. typical work products in CMMI model)
Indirect artefact	Artefacts that are a consequence of performing the process (e.g. meeting minutes), but not necessarily the purpose for which it is performed
Affirmation	Oral or written statements confirming the performance of a practice

discovery activities are concerned with looking for evidence to support practice implementation, and an efficient on-site appraisal will focus more on verification activities rather than on discovery activities.

9.2.5
Prepare for Conducting Appraisal

The appraisal leader will conduct an appraisal readiness review to judge the extent to which the organization is ready for the appraisal. There is no point in going ahead with the appraisal if the organization is not ready or is insufficiently prepared.

The sponsor and appraisal leader will consider the feasibility of the appraisal plan and will decide on whether to continue with the appraisal as planned, to re-plan accordingly, or in a worst case scenario to cancel the appraisal.

The appraisal leader will judge whether the preliminary data are available and whether the appraisal team has been formed and appropriately trained. The logistics will need to be suitably handled and the risks to the appraisal identified and managed.

The PIIDs will detail the coverage of the CMMI specific and generic practices, and it is reasonable to expect few significant coverage gaps prior to the appraisal. The PIID will refer to documents and evidence, and these need to be accessible to the appraisers. The appraisers need a verification strategy to verify the objective evidence that is available for practices, as well as a discovery strategy to find objective evidence for practices that have no available objective evidence. The verification and discovery activities to take place during the appraisal are documented in the data collection plan.

The data collection plan may be documented in a variety of deliverables (e.g. interview schedule and participants and scripted interview questions). It may include a spreadsheet with the CMMI practices or questions listed vertically and sources of information listed horizontally. Data on every practice within the scope of the appraisal are required.[9]

---

[9] Data are required for every project instantiation for practices addressing processes at the project level. One instantiation is sufficient for practices addressing processes at the organization level.

The appraisal leader will determine the participants required at each interview and the documents to be reviewed. The roles and responsibilities of team members in data collection activities will be documented in the data collection plan.

9.3
Conducting the Appraisal

This phase of the appraisal is concerned with on-site activities to gather data on the extent to which the specific and generic practices have been implemented. It involves gathering and examining the objective evidence, as well as documenting and verifying the data. The preliminary findings are generated and presented to the appraisal participants to get feedback in order to validate the data and findings. Additional data are then gathered and the final appraisal results prepared. The activities involved include

– Prepare participants
– Collect objective evidence
– Examine objective evidence
– Verify objective evidence
– Validate objective evidence
– Generate appraisal findings

The appraisal participants will receive appropriate training on the appraisal process and their role in it. The appraisal team members take notes and gather objective evidence during the various data collection activities. The objective evidence is then reviewed and consolidated, related to the specific and generic practices, critically examined and documented, and verified and validated. The extent to which the CMMI practices are implemented is determined.

Preliminary findings are prepared and validated and the final appraisal results are then prepared.

9.3.1
Prepare Participants

The on-site coordinator (this may be the CMMI project manager) will give appropriate orientation to the appraisal participants prior to the appraisal to ensure that they understand the purpose of the appraisal and their role in it. This will be the first experience of an appraisal for many in the organization, and so the participants need to understand the process and the required behaviours:

– Professional behaviour at all times
– Punctuality in attendance for interviews
– Openness and honesty in answering questions
– Acting promptly on requests to provide additional material

- Awareness of the confidentiality requirements
- Awareness that the appraisal findings will not be attributed to individuals or specific projects

The participants need to be aware of the meetings and interviews that they need to attend. All participants will attend the opening and closing sessions and will attend their own specific interview(s) and the feedback session(s).

The sponsor introduces the appraisal leader at the opening session, and the leader will set the context and expectations for the appraisal and describe the activities that will take place in the days ahead. The leader gives a brief overview to the participants on the appraisal process and schedule, and the appraisal team is introduced. The opening presentation will typically cover

- Overview of appraisal
- Appraisals and process improvement
- Process areas within scope of appraisal
- Projects to be reviewed
- Activities in appraisal
- Participants in appraisal
- Confidentiality
- Appraisal schedule
- Output from appraisal

The information provided by participants will be treated in the strictest confidence by the appraisal team, and that none of the appraisal findings will be attributed to individuals or projects. This is important, as otherwise participants may be reluctant to share information.

9.3.2
Examine Objective Evidence

The accuracy of the appraisal findings is dependent on the accuracy of the information collected by the appraisal team. The team needs to collect adequate information on how the organization does its work needs, and the information gathered needs to be related to the CMMI specific and generic practices. This requires that the appraisal team understands how the organization has implemented the CMMI and has objective evidence of specific and generic practice implementation.

The data collection needs to be well planned and tracked and it will be revised appropriately during the appraisal to reflect new information needs. The data collection plan consists of

- Appraisal schedule
- Interview schedule
- Document list
- Interview questions

The appraisal team will continually manage the data collected and plan new data collection in line with information needs. The data collection sources include

– Interviews with appraisal participants
– Reviews of documentation
– Presentations from staff

The interviews need to be well planned as they have a limited amount of time to determine specific evidence (e.g. oral affirmation on the way the process is performed) from the participants. The planning requires the preparation of scripted questions to ensure that the interview is focused and achieves its objectives within the time constraints. Interviews also allow dynamic data gathering, with the interviewer able to branch off to discuss other related topics.

The information provided at an interview is treated in the strictest confidence, and the appraisal findings will not be attributed to individuals or projects. There will be separate interviews for

– Project managers
– Project teams
– Functional area representatives (FAR)
– Managers
– Specific groups (SEPG Team, QA, etc.)

Often, one of the appraisal team members will lead the interview with some or all of the other appraisers being present, listening and taking notes. The planned set of interviews will be defined in the data collection plan, and re-planning will take place as appropriate. There may be a need for extra on-call interviews or some of the planned interviews may be cancelled if sufficient objective evidence is available.

Documentation reviews give the appraisal team a clearer understanding of what practices are performed in the organization. This includes insight into how the process is performed, the extent to which it is performed, as well as allowing explicit deliverables produced to be examined. Most of the direct artefacts used as indicators of practice implementation are documents.

There are three levels of documents that will typically be examined during the appraisal. These are

– Organization documents
– Project documents
– Implementation documents

The organization documents include policies, processes, and procedures; the project documents include the deliverables produced during the project for each project instantiation; and the implementation documents provide an audit trail of the processes used. The appraisal team will maintain an inventory of the documents used.

Presentations allow the organization to explain how particular practices are performed.

The appraisal team will need to analyse the information obtained during the various data collection activities to

- Judge if the information collected is acceptable as objective evidence
- Relate it to the corresponding practices in the model
- Relate evidence to the appropriate part of the organization unit

The results of data collection will often be recorded on electronic tools as the inventory of the collected evidence. The appraisal team will closely monitor progress with the data collection activities, and as appraisals have a limited amount of time available it is essential that the data collection activities are focused and efficient.

Finally, once the team has examined, verified, and validated all of the required data it is in a position to generate the appraisal findings and, where applicable, to generate ratings for the organization.

9.3.3
Document Objective Evidence

This part of the appraisal is concerned with note taking; reviewing and consolidating notes; relating the notes to the corresponding practices in the CMMI model; and documenting practice implementation and the strengths and weaknesses identified. The notes taken by the team members during the data gathering sessions are reviewed at the end of each session and significant items relating to one or more practices tagged. The notes record the particular data gathering session as well as the participants.

The consolidation of the notes allows the appraisal team members to have a common understanding of the data collected to date, as well as identifying further data collection needs. For each project instantiation there is a need to determine the presence or absence of objective data for each specific and generic practice for each process area within scope. The gaps identified in the implemented processes with respect to the practices in the CMMI model are documented.

It is essential that the data collection, consolidation, and documentation activities be conducted in a timely manner. An inventory (usually an electronic spreadsheet tool or a manual wall chart tool) of the objective evidence available for each specific and generic practice for each project instantiation within the scope of the appraisal is maintained.

The inventory allows the status of the data collection and consolidation activities to be determined, and this includes the practices for which there is sufficient objective evidence available and those that have insufficient or missing evidence. The data collection plan needs to be updated appropriately to reflect additional data collection needs. The inventory will record

- Project to which data apply
- Specific or generic practice to which it applies
- Type of evidence (direct, indirect, affirmation)
- Whether implies presence or absence of objective evidence

Often, in large formal appraisals, team members are assigned responsibilities for the collection and documentation of objective evidence for one or more process areas. This usually involves the formation of mini-teams with two or three members to obtain and document the objective evidence for their assigned process areas.

The raw notes taken by the appraisers are treated as confidential information and are not disclosed to anyone outside of the appraisal team. Team members will destroy their notes at the end of the appraisal to ensure that information cannot be attributed to individuals.

9.3.4
Verify Objective Evidence

This is concerned with verifying the implementation of the organization's practices for each project instantiation, as well as determining and documenting the extent to which the practices are implemented. The implementation of each practice is verified for each project instantiation, with exemplary implementations highlighted as strengths to be included in the appraisal findings.

The appraisal team uses the initial objective evidence provided by the organization to understand how the CMMI practices are implemented in the organization. The appraisal team then gathers data to confirm that the practices are actually implemented as defined, and this may reveal gaps in the implementation that were not apparent in the initial evidence provided. The implemented practices are then compared to the specific and generic practices in the CMMI model, and additional gaps may be identified. The gaps in the implementation are recorded and become part of the appraisal findings.

The appraisal team must verify that each project within the scope of the appraisal has objective evidence of implementation of the specific or generic practices (reflecting project activities). The appraisal team will

- Verify the appropriateness of each direct artefact provided for practices within appraisal scope
- Verify the appropriateness of each indirect artefact provided
- Verify appropriateness of affirmations
- Verify that implementation of each practice (within scope) is supported by direct artefacts and corroborated by indirect artefacts or affirmations
- Obtain oral affirmation corresponding to each specific and generic goal within scope of appraisal
- Generate the preliminary findings including the strengths identified and gaps in the implemented practices

Much of the evidence required to perform verification is provided prior to the appraisal. The main focus of the data collection activities is to allow the appraisal team to verify that the intended practices are implemented across the organization unit and to identify any gaps in the implementation.

The appraisal team then characterizes the extent to which the CMMI practices are implemented for each project instantiation and derives an aggregate rating to characterize the extent of implementation in the organization. The extent of implementation of a practice is

- Fully implemented (FI)
- Largely implemented (LI)
- Partially implemented (PI)
- Not implemented (NI)

The extent of implementation of the practice is judged by

- The presence or absence of direct artefacts and their adequacy
- The presence or absence of indirect artefacts and affirmations to confirm the implementation
- Any weaknesses in practice implementation identified

The aggregate organization rating for each practice is determined from the rating of the practice for each project instantiation. For example, if all project instantiations are fully implemented then the organization rating is fully implemented.

9.3.5
Validate Preliminary Findings

The appraisal team will present preliminary findings to members of the organization to ensure that they are an accurate reflection of the organization. This is mainly a data collection activity, and the goal is to validate the appraisal team's understanding of the processes implemented in the organization. Feedback and additional evidence will be requested and used in the formulation of the final findings.

The preliminary findings detail the practice implementation gaps identified as well as strengths noted by the appraisal team. Every model practice characterized at the organization level as not implemented, partially implemented, or largely implemented will have a preliminary finding associated with it.

The appraisal team will issue a request for further information for areas where the appraisal team has insufficient objective evidence available.

9.3.6
Generate Appraisal Results

The appraisal team will rate specific and generic goal satisfaction based on the extent of practice implementation throughout the organization. The extent of practice implemented is judged by the validated data collected, including direct and indirect artefacts and oral affirmation objective evidence. Once the goals have been rated the process areas may be rated and then the overall maturity level determined.

A goal is considered satisfied if the practices associated with that goal are appropriately implemented. Any gaps are considered and the appraisal team makes a judgement on whether these gaps threaten the ability to achieve the associated goal. All associated practices must be rated as largely or fully implemented and any identified weaknesses must not have a significant impact on goal achievement. For any goals that are rated as not satisfied the appraisal team will detail how the weaknesses identified led to this rating.

Once the goals have been rated the team is then in a position to judge the satisfaction of the process areas within the appraisal scope. Process area satisfaction is closely related to goal satisfaction, and a process area is rated satisfied if all of its specific and generic goals up to the targeted maturity level are rated satisfied.

The appraisal team is then in a position to judge the maturity level of the organization. This is based on the ratings of the process areas within the scope of the appraisal. The maturity level determined is the highest level at which all process areas contained at that maturity level and lower levels are satisfied.[10]

The appraisal team is then in a position to prepare the final appraisal findings including

– Documenting the final findings
– Documenting the ratings (where ratings are part of the appraisal)
– Preparing (where applicable) the Appraisal Disclosure Statement (ADS) for the CMMI Stewart at the SEI

9.4
Reporting the Results

The results of the appraisal are presented to the sponsor and the participants. The strengths and weaknesses of the processes are presented, as well as the ratings of the process areas (where these are part of the appraisal). The appraisal results need to be credible, as they will be used for continuous improvement.

The appraisal findings are intended to promote action and occasionally a separate executive session is conducted with senior management. The purpose of this session is to discuss the appraisal results and to facilitate the preparation of an action to address the findings.

9.4.1
Deliver Appraisal Results

The findings will be presented to the participants in the appraisal. The appraisal sponsor is advised of the appraisal results prior to the presentation as a matter of courtesy and to prevent any surprises. The appraisal leader will provide the appraisal findings to the appraisal sponsor, and the findings will be signed by the appraisal leader and team. The appraisal findings will include

– Summary of appraisal process
– Summary of strengths and weaknesses for each process area
– Ratings (where this is part of appraisal)

---

[10]Generic goal 3 must also be rated for all of the level 2 process areas for a level 3 rating.

Any statements of weaknesses will adhere to the confidentiality requirements and will not be attributed to projects or individuals. The appraisal leader and team will sign the appraisal findings to indicate their agreement with them.

An executive session may be conducted between the sponsor and appraisal leader to clarify any issues from the appraisal and to help the sponsor and senior management understand the process weaknesses identified. This helps to ensure that management are sufficiently informed to act appropriately on the findings. An action plan is prepared to act upon the findings.

9.4.2
Archive Appraisal Results

Important data and records from the appraisal will be preserved and confidential information disposed of securely. Any lessons learned from the appraisal will be used to improve the appraisal process.

The information archived will include the appraisal plan and appraisal results. All notes taken by appraisers will be destroyed. The appraisal record will be delivered to the appraisal sponsor and will include

- Dates of the appraisal
- Appraisal input
- Appraisal plan
- Objective evidence to support goal ratings
- Characterization of practice implementation
- Appraisal method
- Final findings
- All ratings (goals, practices, and maturity levels)

The ADS record will be created and submitted to the CMMI Stewart at the SEI for formal SCAMPI Class A appraisals.

9.5
Review Questions

1. Discuss the purpose of appraisals and how they fit into the software process improvement cycle.
2. Discuss the three phases in an appraisal.
3. Discuss the three classes of SCAMPI appraisals.

4. Discuss the difference between data discovery and data verification activities in an appraisal.
5. Describe the activities that take place in planning the appraisal.
6. Describe the activities that take place during the appraisal.

9.6
Summary

Appraisals play a key role in software process improvement and are an essential part of the improvement programme. They allow an organization to understand its current software process maturity, including its strengths and opportunities for improvement. An initial appraisal is generally conducted at the start of the initiative to allow the organization plan and prioritize improvements for the first improvement cycle. Improvements are then implemented, and an appraisal is typically conducted at the end of the cycle to confirm progress.

An appraisal is an independent examination of the software engineering and management practices in the organization and will identify any gaps that exist with respect to the targeted level in the CMMI. There are three phases in an appraisal: planning the appraisal; conducting the appraisal; and reporting the results.

Planning involves identifying the sponsor's objectives and the requirements for the appraisal. The appraisal leader will determine the appraisal objectives in discussions with the sponsor. The type of appraisal to be conducted is determined, and an appraisal plan is developed to meet the sponsor's requirements. The appraisal leader then forms a team to conduct the appraisal and the participants involved in the appraisal receive appropriate training on the appraisal process and their role in it.

Conducting of the appraisal involves on-site activities to gather data to determine the extent to which the CMMI practices within the scope of the appraisal have been implemented. It involves gathering and examining the objective evidence and documenting and verifying the data. The appraisal team makes notes and gathers objective evidence during the various data collection activities (e.g. interviews, presentations, and reviews of documentation). The objective evidence is then reviewed and consolidated, related to the CMMI practices, critically examined and documented, verified and validated. The extent to which the CMMI practices are implemented is determined. Preliminary findings are then prepared and validated by members of the organization. The final appraisal results are then prepared.

The results of the appraisal are then presented to the sponsor and the participants. The strengths and weaknesses identified with the processes will be presented, as well as the ratings of the process areas (where these are part of the appraisal). The appraisal results are used for continuous process improvement. An action plan is prepared to address the appraisal findings.

Glossary

ADS	appraisal disclosure statement
ATM	automated teller machine
BRS	business requirements specification
CAR	causal analysis and resolution
CCB	change control board
CM	configuration management
CMM®	Capability Maturity Model
CMMI®	Capability Maturity Model Integration
COCOMO	Constructive Cost Model
COPQ	cost of poor quality
COTS	customized off the shelf
DAR	decision analysis and resolution
DMADV	Define, Measure, Analyse, Design, Verify
DMAIC	Define, Measure, Analyse, Improve, Control
DOORS	dynamic object-oriented requirements system
DSDM	Dynamic Systems Development Method
EAF	effort adjustment factor
ESA	European Space Agency
ESI	European Software Institute
FAR	functional area representatives
GQM	Goal, Question, Metric
IBM	international business machines
IDE	integrated development environment
IDEAL	initiating, diagnosing, establishing, acting, and learning
IEC	International Electrotechnical Commission
IEEE	Institute of Electrical and Electronic Engineers
IPM	Integrated Project Management
ISEB	Information System Examination Board
ISO	International Standards Organization
JAD	joint application development

G. O'Regan, *Introduction to Software Process Improvement*, Undergraduate Topics in Computer Science, DOI 10.1007/978-0-85729-172-1,
© Springer-Verlag London Limited 2011

LDRA	Liverpool Data Research Associates
MA	measurement and analysis
NATO	North Atlantic Treaty Organization
OID	Organization Innovation and Deployment
OPD	organization process definition
OPF	organization process focus
OPP	organization process performance
OSSP	organization set of standard processes
OT	organization training
PB	project board
P-CMM	People Capability Maturity Model
PI	product integration
PIID	Practice Implementation Indicator Description
PMBOK	project management book of knowledge
PMC	project monitoring and control
PMI	Project Management Institute
PP	project planning
PPM	project portfolio management
PPQA	process and product quality assurance
PSP	personal software process
PVCS	Polytron Version Control System
QA	quality assurance
QPM	quantitative project management
RAD	rapid application development
RD	requirements development
RFP	request for proposal
RM	requirements management
ROI	return on investment
RSKM	risk management
RSM	Rational Software Modeler
RUP	Rational Unified Process
SAM	supplier agreement management
SCAMPI	Standard CMMI Appraisal Method for Process Improvement
SEI	Software Engineering Institute
SEPG	Software Engineering Process Group
SLA	service level agreement
SLOC	source lines of code
SOW	statement of work
SPI	software process improvement
SPICE	Software Process Improvement Capability dEtermination
SQA	software quality assurance
TS	technical solution
TSP	Team Software Process
UML	Unified Modelling Language
VAL	validation

VDM	Vienna Development Method
VDM♣	Irish School of VDM
VER	verification
VOB	version object base
VSS	visual source safe

References

ARC:06   SCAMPI Upgrade Team: Appraisal Requirements for CMMI V1.2. (ARC V1.2).
           TR CMU/SEI-2006-TR-011. Aug 2006

Bas:88   Basili, V., Rombach, H.: The TAME project. Towards improvement-oriented
           software environments. IEEE Trans. Softw. Eng. 14(6), 758–773 (1988)

Boe:81   Boehm, B.: Software Engineering Economics. Prentice Hall, Englewood Cliffs, NJ
           (1981)

Boe:88   Boehm, B.: A spiral model for software development and enhancement. Computer.
           May 1988

Brk:75   Brooks, F.: The Mythical Man Month. Addison Wesley (1975)

Brk:86   Brooks, F.: No Silver Bullet. Essence and Accidents of Software Engineering.
           In: Information Processing. Elsevier, Amsterdam (1986)

CKS:06   Chrissis, M.B., Conrad, M., Shrum, S.: CMMI. Guidelines for Process Integration
           and Product Improvement. SEI Series in Software Engineering, 2nd edn. Addison
           Wesley (2006)

Crs:79   Crosby, P.: Quality Is Free. The Art of Making Quality Certain. McGraw Hill (1979)

Dem:86   Deming, W.E.: Out of Crisis. MIT Press (1986)

Fag:76   Fagan, M.: Design and code inspections to reduce errors in software development.
           IBM Syst. J. 15(3), 182–211 (1976)

Fen:95   Fenton, N.: Software Metrics: A Rigorous Approach. Thompson Computer Press
           (1995)

Glb:76   Gilb, T.: Software Metrics. Winthrop Publishers, Inc., Cambridge (1976)

Glb:94   Gilb, T., Graham, D.: Software Inspections. Addison Wesley (1994)

Hum:89   Humphry, W.: Managing the Software Process. Addison Wesley (1989)

Jac:99   Rumbaugh, J., et al.: The Unified Software Development Process. Addison Wesley
           (1999)

Jur:00   Juran, J.: Juran's Quality Handbook, 5th edn. McGraw Hill (2000)

Lio:96   Lions, J.L.: Ariane 5. Flight 501. Failure Report by Enquiry Board, Paris (1996)

OGC:04   Office of Government Commerce: Managing Successful Projects with PRINCE2 (2004)

ORg:02   O'Regan, G.: A Practical Approach to Software Quality. Springer, New York (2002)

ORg:06   O'Regan, G.: Mathematical Approaches to Software Quality. Springer, London (2006)

Par:72   Parnas, D.: On the criteria to be used in decomposing systems into modules. Commun. ACM 15(12), 1053–1058 (1972)

Roy:70   Royce, W.: The software lifecycle model (waterfall model). In: Proceedings WESTCON, Los Angeles, Aug 1970

Rum:99   Rumbaugh, J., et al.: The Unified Modelling Language. User Guide. Addison Wesley (1999)

SCA:06   Standard CMMI Appraisal Method for Process Improvement: CMU/SEI-2006-HB-002. V1.2. Aug 2006

SEI:06   Software Engineering Institute: CMMI Executive Overview. Presentation by the SEI (2006)

SEI:09   Software Engineering Institute: CMMI Impact. Presentation by Anita Carleton. Aug 2009

Index